"In this important book, Tomáš Profant challenges ideological divisions which have been shaping the post-Cold War development industry. In a compelling manner, this rigorous study addresses socio-political and cultural hierarchization of 'old' and 'new' European donors, demonstrating that the separation is not simply a function of major differences between Eastern and Western aid providers, but instead a reflection of deep, often discriminatory and Orientalising cuts that shape European fabric. A must-read not only for those interested specifically in foreign aid politics, but everyone interested in European issues."

Elżbieta Drążkiewicz, Maynooth University, Ireland

"The author presents a comprehensive analysis in which theoretical and empirical parts are linked in an exemplary manner. It displays lucid, nuanced and sharp observations concerning discursive relations of power in seemingly harmless everyday statements."

Aram Ziai, University of Kassel, Germany

New Donors on the Postcolonial Crossroads

After the collapse of the Soviet Union, Eastern European countries were said to be playing catch up with the West, and in the field of development cooperation, they were classified as 'new donors.' This book aims to problematize this distinction between old and new development donors, applying an East–West dimension to global Orientalism discourse.

The book uses a novel double postcolonial perspective, examining North–South relations and East–West relations simultaneously, and problematizing these distinctions. In particular, the book deploys an empirical analysis of a 'new' Eastern European donor (Slovakia), compared with an 'old' donor (Austria), in order to explore questions around hierarchization, depoliticization and the legitimization of development.

This book's innovative approach to the East–West dimension of global Orientalism will be of interest to researchers in postcolonial studies, Eastern European studies, and critical development studies.

Tomáš Profant is a senior researcher at the Institute of International Relations in Prague, Czechia, and a lecturer at Comenius University in Bratislava, Slovakia.

Routledge Explorations in Development Studies

This Development Studies series features innovative and original research at the regional and global scale. It promotes interdisciplinary scholarly works drawing on a wide spectrum of subject areas, in particular politics, health, economics, rural and urban studies, sociology, environment, anthropology, and conflict studies.

Topics of particular interest are globalization; emerging powers; children and youth; cities; education; media and communication; technology development; and climate change.

In terms of theory and method, rather than basing itself on any orthodoxy, the series draws broadly on the toolkit of the social sciences in general, emphasizing comparison, the analysis of the structure and processes, and the application of qualitative and quantitative methods.

Learning and Forgetting in Development NGOs
Insights from Organisational Theory
Tiina Kontinen

Information Communication Technology and Poverty Alleviation
Promoting Good Governance in the Developing World
Jack J. Barry

Valuing Development, Environment and Conservation
Creating Values that Matter
Edited by Sarah Bracking, Aurora Fredriksen, Sian Sullivan and Philip Woodhouse

Engendering Transformative Thinking and Practice in International Development
Gillian Fletcher

New Donors on the Postcolonial Crossroads
Eastern Europe and Western Aid
Tomáš Profant

New Donors on the Postcolonial Crossroads

Eastern Europe and Western Aid

Tomáš Profant

Routledge
Taylor & Francis Group
LONDON AND NEW YORK

First published 2019
by Routledge
2 Park Square, Milton Park, Abingdon, Oxon OX14 4RN

and by Routledge
605 Third Avenue, New York, NY 10017

First issued in paperback 2021

Routledge is an imprint of the Taylor & Francis Group, an informa business

British Library Cataloguing-in-Publication Data
A catalogue record for this book is available from the British Library

Library of Congress Cataloging-in-Publication Data
A catalog record has been requested for this book

ISBN 13: 978-0-367-78677-9 (pbk)
ISBN 13: 978-1-138-39189-5 (hbk)

Typeset in Times New Roman
by Wearset Ltd, Boldon, Tyne & Wear

In memoriam
Zuzana Profantová
(1953–2018)

Contents

Figures

Acknowledgments

This book would not be possible without the academic guidance of Aram Ziai, to whom I am indebted the most. I am also grateful for his moral support and his belief in this project.

I would like to thank all the respondents for granting me the interviews that constitute half of the empirical material. I dedicate this book to them. If anyone of them will take anything from my arguments, then all this work was not in vain. Despite all the critique, I still believe that they deserve our admiration for engaging in what they believe to be helping less fortunate people.

I would like to thank the following friends and colleagues for the discussions with them and for their advice that improved the book in various ways: Ondrej Gažovič, Miša Krenčeyová, David Schlauß, Nina Molčanová, Martin Zuba, Andrej Findor, Michal Cenker, Michal Šimečka, Stephanie Lettner, Pavel Barša, Ondřej Horký-Hlucháň, Vít Beneš, Karlheinz Spitzl, Walter Schicho, Rudolf Fürst, Ondřej Císař, Veronika Siegl, Alexandra Danišová, Juraj Buzalka, Ivan Buraj, Petra Dannecker, Wolfram Schaffar, Ulrich Brand, Elke Christiansen, Michael Obrovsky, Christoph Gütermann, Romana Sládeková, Hana Ovesná, Gerald Hödl, Peter Brezáni, Jan Daniel, Jakub Eberle, Dan Šitera, Jan Blažek, Jan Hrubín, Zuzana Fialová, and Theo van Leeuwen.

I am grateful to my colleagues at the Institute of International Relations in the conference service, Linda Bergerová, Kristýna Tamchynová, Helena Kolátorová, Eva Husáková, Jiří Mach, Lucie Božková, and Petr Burda, for their help and also to all the interns at the Institute who helped me: Salome Szymanowska, Veronika Kurbelová, Tomáš Kolder, Jakub Kuchař, Emilie Curryova, Zachari Kitt, Dina Krestovská, Roman Oeschger, Adéla Jiřičková, Natália Mrvečková, Tereza Antalová, Vladimíra Dostálová, Jakub Imrich, Pavel Meszároš, Marcela Cimflová, David Navrátil, Veronika Habálová, Jane Ho, Yevgeniya Soldatova, and Karolína Lískovcová.

I would also like to thank Kamil Ivanko, Ondrej Kusý, and Jana Fecenková for helping me with the interview transcriptions.

Finally, this book would not be possible without the moral and material support of my parents, Zuzana Profantová and Milan Profant. Thank you.

This output was realized with the financial support from the Czech Science Foundation within the framework of the project 18–21864S Mainstream and Alternative Economic Discourses in Czechia and Slovakia.

Acronyms

ADA	Austrian Development Agency
BMEIA	Federal Ministry for Europe, Integration and Foreign Affairs
BMF	Ministry of Finance
CARE	Cooperative for Assistance and Relief Everywhere
CDA	Critical Discourse Analysis
CEE	Central and Eastern Europe
CEO	Chief Executive Officer
CGD	Center For Global Development
CIDA	Canadian International Development Agency
CONCORD	European NGO Confederation for Relief and Development
CSR	Corporate Social Responsibility
DAC	Development Assistance Committee
ERP	European Recovery Program
EU	European Union
FCS	Foundation for Civil Society
FDI	Foreign Direct Investment
G7	Group of Seven
GDP	Gross Domestic Product
GNI	Gross National Income
HDI	Human Development Index
HoC IDC	House of Commons International Development Committee
ICT	Information and Communications Technology
IFI	International Financial Institutions
IMF	International Monetary Fund
INGOs	International Non-Governmental Organizations
IO	International Organization
IT	Information Technology
LDC	Least Developed Countries
LIC	Low-Income Countries
MDGs	Millennium Development Goals
MFA	Ministry of Foreign Affairs
MFEA	Ministry of Foreign and European Affairs
MZV SR	Ministry of Foreign Affairs of the Slovak Republic

NDC	Ngorongoro District Council
NDDP	Ngorongoro District Development Programme
NGDO	Non-Governmental Development Organization
NGO	Non-Governmental Organization
NIEO	New International Economic Order
NRSR	National Council of the Slovak Republic
ODA	Official Development Assistance
OECD	Organisation for Economic Co-operation and Development
OEEC	Organization for European Economic Cooperation
ÖFSE	Austrian Foundation for Development Research
PCD	Policy Coherence for Development
PDCS	Partners for Democratic Change Slovakia
PiP	People in Peril
PIPA	Program on International Policy Attitudes
PMVRO	Slovak NGDO Platform
PORLAG	President's Office, Regional Administration and Local Government
PR	Public Relations
SAIDC	Slovak Agency for International Development Cooperation
SAMRS	Slovak Agency for International Development Cooperation
SAP	Structural Adjustment Program
TED	Technology, Entertainment, Design
UK	United Kingdom
UN	United Nations
UNDP	United Nations Development Programme
UNESCO	United Nations Educational, Scientific and Cultural Organization
VSLA	Village Savings and Loan Association
WB	World Bank
WHO	World Health Organization

1 Introduction

On the postcolonial crossroads

Are we still the children of postcommunism? This metaphor for the relation between the East and the West after 1989, which was used by Buden (2010), still haunts this relation. The people living in Eastern Europe were turned from resistance heroes into pupils who needed to be taught how to live in a liberal democracy. The teaching was to be done by the adults who already had the experience. The policy of development aid was no exception to this pattern, and the general hierarchy between the children of postcommunism and their teachers infused this field as well. Both groups were to be donors but not quite in the same way.

The postcolonial critique of development discourse has been mainstreamed during the last decade. More than 30 years after Arturo Escobar (1984) published his first article on development discourse and thereby introduced the postcolonial approach to development studies, the main tenets of postcolonialism can be found in most of the development studies textbooks (Ziai 2017). A whole subfield focused on representations and unequal relations between the Global North and the Global South emerged in recent years. It constitutes an important part of critical development studies.

However, this subfield is incomplete. Its focus on the hierarchy between the donors and their partners or recipients does not include an important postcolonial dimension within development cooperation – the hierarchy among donors. These are ranked as well and this ranking reflects Oriental stereotypes that one may find within development cooperation.

The main aim of this book is to focus on the Orientalist hierarchy among donors and to point to an important gap in the existing postcolonial research within development studies. This gap is also indicative of an unexpected Orientalism within the anti-Orientalist postcolonial critique. The narrow focus on the relation between the Global North and the Global South neglects the nuances of the racialized relations within the Global North (and possibly also within the Global South). These nuances are addressed in this book.

Already in 2010, the then Chairperson of the Slovak Non-Governmental Development Organization Platform, Nora Beňáková, spoke of Slovakia as "one of the *relatively* new donors" (Beňáková 2010: 4, italics by TP). When I asked her why she used the adverb "relatively" she responded that "in general people talk about new EU member countries as 'new donors'; today this is a relative term, as a certain period of time has already passed since our entry into the EU and the OECD" (Beňáková 2013).[1]

Is Slovakia a new donor? Beňáková questioned the term new because in 2010 enough time had already passed for the label "new donor" to possibly no longer be in use. How long can a state be called new in one particular field of public policy? How much time needs to pass in order for a state to catch up with those labeled as old? And are these the right questions to ask?

The distinction in age can be connected with knowledge – the elders are wise, and the youngsters need to learn. Knowledge in turn is connected with power. The elders know the truth about the world and therefore should be followed. Thus, those who have the right to produce knowledge are in a more powerful position than those who are supposed to receive and accept knowledge. There are numerous ways development cooperation could be conducted, but the representation of certain actors as experienced and other actors as inexperienced endows the experienced ones with the power to decide what constitutes the right knowledge – the truth – in development cooperation.

But "the truth isn't outside power" (Foucault 1980: 131). On the contrary, "it induces regular effects of power" (ibid.). The alleged age difference between donors thus translates into a power difference between them. The knowledge produced by particular actors represents their perspective, and if endowed with the power of truthfulness, it may lead to a universalization of their particular perspective. Knowledge can thus have effects in terms of power on the subjects who succumb to it.

The powerful distinction between old and new donors fits well with the Orientalist discourse between East and West. Development cooperation is on the same East–West slope (Melegh 2006) as other policy fields. The societies in the East lack in education, health care, rule of law, social systems, infrastructure, environmental protection, economic performance or technological advancement. Development cooperation is just yet another field in which the Eastern societies lag behind the West.

At the same time the Orientalist slope slides further to the South. Just as the East is inferior to the West, so is the South inferior to the North. The same set of binary dichotomies that constitute the relation between East and West can be applied to the relation between what some still call the developed and the developing world. One of the main differences between the two dichotomies – East–West and North–South – is in the field of development cooperation. Whereas the countries on both sides of the former Iron Curtain are donors, the Global South is defined, among other things, by its position as a recipient of ODA.

The well-known vertical division between North and South is thus complemented with a slope between East and West. The connection between these two axes is development cooperation with its origins in the colonial period. This cooperation constitutes the postcolonial crossroads (see Figure 1.1). It is based, on the one hand, on aid (cooperation) and, on the other, on development. Development ranks countries according to various indices, most prominently the already mentioned World Bank ranking based on the GDP per capita indicator

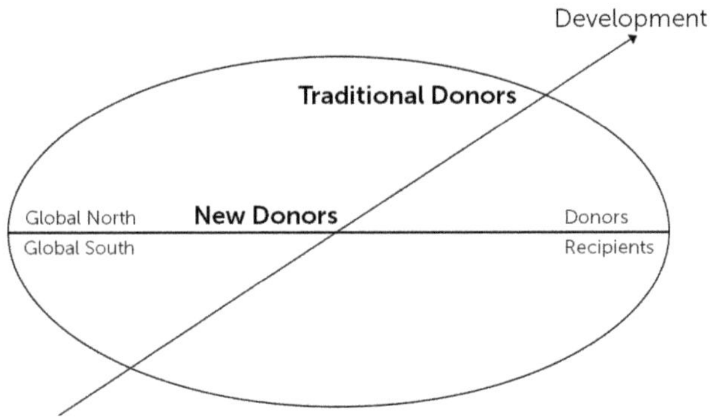

Figure 1.1 The postcolonial crossroads.

and the United Nations' Human Development Index (HDI) based on education, life expectancy and economic performance. These indices create the general difference between all the countries and the societies living in these countries in the world. Official development assistance offers a more rigid indicator – those who give are developed, and those who receive are not yet developed or are underdeveloped.

Development cooperation thus serves as a confirmation that some of the countries from the East belong to the Global North, among the so-called developed countries. This cooperation, however, has another effect. By distinguishing between old and new donors, it confirms the World Bank and UN rankings and divides the donors according to their alleged level of experience. This division complements other fields of public policy in which the East is somehow new, undergoing a transformation in which it has not yet reached the level of the West.

This postcolonial crossroads is the topic of this book. The aim is to use the lenses of postcolonial theory in order to see the continuity of the colonial discourse into the current period in the development discourse in the relation between the Global North and the Global South and in the relation between the East and the West.

In the following I argue that there is such a substantial similarity between Slovakia and Austria as donors that their differentiation into old and new donors is problematic and so is the general old-new donor distinction. Building on this argument I propose several possible divisions of donors that would overcome the current Orientalist distinction based on age.

The next section shows how the postcolonial analysis of the development discourse constitutes the basis for the comparison of new and old donors' development apparatuses in this book. After that the choice of the national development apparatuses and the choice of the analyzed actors are explained. Finally, in the last section an overview of the book is provided.

The comparison and the analysis

The postcolonial crossroads is explored in the book through the analysis of the Slovak and Austrian (i.e., old and new donors') development apparatuses and through their comparison. The comparison focuses on the West–East dimension and is based on an analysis of the North–South relation. The research question stems from this double aim: What kinds of development representations do Slovak and Austrian governmental and non-governmental development actors offer to the public, and what is the difference between them in this regard?

The comparison, as well as the underlying analysis, is informed by the postcolonial and postdevelopment theories. The analysis uses the main analytical concepts derived from these theories – hierarchization of "us" over "them," depoliticization of unequal power relations and legitimization of development. These concepts make it possible to show the ambivalence of the development discourse as opposite representations are also present in the discourse. Deliberate positivism in relation to "them" counters the hierarchizaition of "us" over "them," politicization of unequal power relations counters depoliticization of these relations, and delegitimization of development counters its legitimization. The Slovaks and Austrians offer similar representations in each of these categories, but still differ to some extent, and the aim of this book is to show the similarity as well as the difference. The analysis of discourse is complemented with a comparison of more material elements of the Austrian and Slovak development apparatuses in Chapter 2.

The analysis of both national discourses should contribute to what Arturo Escobar began in 1984 with his first article on development discourse, which introduced the postcolonial approach to development studies. An empirical research on how NGOs and state development agencies follow or deviate from the main tenets of development discourse will move forward the postcolonial analysis within the field of development studies.

The postcolonial critique of the mainstream development perspective is still in need of empirical examination. One is compelled to ask the following questions: to what extent and in what ways is Orientalism still present in the development discourse, or to what extent is Orientalism fought by the producers of this discourse (Said 1979)? How are the subalterns silenced through the development discourse, and how does this discourse enable them to speak (Spivak 1994)? And how are the Austrian and Slovak actors embodying hybrid identities of being developed and at the same time being aware of the problems related to the Western development model that reverses development rankings (Bhabha 2004)? These questions need to be asked, and empirical evidence is required in order to answer them. The postcolonial approach will thus be enriched through the proposed research by a rigorous empirical investigation embedded in the Foucauldian analytical framework.

Escobar has been criticized for offering a "singular" or "monolithic" representation of development discourse (e.g., Cooper and Packard 1997: 10). Agreeing with this argument (Escobar 2000), he states that there indeed are breaks, fissures, or cracks in discourses, and the discourse of development is no exception. It would go against the original aim of suspending "the pre-existing forms of continuity" (Foucault 2002: 28) if one rejected the possibility of discontinuity in a discursive formation empirically constructed by him – or herself. Since the hegemony is never complete, the discourse is inherently incoherent. Yet nowadays the development discourse is more incoherent than in the past (Ziai 2014).

The book examines just how incoherent this discourse is and does so within three already mentioned categories – hierarchization, depoliticization and legitimation – and within three discourse strands – sustainable development, education in development and microfinance. One of the theoretical contributions of the proposed book lies in the discussion of the necessarily incoherent nature of a discourse and the empirical investigation of this incoherence. The three discourse strands have been chosen as generally rather important parts of the overall development discourse and at the same time as particular sectors of development practice in which the analyzed actors are engaged. This enables their comparison.

In order for me to engage in empirical research the rules of formation from Foucault's *Archaeology of Knowledge* are used as the basic methodological concepts. They guide an important part of the research process. The question of how objects, enunciative modalities, concepts, and strategies are formed within the discourse enables me to identify the instances at which the development actors follow or do not follow the rules of formation. These are of great interest to the critical development studies perspective, as they offer space for proposing emancipatory changes inside or outside of the development discourse.

Foucault's *Archaeology* has been chosen due to its overarching approach in relation to a discourse, which is understood in a more complex way than just a text. Defined as "practices that systematically form the objects of which they speak" (Foucault 2002: 55), discourses are more than signs. It is this more that must be revealed and described (ibid.). The rules of formation focus not only on the way concepts, theories or arguments are formed by the rules of formation, but also on how particular objects appear as objects, who is authorized to speak within a discourse, and from which position, and also on the function "that the discourse under study must carry out in a field of non-discursive practices" (ibid.: 75). All these analytical tools make Foucault's approach more useful than the narrower, even if more practical, approaches that one may find within analytical methods focused on discourses.

The lack of clarity in terms of the practical conduct of the analysis in Foucault's complex *Archaeology* is remedied by the use of the much more concrete Critical Discourse Analysis as formulated by van Leeuwen, who is focused on agency rather than structure and whose approach is based on a detailed linguistic analysis (Wodak and Meyer 2009: 22).

The term Critical in Critical Discourse Analysis also represents the basis of my own ethical stance. Foucault has been criticized by his opponents for his "relativism" (Habermas 1987: 279) and "normative confusion" (Fraser 1981). Indeed, his perspective comes very close to the positivist notion of an outsider looking at the world (or discourse) from above and he presents his normative position only occasionally, such as, for example, when he speaks of a left governmentality (Foucault 1988: 11–13). CDA rectifies this problem as the discourse analysts from within this school often make their ethical stances explicit. The term Critical comes from the Critical Theory of the Frankfurt School, which has a "concern for the abolition of social injustice" (Horkheimer 2002: 242). The general aim of critiquing and changing society rather than just understanding or explaining it (Wodak and Meyer 2009: 6) is also the aim of this book – to problematize (and, if possible, contribute to a change of) unequal relations not only between the Global North and the Global South, but also between East and West within the field of development cooperation. The ethical stance of the author is to be found within the radical democratic perspective of Laclau and Mouffe (2001; see also Bowles and Gintis 1987; Lummis 1996; Wolin 1981) and within development studies, where he sides with Cowen and Shenton's (1996, 1999) critique of trusteeship.

This approach is in accordance with Foucault's understanding of the role of the intellectual, which is to question what is postulated as self-evident and thereby ascertain "the possibility of constituting new politics of truth" (Foucault 1980: 133). These new politics should be emancipatory for either the subaltern from the Global South or the Orientalized Others in Eastern Europe (see also Profant 2013). These, I hope, could be the ethical and political implications of this research.

The postcolonial approach further contributes to the study with three well known theoretical concepts – Orientalism, hybridity and the subaltern. Orientalism (Said 1979) as a conceptual tool is operationalized into the category hierarchization, which includes a variety of representations. My main concern is the strength of the hierarchy. The weaker the hierarchy, the greater the space that is created for hybridity. Hybridity (Bhabha 2004) serves to problematize the identities of the Northern selves as the respondents show many cracks in the development discourse, casting a clear doubt on their alleged superiority. The research also focuses on who gets to speak and what these actors say in the discourse, thereby engaging with a still pertinent question: can the subaltern speak (Spivak 1994)? The operationalization of Spivak's question is based on the institutional sites from which the actors speak, on the positions of the speaking actors in terms of power and on the content of what they say.

The research thus fits among similar analyses of discourses that focused on different corpora of different sizes and used similar methods with differing amounts of rigor (see, e.g., Noxolo 2006; Ziai 2004; Dogra 2014; Eriksson Baaz 2005; Goudge 2003).

The critical perspective on the East–West relation is based on the postcolonial approach as well. Following earlier studies criticizing the (post)colonial nature of this relation (e.g., Wolf 1994; Melegh 2006; Todorova 2009; Zarycki 2014; Bakić-Hayden 1995), this book extends the analysis of Orientalism to *demi-Orientalism* (Wolf 1994) or *Balkanism* (Todorova 2009), both of which depart from Said's (and Abdel-Malek's [1963]) groundbreaking insights.

The hierarchy between the West and Said's Orient differs from the hierarchy between Western and Eastern Europe or that between the West and the Balkans. Both Eastern Europe and the Balkans have been considered a bridge or a crossroads between the West and the actual Orient. Eastern Europe was paradoxically constructed through its simultaneous inclusion and exclusion as an entity that was supposed to mediate between Europe and the Orient (Wolf 1994: 7). If the Orient was considered uncivilized, Eastern Europe and the Balkans were considered semi-civilized, semi-Oriental, and even semi-developed (Todorova 2009: 16).

It is this special place of Eastern Europe that fits well with Bhabha's expression of the colonial mimicry as the Other, who, in the case of Eastern Europe, is never completely different; this Other becomes almost the same but not quite (Bhabha 2004: 122). The ambiguity of the Orientalist discourse gains another dimension by creating an East–West slope (Melegh 2006). Postcommunist countries have become "almost the same" in terms of becoming donors, but "not quite" as they are still not quite full-fledged donors and therefore still keep the label "new."

I will try to point to the power relation behind the new-donor/old-donor distinction in development cooperation and problematize this distinction on the basis of my research (on this topic see also Oprea 2012; Drążkiewicz-Grodzicka 2013; Horký-Hlucháň 2015). The aim will be to consider the idea of dispensing with the old-new distinction. This may contribute to a discussion on the way power works within this discourse.

More specifically, I will try to contribute to the current thinking about development discourse with the introduction of one specific postcolonial dimension. Whereas the critical development studies focus on the North–South postcolonial dimension, they often miss the East–West postcolonial dimension. The new donors subfield of development studies occasionally offers a critical perspective on the postcolonial East–West relation, but does not do so through a postcolonial comparison focused on the North–South relations. This North–South – East–West double postcolonial analytical connection is the core contribution of the book to the field of development studies. These two basic postcolonial geographic dichotomies create the postcolonial crossroads that is exposed within the development cooperation of the new donors.

Therefore, the research is unique not only within the general field of development studies, but also within the new donors sub-field. So far there has not been any attempt to compare the new – post-communist – donors with the old – Western – donors. The new donors have generally been analyzed as a group (see, e.g., Szent-Iványi and Lightfoot 2015) or separately (see, e.g., Horký-Hlucháň and Lightfoot 2013, 2015), but there is no rigorous comparative study of old and new donors.

It should also be mentioned that different theoretical approaches inspired the researchers who focus on the new donors. One approach is focused on Europeanization and there is a normative position toward the relationship between donors. European Union norms are perceived in a positive way as contributing to poverty reduction and development in the Global South, and at the same time CEE donors are represented as being on the path to reaching the qualities of traditional donors, but without having done so yet. According to two representatives of this approach: "These new international development policies however are still rather in their infancy in terms of both quantity and quality, and thus are difficult to compare with the policies of leading established donors such as the UK or Sweden" (Szent-Iványi and Tétényi 2013: 819–820). At the beginning of a more serious engagement with the new donors an optimism was expressed in relation to Europeanization: "Spain is now a significant aid donor and optimists hope that in the future a country like Poland or the Czech Republic could follow suit" (Lightfoot 2008: 140). The new donors were to become "mature" (Lightfoot 2010: 347). In these cases the potentially Orientalist hierarchy between old and new donors is openly expressed and accepted. Some authors even seem to have gone through a period of self-reflection, having written about the new donors within the Europeanization paradigm (Horký 2010) and then discussed the matter from the postcolonial perspective (Horký-Hlucháň 2015: 10), claiming that this approach contains an underlying 'development ladder' associable to the 'East–West slope' and arguing that "these different identities give higher legitimacy to the Western models and influence policy-making in Central and Eastern Europe" (ibid.).

The seemingly neutral approach that analyzes the progress in achieving the fulfilment of European norms among the new donors is thus normatively clearly anchored in the positive understanding of these norms. The actual normativity of any approach is not problematic, but from a poststructuralist perspective it is considered as an inevitable result of the way our societies function. One cannot be normatively neutral.

The academic response to the normative orientation of Europeanization research is the more recent research that questions the division of donors. It questions the linearity of development not only in the relationship between the Global North represented by the CEE donors and the Global South (see Fecenková 2013; Pavlicová 2012; Horký 2011; HorkýHluchář 2015; Profant 2010, 2015), but also in the hierarchic relationship between old and new (CEE) donors (Oprea 2012; Drążkiewicz-Grodzicka 2013).

This book is, to a certain extent, a response to the already mentioned argument that old and new donors are difficult to compare (Szent-Iványi and Tétényi 2013: 820) and puts forth an argument that such a comparison is necessary to show the particular normativity of the very distinction that allegedly makes the comparison impossible. The comparison is made from the postcolonial perspective and enters the (rather unspoken) debate between the Europeanization approach and the postcolonial approach.

As such the book is part of a wider scholarship. Not only does it belong to the already mentioned postcolonial approach within development studies that focuses on the North–South relations and within the postcolonial approach that focuses on the East–West relations, but it also belongs to the emerging field that focuses on the new donors that, apart from the CEE donors, also include countries such as China, India, or Brazil, and questions the hierarchy between old and new donors (see, e.g., Mawdsley 2012; Woods 2008; Oh-Seok and Arnold 2010).

This book should be a contribution to this literature. However, it should be noted here that the challenging of the Orientalist hierarchy need not be on the agenda of CEE development workers. As already two reviewers (see Profant 2018) pointed out to me, they may accept and even welcome European (or OECD) norms within development cooperation. This book does not provide empirical material to prove or refute such a claim (even though I encountered CEE development workers complaining about the hierarchy between NGDOs from old donor countries and themselves). The stronger declaratory resistance against old colonial ways of doing things connected with the Western donors among, e.g., Indian and Chinese state representatives (see Eyben and Savage 2012) can be present to a much lesser degree among (self-)Orientalized CEE development workers. Their acceptance of inferiority can also be based on the capacity to engage in "shallow Europeanization" (Horký 2012a) and other types of resistance such as low financial commitments (Profant 2018) or even on the promotion of their own interests as respected norms in regard to the European soft law – e.g., the norm of effectiveness and coordination that enables CEE donors to focus within development cooperation on the neighbourhood countries that also belong to their national interest (ibid.).

The "actual" relation between old and new donors is a complex one and the data from this research only make it possible to challenge the very distinction between them. The basis of the specificity of these socially constructed groups of donors needs to be questioned.

A similar argument to the one made about Europeanization research can be made about research focused on the transition experience (Hanšpach 2004; Szent-Iványi and Tétényi 2008). This experience is in general perceived in a positive light as something that should be exported. The postcommunist donors allegedly have a very specific knowledge in several fields and are in a position to provide this knowledge to those below them on the development ladder. One can read about Slovakia being able to share its experience with health sector transformation, social and economic reforms, infrastructure building, civil society development, good governance, and rule of law (see Profant 2018). Slovakia has experience to offer in all these fields. The quality of the experience that makes it suitable for export has a discursive effect of perceiving the Slovak transition experience as positive. The export of the transition experience through development cooperation contributes to the image of a problematic, totalitarian communist past and its binary opposite – a present that managed to achieve positive results on its developmental way to the traditional Western-type democracy. It should be noted that mistakes are often admitted to, even if to a considerably lesser extent in official documents. However, the overall effect of the transition experience discourse remains an ideological support for the current regime. Again, this book is a critical intervention into this type of literature as it problematizes the whole concept of development, whose Orientalist basis contributes to the perception that there is an ideal to which a transition can lead and that there are other states which can be helped by less developed donors like Slovakia. A non-Orientalist perspective on donors and recipients alike casts a doubt on the meaningfulness of the idea that the postcommunist donors should always be in the position of exporting their transition experience rather than being in a position in which they can learn from the recipient or teach other donors.

Overall, my aim is to build on research informed by postcolonial and post-structuralist perspectives (Drążkiewicz-Grodzicka 2013, 2015; Oprea 2012; Horký 2011, 2012b; Gažovič and Profant 2015; Profant 2018, 2015). I share many assumptions with the authors of this research and hope to contribute to this small subfield by offering a comparison of an old and a new donor, which so far has not been attempted.

Why Slovakia and Austria?

It is legitimate to ask why Austria should represent the old donors and why Slovakia should represent the new donors. The first point to be made is that both countries are perfectly legitimate representatives of the respective groups. There is little doubt that Austrian development workers perceive Austria as belonging among the traditional DAC donors and that Slovak development workers perceive Slovakia as part of the group of post-communist or Eastern and Central European new donors.

As the quote in the beginning of the introduction from the former NGDO Platform director shows, however, the perspective that these donors are also new may be crumbling. Still, the division of donors into groups is accepted in general and so are the positions of Austria in one group and Slovakia in another.

The actual choice of donors that enabled a more detailed analysis should therefore not be considered of great importance. Yet, there were reasons to choose these two particular actors and they stem from J. S. Mill's method of difference (also known as the most similar systems design, see, e.g., Gerring 2008; George and Bennet 2005) as this is the most suitable method for the aim of problematizing the current differentiation of donors into old and new ones rather than making a much stronger argument, e.g., that all donors are the same and there should be no differentiation between them at all.

The method of difference focuses on very similar cases with different outcomes – in this case the allocations of two similar donors to two different particular groups of donors (an outcome that could be considered a dependent variable). The aim of this book is to compare Austria and Slovakia, and the result of this comparison is the finding that there is a great similarity between the two donors, which begs the question of why should they be put into different groups. In more positivist terms, if the dependent variables are the same, why is the independent variable not the same as well? I refrain from going one step further to empirically look for the one independent variable that determines the allocation of the donors. The postcolonial perspective has an answer as this should be the Orientalist perspective that perceives the world as hierarchically divided into the West and the East, and development cooperation simply follows this division. However, this suggestion goes one step further than the actual empirical analysis conducted here. I merely aim at problematizing the existing division.

So, what are the reasons for choosing Austria and Slovakia – what makes them look similar and therefore suitable for a comparison while we have the already mentioned research question in mind? Both Slovakia and Austria are somewhat peculiar in their respective groups of donors. With regard to the peculiarity of Slovakia as a new donor, one of the arguments of some of the abovementioned books and articles is that quite a few of the new donors have a history of international aid during the communist era (see, e.g., Oprea 2012; Horký-Hluchâň 2015: 7; Szent-Iványi and Lightfoot 2015: 1). Czechoslovakia was one of the more active donors of that period, and its aid at the time was much greater than today (Mesík 2012: 182), not only in terms of the number of recipient countries, but also in the amount of aid. In the 1980s, Czechoslovak aid was received by 124 countries, including Vietnam, Cuba, Ethiopia, and Libya (Benč 2005: 75; Brzica 2002: 107), and the provided sum was from "0.7–0.9% [of the] GDP" (Szép 2004: 10). "[The f]ormer Czechoslovakia thus belonged among the biggest donors" (Szép 2004). Czechoslovakia engaged in the usual aid projects of the period as it built elementary schools in the recipient countries, provided help with irrigation, provided technical gear and engineers, etc. (Benč 2005: 75; Brzica 2002: 107). There is no discussion between academics about whether Czechoslovakia was or was not a donor before 1989. This is clearly accepted. However, it is equally accepted that Slovakia is a new donor.

What arguments can be used to support the claim that Slovakia is a new donor despite its history? One may say that the tradition of international aid during socialism has been lost, and therefore the new character of the Slovak development cooperation is, in general, accepted in the Slovak development apparatus (Profant 2018). The question then is, what can be said about the path-dependency of the international aid of the formerly socialist donors?

The argument that there is a path-dependency connected to the communist past may apply to the Czech Republic (Horký-Hluchâň 2015), but the corresponding path-dependency might be more difficult to decipher in the Slovak case. This should make it easier for Slovaks to Europeanize, as the research on the geographical disbursement of aid seems to suggest (Szent-Iványi 2012). However, more recent research problematizes the use of the Europeanization concept in new donors research (Horký-Hluchâň 2015; Drążkiewicz-Grodzicka 2015), and also more recent data shows difficulties in dealing with the concept (Gažovič and Profant 2015). Slovakia behaves as other CEE donors, sending ODA mainly to European countries. Indeed, the question becomes, what is Europeanization? Still Slovakia is in a peculiar position of having a history of international aid while at the same time being less path dependent than, e.g., the Czech Republic. Its "newness" therefore seems to be more authentic and makes Slovakia more of an outlier and therefore a more suitable candidate for a comparison with an old donor that could question the old-new distinction. Slovakia seems to be less of a new donor with a different tradition of international aid and more of a new Europeanized donor.

Austria is also a peculiar member of the old donors group. It is not one of the countries with a strong colonial heritage, nor is it a trend-setter in development policy such as the Netherlands or Denmark. Being a follower, Austria is still recognized as one of the old donors, yet at the same time it might be considered an outlier in several dimensions and therefore more apt for a comparison that could question the analyzed distinction between old and new donors. As the next chapter shows, Austria lags in many ways behind other traditional donors. For example, in the part of the Commitment to Development Index that assesses the quality and quantity of aid, Austria is one of the worst performing old donors (18th out of 27 in the DAC OECD; CGD 2018).

The difference from traditional donors may bring Austria close to the non-traditional donors. Their geographical closeness and their similar geopolitical interests show that Slovakia and Austria as donors may have more in common than Austria and other traditional donors. The similar histories of the two countries are further explored in the next chapter. The distinction between old and new donors thus may be questioned on the basis of a very practical similarity in issues directly related to development cooperation. A group of donors with a focus on neighbouring European countries, either in the Balkans or in the Eastern Partnership, might offer a better way of distinguishing among donors. The aim here is not to claim that, for example, there should be a group of Central European donors because these have common interests within the field of development cooperation, but merely to problematize the seemingly natural distinction between old and new donors based on age and show that this distinction could be replaced if different criteria were applied. As the research shows, an analysis of Austria and Slovakia enables such a critical perspective.

The politics of labeling is an important feature of power relations in any public policy field. The differentiation of donors is no exception. The most common label for donors, which is also used in the title of this book, is "new donors" as opposed to "old donors." This category includes all non-DAC donors and Czechia, Slovakia and Poland from DAC. "The non-DAC donors" could also be used as a label just like narrower labels such as CEE donors, emerging donors, Gulf donors, etc.

One of the basic arguments of this book is that there is no label that could be considered the correct one. All labels have their normative connotations and all are based on power relations. Simply put, all are the result of the politics of labeling. Szent-Iványi and Lightfoot (2015) opt for the label East Central European donors to cover the Czech Republic, Slovakia, Poland, Hungary, and Slovenia, after discussing the problems related to any geographical term concerning "Central Europe."

They also consider the label EU-13, which, however, covers too many donors and does not suit their analytical purposes. It is this technocratic labeling that is gaining primacy in European institutions. Numbers have the power to disguise political choices and represent issues through technocratic means. There are traces of politics in the EU-13 label, the most obvious being the exclusion of the countries from the 1995 enlargement – Austria, Sweden, and Finland. It seems that the bureaucrats and decision makers are aware of the problems related to the normative labeling that uses words and opt for the seemingly least normative choice – to use numbers.

Whereas the move away from the terms such as backward or underdeveloped to terms such as the Global South or the majoritarian world may be meaningful, as these new terms lose the obvious negative connotations of the previous terms while keeping the distinction in terms of power or wealth, the same attempt in the case of the division of donors may be problematic due to the similarity between the donors. Keeping the distinction between those who, in general, profit and those who lose because of the global division of the world makes it easier to point to the unfair gains of the former. But, keeping the distinction between the EU-15 (or the EU-14 without the UK) and the EU-13 is not only problematic on empirical grounds, as I will argue throughout the book, but, more importantly, it also reproduces an old Orientalist distinction between East and West without using these terms.

The aim here is to destabilize both labels – "old-new" and "EU-13" – and point to the normative Orientalist assumptions that constitute the basis of these labels. The same could apply to the label ECE donors used by Szent-Iványi and Lightfoot. This label should not include Austria, which was never considered a part of Eastern Central Europe. On the other hand, Austria is sometimes considered part of Central Europe and thus could be part of a group of Central European donors. More importantly, how is it so that there is still a need to distinguish ourselves on the basis of the division of the world into East and West? It is much easier to merely criticize the labels that are currently being used, which is the aim of this book. In the following chapters, however, I will also propose a differentiation of donors based on other distinctions that dispense with Orientalism.

The analyzed actors

In the research I analyzed texts and interviews from six institutions: two Slovak NGDOs – the Pontis Foundation and People in Peril (PiP); two Austrian NGDOs – Austroprojekt and CARE Austria; and two state agencies from the two countries – the Slovak Agency for International Development Cooperation (SAIDC) and the Austrian Development Agency (ADA).

The Pontis Foundation was established in 1997. It is a successor of the Foundation for a Civil Society that was founded as Charter 77 New York in January 1990 with offices in New York and Prague. Its goal was "to respond to the needs Czechoslovakia faced as it transitioned to democracy" (FCS n.d.). The Pontis Foundation took over its position in 1997. Pontis' mission is "[t]o motivate individuals, communities and companies to be responsible for themselves and the wider world" (Pontis n.d.).

Pontis has three areas of activity: sustainability of nonprofit organizations; philanthropy and corporate social responsibility; and democratization and development abroad. In the first area they support Slovak non-profit organizations by providing grants, loans, and expert consultancy. In the second they support corporate philanthropy and corporate social responsibility. In this field Pontis works as an actor who administers funds to provide grants to other NGOs in Slovakia and at the same time helps companies with their CSR.

In the third area Pontis behaves as a "normal" non-governmental *development* organization and competes for grants from the government. It engages with the civil society in the non-democratic and transition countries but also works in Kenya in projects such as the educational one that I analyze in this book.

People in Peril is a Slovak NGO that was established in 1999 and is active in the field of humanitarian aid, development cooperation, human rights advocacy, and global education and awareness raising. According to their site, their mission is "to provide effective support to those who suffer the consequences of natural catastrophes, conflicts and authoritarian regimes, [and they also] strive to contribute to forming [an] open, tolerant and solidary society" (PiP 2012a).

People in Peril began their work in the war-stricken Kosovo. In financial terms the most important work they do is in development cooperation. They are active in Kenya, South Sudan, Afghanistan, Moldova, Bosnia and Herzegovina, and several other countries.

People in Peril are thus different from the Pontis Foundation in that they are not as business-oriented. Their Annual Report (PiP 2013) shows this in financial terms as well. Whereas Pontis received from companies 72% of their budget, PiP received from corporate bodies less than 21% of their budget. PiP are much more financially dependent on the state. However, regarding the development cooperation sections, there is not much of a difference as in both organizations these sections are supported mainly by the state. I interviewed five relevant employees and the director of Pontis and four relevant employees from PiP. These respondents represented almost all members of these two NGDOs who deal with development cooperation.

The reason for choosing Pontis and PiP is their salience in the Slovak non-governmental sphere. They are both well known and often present in the media, where they get much more attention than other NGDOs. Another reason was the focus on microfinance and sustainable development in the case of PiP and the focus on education in the case of Pontis that made a comparison with the Austrian actors possible.

Austroprojekt GmbH used to be a company. Since then, however, its owners and employees from that period retired. It started in 1962 as part of Austrovieh, an Austrian company specialized in pure breed livestock exportation (Austrovieh n.d.; see also Developmentaid.org n.d.). Later, in the 1980s, the company focused on rural development, including sustainable agriculture, decentralization, the promotion of small and medium artisan enterprises, public health services, and water management (Developmentaid.org n.d.).

In 1995, Austroprojekt took over all running projects from the development department of Austrovieh. However, Austroprojekt did not become an NGO, but remained a company owned by, among other people, its CEO, Christoph Gütermann, and its managing director, Wolfgang Achleitner. According to Gütermann, they worked in the for-profit framework because they were used to it in Austrovieh and also because "it was easier in some respects with taxes" (Gütermann 2014a). There were five to six people working for Austroprojekt in Vienna and many other local employees in the recipient countries. Gütermann claims that since 2004 "there were less and less projects and now there are almost no projects of this kind [i.e., ADA projects executed by companies]" (ibid.).

Austroprojekt was thus a company that competed with NGDOs by offering its expertise and consulting services (Obrovsky 2006: 256) and in many ways resembled them. Regarding the development discourse, the fact of Austroprojekt being a company should not in any way make it different from other Austrian NGDOs.

However, it was not possible to find any of Austroprojekt's public relations material. On its website, there were only very short descriptions of its projects without much detail. Articles such as those from CARE, Pontis, or PiP were completely missing. Austroprojekt did not try to educate Austrians or persuade them that they should contribute with a small sum of money. Its main purpose of existence was to conduct projects in the Global South contracted from ADA.

The lack of the PR materials creates the problem of compatibility with the texts from other NGOs, but, on the other hand, it enables an analysis of a greater variety of material. As the results show, however, there is no substantial difference between the two genres. Both types are part of the development discourse. I interviewed only two members of Austroprojekt, as I did not have the chance to talk to any more of its members.

CARE International is one of the largest international NGDOs. It was established in 1945 (as the Cooperative for American Remittances to Europe) in order to deliver packages of food and relief supplies across Europe. After that it changed its focus to help in the Global South (CARE International 2014).

CARE Austria was established in 1986 and since then was active in 50 countries. CARE works towards achieving a world in which poverty is overcome and people live in dignity and security (CARE 2014).

In 2015, 43% of the funds for CARE came from the EU, 39% from private donors, and 18% from domestic public funds (CARE 2016: 24). According to Jaklin, Wank and Wolfram (2013: 8), CARE is in a "situation of being less dependent on governmental support." This gives CARE freedom in "decision-making, especially in choosing its project-countries, although it has to follow the requirements of CARE International" (ibid.), and the authors favorably compare it in this regard to another of the two largest Austrian NGDOs, Horizont 3000, which gets 50.5% of its budget from ADA (Horizont 3000 2014: 29). I interviewed four CARE employees that were selected from within the organization.[2] It was not possible for me to get more interviews, but these were in many ways sufficient in terms of the saturation criterion. There are currently 32 employees working in CARE Austria.

CARE Austria is thus one of the largest Austrian NGDOs and at the same time it is part of an international NGO. The two Austrian actors were chosen on the basis of their different sizes, and CARE Austria was specifically selected with the aim to analyze one NGDO with a somewhat more international character. Just like the two Slovak NGDOs, these two actors are in many other aspects random representatives of the Austrian development discourse at the NGDO level.

The Slovak Agency for International Development Cooperation (SAIDC) was established in 2007 as an administrative and contracting unit of the Ministry of Foreign Affairs. It is responsible for managing, i.e., contracting, the implementation, monitoring, and evaluation of the Slovak development cooperation. Its yearly budget is almost six million euro, which included 5.65 million euro of ODA in 2015 (SAIDC 2016: 32). I interviewed four (i.e., almost all of the) relevant respondents responsible for development cooperation at SAIDC. Altogether, there are 16 employees in SAIDC.

The Austrian Development Agency (ADA) was established in 2004 with similar tasks as SAIDC. Its main difference from SAIDC is in the size of the organization. The yearly budget of ADA in 2015 was around 85 million euro, and the ODA in this year was 74 million euro (ÖFSE 2016: 67). I interviewed five senior employees of ADA, as I was allowed to interview only these five by one of them, who chose the other four and acted as a gatekeeper. Altogether, there are 160 ADA employees working in Vienna (85) and also abroad (75).

The corpus contained various more or less closely analyzed articles. For the more thorough analyses of the selected texts, Leeuwenian Critical Discourse Analysis was used, which included an analysis of social actions and social actors, and an analysis of the discursive constructions of legitimation. I closely analyzed one PR text from Pontis (2010), which focused on education, two from People in Peril (PiP 2009, 2012b), which focused on sustainable development and microfinance, and two from CARE (2006, 2012), which focused on education and microfinance. I also analyzed the Introduction to Austroprojekt's Plan of Operation for the Ngorongoro District Development Programme (NDC-Austroprojekt and Orgut 2002: 4), which focused mainly on sustainable development. Furthermore, I closely analyzed sections of the state three-year strategies that focused on more global relations (MFEA 2013: 4–6; BMEIA 2012: 9–13). In a less detailed manner, by using categories found in the previous analysis, I analyzed all the PR texts I could find on the abovementioned topics from the NGDOs and the state agencies, and the other remaining sections of the three-year strategies, the Plan of Operation and CARE's report "Banking on Change" (Plan UK, CARE International UK and Barclays 2013). Furthermore, I also analyzed articles that one could put into the critical development genre, acts on development cooperation, reports related to Austroprojekt's project and blogs written by the employees of the NGDOs and state agencies that I found. Altogether the corpus included 168 documents.

The findings are based also on an analysis of the semi-structured interviews with employees from all the NGDOs and state agencies that focused on hierarchization, depoliticization, the meaning of development, education, sustainable development, and microfinance. Altogether I interviewed 24 respondents from all six organizations. Furthermore, I analyzed publicly accessible interviews given by the NGDOs' employees, interviews with the respondents that were conducted after they read the first drafts of the chapters, and expert interviews with Austrian scholars, and I occasionally also engaged in personal email communication to clarify particular issues.

A caveat regarding the claim that I focus on Slovak and Austrian development discourses is necessary here. In the case of each of the examined countries, the analysis focuses on three particular actors and their discourses, and it does not deal with the whole national development discourses. Thus, whenever I refer to the Slovak development discourse, I am in fact referring to the discourse of three actors, and the same applies to the Austrian development discourse.

An overview of the book

This book argues that there are differences between Austria and Slovakia as donors, but these are of degree and not of substance. The similarities between them are so great that the division into old and new donors should be questioned. The argument made in this book can also serve to problematize the current distinction that follows the Orientalist East–West slope.

The book is divided into six chapters. Chapter 2 focuses on more material differences between Austria and Slovakia, and the remaining chapters offer an analysis of development discourses organized according to the already mentioned main analytical categories – the hierarchization of "us" over "them" (Chapter 3), the (de)politicization of unequal power relations (Chapter 4), and the (de)legitimization of development (Chapter 5). An analysis shows that mainly the respondents (but also a small number of texts) both follow and disrupt the main tenets of the development discourse.

Chapter 2 focuses on more material issues and provides a comparison of the Austrian and Slovak development apparatuses with regard to these issues. The comparison is concerned with the origins of the respective development apparatuses, the commitment to aid on the side of the governments and on the side of the populations, the relation between the national interest and the regional focus of the Austrian and Slovak ODAs, the non-governmental sphere, and the motivations for development cooperation. The chapter also problematizes the distinction of donors into old and new donors.

Chapter 3 analyzes the hierarchization of "us" over "them." It asks how Austrian actors and Slovak actors hierarchize "us" over "them" and what the differences between the two are in this regard. The chapter focuses on the hierarchy as well as the anti-hierarchic moments in the analyzed texts and interviews. It problematizes the perspective that there is a clear hierarchy between "us" and "them" and shows the various forms of deliberate positivism (Lidchi 1999: 96), of deliberately positive representations of the Other (this is not to be confused with epistemological positivism).

The chapter first shows the basic logocentric pattern and the general law of development in the development discourse and their disruptions and then moves on to show more particular hierarchic representations of "us" and "them" – "our" positive and "their" negative representations and the one-way (inter)actions between "us" and "them." This chapter also asks whether the subaltern can speak, what the institutional site of the speaking actors is and who the speaking actors are, showing again a hierarchy between "us" and "them." Finally, the way power operates in a partnership is analyzed using one particular example.

This chapter also disrupts the hierarchic image of the development discourse with empirical evidence showing that the logocentric pattern and the general law of the development discourse do not always hold. In particular, the various ways deliberate positivism can be enacted are shown as "their" negative representations are softened by several actors, other actors actively fight negative stereotypes, some represent "them" positively both within and outside the development discourse and represent "us" as enabling "their" progress, and some actors put stereotypes into context and refuse to generalize or compare societies. These various forms of deliberate positivism were strongest in an interview with one respondent from CARE Austria that is analyzed in a separate section. The analysis further shows that "they" are represented as learning and sometimes even as knowledgeable actors, and that "they" are represented also through respectable functions and as active actors. The aim of the chapter is to show the positive ways in which the Other is represented in the analyzed texts and interviews. The comparison shows that Slovaks hierarchize more often and in a sharper way than Austrians, but the difference is one of degree and not of substance.

Chapter 4 analyzes depoliticization and politicization of unequal relations of power. The main questions this chapter responds to are the following: in which ways do the analyzed actors politicize and depoliticize unequal relations of power? What is the difference between Slovakia and Austria in this regard? The response to the former lies in the operationalization of depoliticization and politicization that enables the analysis of the various kinds of both practices.

Chapter 4 thus shows a spatial depoliticization that is based on an ignorance of different political and geographical scales through a focus on the local reasons for poverty, local legitimation of development intervention, and local instruments that are supposed to solve the local problems – access to an inherently benign market, microfinance, and education. Depoliticization of unequal power relations is further achieved through technological rather than political solutions, the use of different temporal dimensions, the omission of agents, and an explicit consensus invocation.

The chapter continues by identifying the variety of potential politicizations whose potential is not used. These include politicization through good governance and the Policy Coherence for Development, the problematization of unequal gender relations, and cultural politicization (as well as depoliticization) in archipolitics through education, which analyzes the Global Development Education. The last section of the chapter shows both weaker and stronger types of engagements of the respondents in politicization. This section shows the greatest difference between the Austrians and the Slovaks with regard to (de)politicization. Overall, however, the difference is one of degree and not of substance, and there is almost no difference in the texts with regard to (de)politicization.

Chapter 5 analyzes legitimization and delegitimization of development. The question posed in this chapter is: how are development and development cooperation legitimized and delegitimized? An additional analysis focuses on an explanation of this discursive practice of legitimization and delegitimization, but also of hierarchization and depoliticization. The main form of legitimization is achieved through the positive connotation of the term development, which is understood without having any content or understood as progress or as a higher quality of living, and also through more particular forms of development such as the reduction of poverty. The analysis shows numerous other ways development cooperation is legitimized in the corpus as well. A more critical perspective comes mainly (but not only) from the respondents, as they distance themselves from development by invoking the need for partnership or distinguish between the problematic "real" development and sustainable development by criticizing Westernization and environmental issues.

Overall, the comparison between Austria and Slovakia shows a much greater similarity between them than the division of donors into old and new suggests and thereby questions this normative division. The conclusion then summarizes the results and offers a tentative explanation for them.

Notes

1 I would like to kindly ask the reader to consider the terms "new," "old," and "development" to be within inverted commas throughout the text as these terms are contested. In order not to annoy the reader I drop the commas.

2 One of them, who focuses on microfinance, is a member of CARE International and is a head of CARE in one African country, was recommended to me as a better fit to discuss the issue of microfinance.

Bibliography

Abdel-Malek, Anouar 1963: Orientalism in Crisis. *Diogenes* 11(44), 103–140.

Austrovieh n.d.: austrovieh - Die Geschichte, www.austrovieh.com/infoseiten/ueber-uns/geschichte.html.

Bakić-Hayden, Milica 1995: Nesting Orientalisms: The Case of Former Yugoslavia. *Slavic Review* 54(4), 917–931, doi:10.2307/2501399.

Beňáková, Nora 2010: SlovakAid – an Unemployed Foreign Policy Tool. *International Issues and Slovak Foreign Policy Affairs* 19(3), 3–22.

Beňáková, Nora 2013: Personal email correspondence.

Benč, Vladimír 2005: Ekonomické aspekty rozvojovej pomoci. *Rozvojová pomoc a spolupráca*. Prešov: Slovenská spoločnosť pre zahraničnú politiku, 64–87.

Bhabha, Homi 2004: *Location of Culture*. London and New York: Routledge.

BMEIA 2012: Three-Year Programme on Austrian Development Policy 2013–2015. Federal Ministry for European and International Affairs, Directorate-General for

Development Cooperation, www.entwicklung.at/fileadmin/user_upload/Dokumente/Publikationen/3_JP/Englisch/2013-2015_3-YP.pdf.

Bowles, Samuel and Gintis, Herbert 1987: *Democracy and Capitalism. Property, Community, and the Contradictions of Modern Social Thought*. Basic Books.

Brzica, Daneš 2002: Slovensko v medzinárodnom systéme rozvojovej spolupráce. *Rozvojová pomoc a spolupráca*. Bratislava: Slovenský inštitút medzinárodných štúdií, 107–120.

Buden, Boris 2010: Children of postcommunism. *Radical Philosophy*, 159, January–February, 18–25.

CARE 2006: CARE: AIDS bewirkt Bildungsmissstände. CARE, www.care.at/news/presseaussendungen/care-aids-bewirkt-bildungsmissstaende/.

CARE 2012: Ein Dorf zieht an einem Strang. CARE, www.care.at/news/news/ein-dorf-zieht-an-einem-strang/.

CARE 2014: Über CARE. CARE Österreich, www.care.at/ueber-care.

CARE 2016: Annual Report 2015. CARE Österreich, www.care.at/wp-content/uploads/2015/12/care_jb_15_e_final.pdf.

CARE International 2014: CARE's History, www.care-international.org/who-we-are-1/cares-history.

Cooper, Frederick and Packard, Randall 1997: Introduction. In: Cooper, Frederick and Packard, Randall (ed.): *International development and the social sciences: essays on the history and politics of knowledge*. Berkeley, Los Angeles and London: University of California Press, 1–41.

Cowen, Michael P. and Shenton, Robert W. 1996: *Doctrines of development*. London and New York: Routledge.

Cowen, Michael P. and Shenton, Robert W. 1999: The Invention of Development. In: Crush, Jonathan (ed.): *Power of Development*. London and New York: Routledge, 25–41.

Developmentaid.org n.d.: *developmentaid.org – organizations*, http://developmentaid.org/view_organization?org_id=2161.

Dogra, Nandita 2014: *Representations of Global Poverty. Aid, Development and International NGOs*. London and New York: I.B. Tauris.

Drążkiewicz-Grodzicka, Elżbieta 2013: From Recipient to Donor: The Case of Polish Developmental Cooperation. *Human Organization* 72(1), 65–75.

Drążkiewicz-Grodzicka, Elżbieta 2015: Poland: Attempts at Defining Aid by Solidarity, Democracy and Development. In: Horký-Hlucháň, Ondřej and Lightfoot, Simon (ed.): *Development Cooperation of the 'New' EU Member States. Beyond Europeanization*. Basingstoke and New York: Palgrave Macmillan, 43–63.

Eriksson Baaz, Maria 2005: *The Paternalism of Partnership: a Postcolonial Reading of Identity in Development Aid*. London: Zed Books.

Escobar, Arturo 1984: Discourse and Power in Development: Michel Foucault and the Relevance of his Work to the Third World. *Alternatives: Global, Local, Political* 10(3), 377–400.

Escobar, Arturo 2000: Beyond the Search for a Paradigm? Post-Development and Beyond. *Development* 43(4), 11–14.

Eyben, Rosalind and Savage, Laura 2012: Emerging and Submerging Powers: Imagined Geographies in the New Development Partnership at the Busan Fourth High Level Forum. *Journal of Development Studies*, 49(4), 457–469, doi:10.1080/00220388.2012.733372.

FCS (n.d.): About Us. The Foundation For A Civil Society, n.d., http://fcsny.org/?page_id=6.

Fecenková, Jana (2013): "Rozvinuté" Slovensko vs. "rozvojová" Afrika. *JeToTak.sk – Blog Kritická Ekonómia*, 22. 8. 2013, http://blog.jetotak.sk/kriticka-ekonomia/2013/08/22/jana-fecenkova-%E2%80%9Erozvinute%E2%80%9C-slovensko-vs-%E2%80%9Erozvojova%E2%80%9C-afrika/.
Foucault, Michel 1980: *Power/Knowledge: Selected Interviews and Other Writings 1972–1977. ed. Colin Gordon*. New York: Pantheon Books.
Foucault, Michel 1988: Power, Moral Values, and the Intellectual (interview with Michael Bess). *History of the Present* 4(Spring), 1–2, 11–13.
Foucault, Michel 2002: *Archaeology of Knowledge*. London: Routledge.
Fraser, Nancy 1981: Foucault on Modern Power: Empirical Insights and Normative Confusions. *PRAXIS International* 1(3), 272–287.
Gažovič, Ondrej and Profant, Tomáš 2015: Slovakia: A Donor Against its Will? In: Horký-Hluchááň, Ondřej and Lightfoot, Simon (ed.): *Development Cooperation of the 'New' EU Member States. Beyond Europeanization*. Basingstoke and New York: Palgrave Macmillan, 64–81.
George, Alexander L. and Bennet, Andrew 2005: *Case Studies and Theory Development in the Social Sciences*. Cambridge and London: MIT Press.
Gerring, John 2008: Case Selection for Case-Study Analysis: Qualitative and Quantitative Techniques. In: Box-Steffensmeier, Janet M., Brady, Henry E. and Collier, David (ed.): *The Oxford Handbook of Political Methodology*, www.oxfordhandbooks.com/view/10.1093/oxfordhb/9780199286546.001.0001/oxfordhb-9780199286546-e-28.
Goudge, Paulette (2003): *The Whiteness of Power: Racism in Third World Development and Aid*. London: Lawrence And Wishart.
Gütermann, Christoph 2014a: Interview with Christoph Gütermann led by Tomáš Profant.
Habermas, Jürgen 1987: *The Philosophical Discourse of Modernity: Twelve Lectures*. Cambridge: MIT.
Hanšpach, Daniel 2004: V4 countries and development cooperation: (Re)emerging donors in (re)united Europe and the role of UNDP. *International Issues and Slovak Foreign Policy Affairs* 13(4), 13–41.
Horizont 3000 2014: Jahres Bericht 2013, www.horizont3000.at/wp-content/uploads/2015/07/H3000_JB_2013.pdf.
Horkheimer, Max 2002: *Critical Theory. Selected Essays*. New York: Continuum.
Horký, Ondřej 2010: *Česká rozvojová spolupráce. Diskurzy, praktiky, rozpory*. Praha: SLON.
Horký, Ondřej 2011: Depoliticization, instrumentalization and legitimacy of Czech development cooperation: A case of imposed altruism? *Éthique et économique/Ethics and Economics* 8 (1), 120–132.
Horký, Ondřej 2012a: The Impact of the Shallow Europeanisation of the "New" Member States on the EU's Actorness: What Coherence between Foreign and Development Policy? *The European Union and Global Development: An "Enlightened Superpower" in the Making?* Basingstoke: Palgrave Macmillan, 57–73.
Horký, Ondřej 2012b: The Transfer of the Central and Eastern European "Transition Experience" to the South: Myth or Reality? *Perspectives on European Politics and Society* 13(1), 17–32.
Horký-Hluchááň, Ondřej 2015: Introduction: Diverging Theoretical Approaches to a Normative Research Field. In: Horký-Hluchááň, Ondřej and Lightfoot, Simon (ed.): *Development Cooperation of the 'New' EU Member States. Beyond Europeanization*. Basingstoke and New York: Palgrave Macmillan, 1–21.
Horký-Hluchááň, Ondřej and Lightfoot, Simoned 2013: *Development Policies of Central and Eastern European States. From Aid Recipients to Aid Donors*. London and New York: Routledge.

Horký-Hlucháň, Ondrej and Lightfoot, Simoned 2015: *Development Cooperation of the "New" EU Member States: Beyond Europeanization*. Basingstoke and New York: Palgrave Macmillan.

Jaklin, Ulrike, Wank, Lukas and Wolfram, Marion 2013: Changes in funding of Austrian development NGOs. Shabka, www.shabka.org/2013/05/20/changes-in-funding-of-austrian-development-ngos/.

Laclau, Ernesto and Mouffe, Chantal 2001: *Hegemony and Socialist Strategy. Towards a Radical Democratic Politics*. London and New York: Verso.

Lidchi, Henrietta 1999: Finding the right image. British development NGOs and the regulation of imagery. In: Skelton, Tracey and Allen, Tim (ed.): *Culture and Global Change*. London and New York: Routledge, 87–101.

Lightfoot, Simon 2008: Enlargement and the challenge of EU development policy. *Perspectives on European Politics and Society* 9(2), 128–142, doi:10.1080/15705850801999602.

Lightfoot, Simon 2010: The Europeanisation of international development policies: the case of Central and Eastern European States. *Europe–Asia Studies* 62(2), 329–350.

Lummis, Douglas C. 1996: *Radical democracy*. Ithaca: Cornell University Press.

Mawdsley, Emma 2012: *From Recipients to Donors. Emerging Powers and the Changing Development Landscape*. ZED Books.

Melegh, Attila 2006: *On the East–West Slope. Globalization, Nationalism, Racism and Discourse on Central and Eastern Europe*. Budapest and New York: Central European University Press.

Mesík, Juraj 2012: *Obor a trpaslík. Slováci, Česi a perspektívy Afriky*. Bratislava: Nadácia Pontis.

MFEA 2013: Medium-Term Strategy for Development Cooperation of the Slovak Republic for 2014–2018. Ministry of Foreign and European Affairs of the Slovak Republic, https://issuu.com/slovakaid/docs/strednodoba_strategia_oda_sr_2014-2_83963017c1b288.

NDC-Austroprojekt and Orgut 2002: Plan of Operation for Ngorngoro District Development Programme. Phase 1. Ngorngoro District Council and Austroprojekt and Orgut Consortium.

Noxolo, Patricia 2006: Claims: A Postcolonial Geographical Critique of "Partnership" in Britain's Development Discourse. *Singapore Journal of Tropical Geography* 27(3), 254–269.

Obrovsky, Michael 2006: "Von der Solidarität zur professionell verwalten Wohltätigkeit": Entwicklungspolitisische NGOs in Österreich auf Identitätsuche. In: Gomes, Bea, Maral-Hanak, Irmi and Schicho, Walter (ed.): *Entwicklungszusammenarbeit. Akteure, Handlungsmuster und Interessen*. Wien: Mandelbaum, 249–270.

ÖFSE 2016: 2016 Österreichische Entwicklingspolitik. Fluchtbedingte Migration – Herausforderung für die EZA. Österreichische Forschungsstiftung für Internationale Entwicklung, www.oefse.at/fileadmin/content/Downloads/Publikationen/Oepol/OEPOL2016_web.pdf.

Oh-Seok, Hyun and Arnold, David 2010: *Emerging Asian Approaches to Development Cooperation*. Seoul: KDI and The Asia Foundation.

Oprea, Mirela (2012): Development Discourse in Romania: From Socialism to EU Membership. *Perspectives on European Politics and Society* 13 (1), 66–82.

Pavlicová, Vendula 2012: Stereotypical Images of the Global South in the Media: The Role of the Development Actors. In: Tůmová, Jana (ed.): *Crucial Problems of International Relations through the Eyes of Young Scholars "Actors and Actorness in International Relations: State and Their Discontents."* Praha: Nakladatelství Oeconomica, 97–110.

PiP 2009: Podpora podnikania vidieckych žien v západnej Keni (2008–2009). People in Peril, https://clovekvohrozeni.sk/podpora-podnikania-vidieckych-zien-v-zapadnej-keni-2008-2009/.

PiP 2012a: About Us. People in Peril, www.clovekvohrozeni.sk/en/about-us.

PiP 2012b: Poľnohospodárstvo rozvíjame aj na východnom pobreží Kene. People in Peril, https://clovekvohrozeni.sk/polnohospodarstvo-rozvijame-aj-na-vychodnom-pobrezi-kene/.

PiP 2013: Annual Report 2012. People in Peril.

Plan UK, CARE International UK and Barclays 2013: Banking on Change: Breaking the Barriers to Financial Inclusion, www.care.org/sites/default/files/documents/Banking_on_Change_Breaking_Barriers__April2013.pdf.

Pontis 2010: slovak teachers taught their colleagues from kenya how to use information technologies. Pontis Foundation, www.nadaciapontis.sk/article/slovak-teachers-taught-their-colleagues-from-kenya-how-to-use-information-technologies/277?lang=en_US.

Pontis n.d.: Who we are. Pontis Foundation, n.d.-a, www.nadaciapontis.sk/who-we-are-en.

Profant, Tomáš 2010: Fair Trade z pohľadu postrozvojového prístupu. *Mezinárodní vztahy* 45(2), 71–98.

Profant, Tomáš 2013: On the role of an intellectual. *Studia Politica Slovaca* 6(1), 50–59.

Profant, Tomáš 2015: The Pontis Foundation: Partly Disrupting the Development Discourse Through Partnership. *Forum for Development Studies* 42(2), 265–287.

Profant, Tomáš 2018: The Social Construction of Slovakia as a Donor and its Power Effects. *Europe–Asia Studies* 70(3), 365–387, doi:10.1080/09668136.2018.1453486.

Said, Edward 1979: *Orientalism*. New York: Vintage Books.

SAIDC 2016: Výročná správa 2015. Slovak Agency for International Development Cooperation, www.slovakaid.sk/sites/default/files/vyrocna_sprava_2015_final_web.pdf.

Spivak, Gayatri Charkravorty 1994: Can the Subaltern Speak? In: Williams, Patrick and Chrisman, Laura (ed.): *Colonial Discourse and Post-colonial Theory: A Reader*. New York: Columbia University Press, 66–111.

Szent-Iványi, Balázs 2012: Aid Allocation of the Emerging Central and Eastern European donors. *Journal of International Relations and Development* 15(1), 65–89.

Szent-Iványi, Balázs and Lightfoot, Simon 2015: *New Europe's New Development Aid*. Oxon and New York: Routledge.

Szent-Iványi, Balázs and Tétényi, András 2008: Transition and foreign aid policies in the Visegrád countries. A path dependent approach. *Transition studies review* 15(3), 573–587.

Szent-Iványi, Balázs and Tétényi, András 2013: The East–Central European New Donors: Mapping Capacity Building and Remaining Challenges. *Journal of International Development* 25(6), 819–831, doi:10.1002/jid.2922.

Szép, Attila 2004: Oficiálna rozvojová pomoc Európskej únie a Slovensko. *Medzinárodné otázky* 13(4), 3–22.

Todorova, Maria 2009: *Imagining the Balkans*, Oxford: Oxford University Press.

Wodak, Ruth and Meyer, Michael 2009: Critical Discourse Analysis: History, Agenda, Theory and Methodology. In: Wodak, Ruth and Meyer, Michael (ed.): *Methods of Critical Discourse Analysis*. London: SAGE, 1–33.

Wolf, Larry 1994: *Inventing Eastern Europe: The Map of Civilization on the Mind of the Enlightenment*. Stanford: Stanford University Press.

Wolin, Sheldon S. 1981: The People's Two Bodies. *Democracy* 1(1), 9–24.

Woods, Ngaire 2008: Whose aid? Whose influence? China, emerging donors and the silent revolution in development assistance. *International Affairs* 84(6), 1205–1221, doi:10.1111/j.1468–2346.2008.00765.x.

Zarycki, Tomasz 2014: *Ideologies of Eastness in Central and Eastern Europe*. London and New York: Routledge.

Ziai, Aram 2004: *Entwicklung als Ideologie? Das klassische Entwicklungsparadigma und die Post-Development Kritik zur Analyze des Entwicklungsdiskurses.* Hambrug: Deutsches Übersee-Institut.

Ziai, Aram 2014: Progressing towards incoherence: Development discourse since the 1980s. *Momentum Quarterly: Zeiotschrift für sozialen Fortschritt* 3(1), 3–14.

Ziai, Aram 2017: 'I am not a Post-Developmentalist, but ...' The influence of Post-Development on development studies. *Third World Quarterly*, 38(12), 2719–2734, doi: 10.1080/01436597.2017.1328981.

2 Slovakia and Austria as development donors

The current development discourse distinguishes between the donors on the basis of their temporal origin. If old and new donors differ, so should Austria and Slovakia. But how different are the new and the old donors? The aim of this chapter is to analyze the differences between Austria and Slovakia as donors with regard to several rather material issues. The analysis shows many similarities between the two donors. The underlying argument of this chapter as well as the whole book is that the perception of a substantial difference between various donors is problematic due to important similarities. In the case of Austria and Slovakia, these similarities can be based on their shared history in the Austro-Hungarian Empire that lasted until 1918. Also, until 1948, there were similar democratic/authoritarian economic and political developments in Czechoslovakia and Austria. The modernization paradigm in both countries lasted beyond 1989. These shared histories are the basis for the problematization of the strong division not only of Austria and Slovakia as an old and a new donor, but also of Austria and Slovakia as embodiments of the West and the East, respectively. There is no doubt that there are differences between these two countries (as well as other donors), but the geographical distinction may serve as a racial explanation of phenomena whose origin may simply lie elsewhere than in the 1948 transition to communism in Czechoslovakia.

The chapter will focus on a comparison of the origins of the two development apparatuses, the commitments to development cooperation in the two countries, their levels of popular support for this cooperation, the regional and sectoral focuses of the two donors, the positions of their non-governmental spheres in the field of development cooperation, and the motivations at the governmental as well as the personal level within the Austrian and Slovak development apparatuses.

The origins of development apparatuses: development induced from the outside

There are similarities in the ways the Austrian and Slovak development apparatuses (re)emerged after the Second World War and after the Cold War. The first similarity between these two countries is in the way this policy field has been induced from the outside and brought upon both of the societies. Just as Slovakia became a recipient of aid after the Cold War ended in 1989, so was Austria a major recipient of foreign aid after the Second World War. It was the Marshall Plan that helped to initiate the economic recovery after the war, and at the same time the Plan created a sense of solidarity towards others (Eder and Krobath 1972: 15). It enabled Austria to become a donor. But, not only did the Plan create the necessary conditions for Austria to become a donor, it also demanded this in its Article III (Hödl 2013).[1]

Slovakia, as part of Czechoslovakia, became a donor under the Soviet leadership. The international aid of the Eastern bloc was just as tied politically as Western aid. (Potential) socialist allies received aid from it from the 1950s (Olša 2003:21). Historians of aid speak of an important similarity based on the dominant modernization paradigm between Eastern and Western aid in this period (Unfried and Himmelstoss 2012). Experts from Eastern bloc countries were building factories, dams or schools in the aid-receiving states. They helped with irrigation, health care, or technical issues (see Profant 2018). Similar activities were undertaken by Western donors, including Austria (see Hödl 2004), in countries oriented more to the West than to the East.

The story of the re-emergence of the Slovak development aid after 1989 is similar to the Austrian story from the 1950s. Between 1993 and 1998 Slovakia was a recipient country governed by the semi-authoritarian (but legitimately elected) leader Vladimír Mečiar, whose government leaned toward Russia rather than toward its Western neighbors. For the NGO sector, these were "the years of learning" (Brezáni 2013) as this sector just began to emerge. The NGOs were heavily supported by the funds coming from the EU and the USA such as those of the Heritage Foundation or the German Marshall Fund, especially in their actions against the government. Some of these were the NGOs that would later become non-governmental development organizations (NGDOs). The only development aid during this period covered foreign students' grants or humanitarian aid, and if it did not come from the state, it came from Christian organizations (Brzica 2002: 116–117). It was the support of the Slovak civil society from the West that contributed to the creation of the NGO sector that would later turn its attention to the Global South.

The second external factor that led Austria and Slovakia to (again) become development donors came from the OECD. The OECD, the organization originally known as the OEEC (Organization for European Economic Cooperation), which was in charge of the Marshall Plan, also formally obligated Austria to become a donor (Hödl 2013). Eder and Krobath note that next to politicians' personal motivations and goals, which were stated in various international treaties, "the legally binding obligation can also be seen as a motive of the Austrian development aid" (Eder and Krobath 1972: 20). Gažovič (2012: 40) claims the same thing about Slovakia, which gives "because it *has to*." His analysis of official documents shows that in these documents "the argument of obligation often contained a reference to international commitments that Slovakia accepted instead of an emphasis on some kind of an internal duty" (ibid.).

In the case of Austria, being part of the UN also served as a "major impulse for subscribing to the global developmentalism of the post-war decades" (Hödl 2013), and several other international agreements obligated Austria to provide aid as well.[2] Simply put, the membership in the US-led "free" world was supported by the Austrian public as well as its political parties (apart from the small Communist Party), and this required the country's participation in the dispersion of development assistance.

With Slovakia's accession to the OECD in 2000, the Slovak government started to pay at least formal attention to the development aid topic. However, the situation was similar to the one in Austria in the 1950s. According to Szép (2004: 11)

> apart from the influence of the international environment and not least due to the termination of the original organizational infrastructure, the new system of development aid provision was created without much activity and interest on the side of the political and economic elite [...] development aid did not belong among the priorities of the Slovak foreign policy.

The first step was the passing of the *Concept of Development Aid* and the *Charter of Active Development Aid and Cooperation* by the government in 1999. The development aid was spread between various ministries and their departments, and was in general "non-systemic and ineffective" during this period (Brzica 2002: 117). In 2001, Slovak ODA was first measured according to the DAC OECD statistical directive for the years 1999 and 2000. The amount then was between 0.02 and 0.04% of the GNP (OECD 2011).

During this period there were significant cuts in the funding for the Slovak NGOs coming from abroad, as the already mentioned semi-authoritarian ruler Vladimír Mečiar was unable to form a government after the election in 1998, and Slovakia turned into a pro-European democracy in the eyes of the foreign donors. Some of these NGOs decided to turn their attention to new activities in order to secure further funding. They focused on transferring the Slovak transition experience or, as the Christian organizations did, they joined the mostly Austrian charitable institutions working in Africa (Brezáni 2013; Szép 2004: 12).

The period from 2002 onwards was characterized by Brzica in 2002 as "the growing period" (Brzica 2002: 118). Today, though, given the current figures, one would be more careful before uttering such an overly optimistic term. The MFA together with the NGDOs started to shape the ill-financed policy and polity at the time. The most influential donors from abroad then were the UNDP Bratislava Regional Center and the Canadian International Development Agency (CIDA). They prepared special programs to build Slovak capacities in "development" aid – especially technical aid and training programs. "The goal was to build mechanisms of development aid provision [in the emerging donor countries from Eastern Europe] that would be compatible with standard mechanisms of the advanced donor countries and with the EU aid provision system" (Szép 2004: 13; see also Hulényi (2004) on the trilateral cooperation with Western donors). The influence of the foreign donors was possible only with the creation of the myth that Slovakia is a new donor.

Here it should be noted that the influence of the UNDP or the CIDA might have been welcomed by many Slovak development workers, who perceived these organizations and donors as more experienced (but I should add that I keep on hearing complaints about inequality between NGDOs from the East and the West). Such an acceptance of the inferior position of the Self may have also been empirically correct with regard to the personal experiences of the particular development workers. The aim here is not even to claim that such an influence was necessarily problematic, but merely to say that it was made possible only with the myth that Slovakia is a new donor and that this unequal relation within the field of development cooperation is part of a wider Orientalist inequality between the East and the West.

Finally, the issue of Europeanization of the new member states' development cooperation has been thoroughly analyzed, and the analysis showed mostly only a shallow level of Europeanization (Horký 2012a; Lightfoot 2010; Lightfoot and Szent-Iványi 2014). This is an important insight that shows the possibility of resistance in unequal power relations as theorized by Foucault (Foucault 1982). Once the EU-related responsibilities, including the necessity to accept the EU acquis, were induced from the outside, Slovakia and other new members ceased adopting EU norms, and the socialization was progressing rather slowly (Lightfoot and Szent-Iványi 2014).

In sum, becoming a donor country "was to a significant extent imposed on Austria by external actors and exigencies" (Hödl 2013). The Slovaks also give aid, because they have to. The external influence remains crucial for both countries still today. In the case of Austria, the changes it went through after joining the EU show that even after 30 years of being engaged in this business, it was still the rest of the Western world that determined the Austrian aid, and not its internal drive for foreign engagement. The importance of external actors is further evident in the weak national commitment to aid of both countries, as the next section shows.

Weak commitment to aid

An important actor that strongly influenced the financial level of the Slovak and the Austrian development cooperation was the EU. Between the years 2002 and 2005 (two years before and one year after Slovakia's accession), the Slovak ODA rose from 0.024% to 0.12% of GNI (Čaučík, Krátka, and Pastorová 2007: 128). The Austrian aid rose from 0.11% of GNI in 1993 to 0.27% of GNI in 1995, the year of the Austrian accession (Hödl 2013). In both cases, the aid decreased in the years after the sharp increases, and in 2015 the ODA was at 0.103% of GNI in Slovakia (PMVRO 2016: 6) and at 0.35% of GNI in Austria (ÖFSE 2016: 55). This puts Austria among the worst performing old EU donors (only Italy, Portugal, Greece and Spain fare worse) and well below the EU average of 0.47% of GNI.

With regard to the ODA level, it is necessary to mention the social construction of the new donors influencing the actual performance of this group. As soon as the "new" donors group is discursively constructed, it emerges into existence and starts acting as a group according to its own specific norms. According to Ghica (2013),

> it is more likely that policy makers [from this group] use the regional labeling rhetorically for either not committing themselves to substantive ODA or for creating identity markers and thus justify internally their position not as an international donor but as the more 'handsome' country in the neighbourhood.

One of the main arguments in this regard is related to the amounts of development aid. Whereas the richer donors have set their targets for development aid at 0.7% of their GNI already in 1969 (Pearson et al. 1969), the UN in the 2002 Monterrey Conference and the European Council in 2005 set the targets for new member states at 0.17%, which was to be reached in 2010, and 0.33%, which was to be reached in 2015. This was mainly due to the perception that "the new member states were not able or expected to do the same thing as the old member states did in a time span of 50 years" (Lightfoot 2010: 337). The commitment was weakened also by the wording as it required the states to "strive to increase" the ODA level (in ibid.). The new member states in general thus perceived themselves more as in need of funds than as donors who should give aid.

Thus, it is not surprising that they are not capable of reaching even the 0.17% target and compete at the level of 0.05–0.15% over who is "the more handsome" country in the region. It is impossible to determine what the actual ODA would be if the new donors group never existed, but there is clearly a group behavior influenced by the existence of the group, as the countries can compete with each other and do not have to worry about other comparisons as the lack of commitment of each member of the group legitimizes the others' lack of commitment. Simply put, the discursive effect of the label "new donors" may be found not only in the realm of financial commitments, but possibly also in the actual financial performance.

The increase of ODA in relation to the entrance to the EU was the only political event that influenced the ODA level in Austria. Another temporary increase was due to debt relief. Similarly to the case of Slovakia in 2008, where the cancellation of the Liberian debt increased the Slovak ODA from 0.094% of GNI in 2007 to 0.102% of GNI in 2008, the debt relief for Iraq and Madagascar in 2005 changed the Austrian ODA figures as well, increasing the ODA from 0.23% of GNI in 2004 to 0.52% of GNI in 2005. Austrian ODA levels thus "do not reflect political decision-making and concrete planning but rather have been the result of peculiarities in Austria's reporting practice or the respective dates when contributions to replenish the funds of international financial institutions fell due" (Obrovsky 2005: 114, see also Obrovsky 1993: 80). Apart from reporting practices, it was the rise of asylum seekers and, in one case, a specific financial commitment to the World Bank that actually had an influence on the ODA levels. Hödl makes a similar argument based on his research that went until 2009: "no clear-cut overall trend can be identified" (Hödl 2013) with regard to the ODA levels.

To claim a significant similarity, one would need to do a closer analysis of the Slovak case, but the stable level in the Slovak ODA suggests that the influence of political changes is limited there as well. Both countries fail to fulfill the ODA target of 0.7% of GNI. Slovakia still fails to fulfill its older target – to reach 0.33% of GNI in 2015 – and it even fails to reach the 2010 target of 0.17% of GNI. The low ODA figures suggest that there is a weak political commitment to development cooperation at the level of the national governments in both countries. The higher political commitment in other countries – e.g., the Nordic countries – translates into higher ODA figures.

It is not just the level of ODA that shows a weak commitment to development cooperation. Not only was the Austrian development cooperation induced from the outside, and not only is Austria changing its ODA due to outside pressures, but the Austrian development cooperation is in no way original in its approach and merely follows other donors. According to Walter Schicho (2013), "the Austrians, they follow the mainstream. There is so much talk on those principles, but everything which comes up in the global discourse immediately enters local discourse." He specifically mentioned that Austrians follow strategies coming from the Danes, the Dutch, or the Irish: "[Austrians] don't develop their own strategies" (ibid.). These donors, according to Schicho, try to have an influence on the global discourse, have their own think tanks, and have a political interest in taking a lead. Obrovsky argued in a similar manner that "Austria is more oriented on the German development activities" (Obrovsky 2013). As an example he offered the current preference for reaching "development" through the economy (again): "Germany already changed the structure and already started to spend much more money on development economic activities and private public partnership, [and] Austria is doing the same" (ibid.).

Austria is, in this sense, in a similar position to Slovakia. Slovakia as a "new" donor is supposed to follow the "old" donors, who are allegedly more experienced and therefore superior to the "new" ones. Yet, Austria is also following the old donors despite being one. In this sense, Austrians and Slovaks are both followers of the leading donors. The distinction between "old" and "new" donors can thus be questioned, and a different distinction between *leaders* and *followers* seems a better fit to describe the relation among the donors in the EU. One could use the leaders-followers distinction not only with regard to originality, but also with regard to more particular norms, such as the overall quality of aid or the norms of the Paris Declaration.

What could be of use here is the Commitment to Development Index that ranks the richest countries in terms of their alleged "dedication to policies that benefit people living in poorer nations" (CGD 2018). It focuses on the quality of aid (e.g., penalizing tied aid), trade with poorer countries (especially barriers to imports and subsidies), FDIs and their quality, migration, and environmental and security policies, as well as the creation and dissemination of new technology. Overall, Austria is 11th and Slovakia is 21st out of the 27 donors listed in the Index. It is interesting to note that, whereas Slovakia is last in terms of technology creation and knowledge sharing, Austria is third. However, in terms of environmental policies, Slovakia is second and Austria is 15th, and in the case of trade Austria is 17th and Slovakia 18th (ibid.). Most of all, these numbers tell us that there are numerous ways to classify donors, and some donors may be better in one policy and others in another; hence there is the question, why should the old-new distinction (or its expression in numbers) be used? We could have donors who are good at trade and are thus more beneficial to the recipients or donors who are good at knowledge sharing.

In fact, for example Carbone (2015) distinguishes between regionalists who emphasize strategic links between Europe and its former colonies (France, Belgium, Italy, Spain, Portugal) and globalists who place greater emphasis on levels of poverty (Germany, the Netherlands and the Nordic countries). Another division is based on the promotion of the idea that development cooperation should be carried out to a greater extent through the EU and on the promotion of the opposite idea that development cooperation should remain within the national member states of the EU.

More importantly, the old-new distinction could be reversed following the problematic practice of the representation of the Other as a noble savage, or in this particular case, a noble donor savage. Eyben and Savage (2013) show how new donors distance themselves from the old ones because (among other things) of their colonial past. Regardless of who is actually better at maintaining an equal partnership with the recipients that is rhetorically praised by all donors, the past can determine the positioning of the donors in exactly the opposite way to that of the old-new distinction. Suddenly some of the old donors are the problematic ones with their history of colonial oppression, and the new donors are represented in a positive way as those engaged in the allegedly equal South–South cooperation. This finding is important, not because it may point to some kind of true division of donors, but merely because it shows that the old-new distinction between donors is a social construction and that there could even be a complete reversal of this construction. If this is the case, then, one may wish to dispense with the Orientalist old-new division and seek new ways of ordering the world of donors.

There are other aspects of the way donors can be judged in which Slovakia and Austria show important similarities. Both development apparatuses face problems with the fulfillment of the Paris Declaration norms. According to Obrovsky and Raza, only about 18% of the Austrian ODA follows the principles of the Paris Declaration (Obrovsky and Raza 2012: 17).[3] According to an analysis conducted by the representatives of the Slovak NGDOs,

> democratic ownership and active participation of the people, for whom we work, is not the strongest side of most of the organizations […] it is not

> unusual that an idea emerges in Slovakia and after that a partner and a suitable target group [are] sought.
>
> (Fialová 2011: 7; see also Profant 2015: 131)

These are just two examples that show that there is no hard divide between old and new donors. Not only do both types of donors tackle similar problems, but new donors may even fare better than the allegedly more experienced ones, reversing the traditional Western-centric hierarchy.

Austria has been known for inflating its statistics as much as it could throughout the history of its "development" aid and cooperation. In the statistics of the Genuine Aid concept[4] calculated by Concord, Austrian genuine aid as part of the total aid was 74% in 2015, and as part of the bilateral aid it was 44%, making Austria the worst performing member of the EU in this respect (Concord 2016: 13). For Slovakia these figures were 24% and 5%, respectively (it was the fifth best performing member in the EU) (ibid.). Again, one could simply say that the East–West slope (Melegh 2006) embodied in the distinction between the old and new donors is here being reversed, and Slovakia is one of the leaders, whereas Austria is clearly lagging behind.

Finally, the population's commitment to aid seems to be quite high in both countries. In Austria, 86% of the respondents in 2015 believed that it was very or fairly important "to help people in developing countries" (Eurobarometer 2016: 14). In Slovakia, the figure was 79%. A greater difference was to be found among those who believed that it was "very important [...] to help the people in the developing countries" (ibid.). In Austria this was 38% and in Slovakia 22% of the respondents (ibid.). These figures seem to confirm the distinction between the old and new donors despite the Austrian population being among the least willing to help from among the populations of the old donors. For example, 53% of Germans find helping people in the poor countries of the Global South to be very important. Yet, so do 45% of Romanians.

The problem with these figures, however, is that this support seems to be "a mile wide and an inch deep" (Smillie 1999). Research conducted in the UK and inquiries in the USA show that the generic questions asked by Eurobarometer usually bring rather positive answers, portraying the respondents as willing to give.[5] However, relative questions asking about the support for aid in relation to other policies bring different results (Darnton 2009; Hudson and van Heerde-Hudson 2012; HoC IDC 2009; Henson et al. 2010; PIPA 2001). This is the case, not just in the UK or the USA, but also in Austria. As soon as the question of financing the aid was connected with a compensation in the form of lower social welfare expenditures in the survey, only 33% of the Austrian respondents were for more money being spent on development cooperation (Maral-Hanak 2008: 110; see also Profant 2018).

There is no research that would contrast answers to generic questions with answers to relative questions in connection with this issue for Slovakia. However, statements made by the leading figures from the NGDO sector suggest that the level of support is not as great as Eurobarometer suggests. Despite the level of support for SlovakAid activities being 84% according to Eurobarometer (2011: 9) in the year of the interview, former NDGO Platform director Nora Beňáková claimed that the Slovaks are unwilling to help in this respect (Beňaková 2011). The current director of the Slovak NGDO People in Peril, Braňo Tichý, in an article on the refugee crisis, qualified the results from Eurobarometer with the low amount of money Slovaks actually give from their own pocket for development and also stated that our aid is limited "by the willingness of Slovakia and its people to support this aid" (Tichý 2015). Whereas Tichý uses a particular statistical figure for donations during the Syria crisis (personal communication), Beňáková's claim rests only on her own perception or experience and therefore cannot be taken as more than just that. The backing of their argument that goes against Eurobarometer's hard data is that what they claim goes against their own material and probably also their personal interest. Should the Slovak government follow their belief that Slovaks are unwilling to help, they would lose their jobs as their NGDOs would not be getting any funds from the government. Thus, one could argue that the "common sense" view of the Slovak willingness to help might differ from the surveys' results.

There are further problems related to the official surveys (see Profant 2018). The argument here is that different questions would bring answers that would indicate much lower support in both countries. The support would, however, probably be higher in Austria than in Slovakia. The question is whether this has anything to do with the tradition of giving that existed in both countries for a very long period or with other factors, for example, the levels of wealth. The perception of oneself as being either developed or not so developed may also influence the decision to give. An exposure to a more anti-racist education at school can lead to a greater propensity to give among the educated part of the population, and this propensity is larger in Austria than in Slovakia as well. Simply put, the alleged difference in the popular support for development cooperation between old and new donors need not be based on the alleged maturity of the donors, but can be related to different issues. This again casts doubt on the distinction itself. Overall, there is a rather weak commitment to aid on both sides of the Danube River.

The regional focus and the national interest: a possible ranking based on the recipients

The Austrian and Slovak ODA allocations in terms of regional focus move within the dichotomy of the national interests and altruists' motivations, and this dichotomy has been recently complemented by the discourse of effectiveness and complementarity and coordination of donors (see Profant 2018). In both national apparatuses, the discussion also revolved around the number of recipients.

This number was narrowed down in Austria due to the pressure "from above, from the DAC level" (Schicho 2013). In Slovakia, a similar narrowing was due to the shaming of Slovak officials in international fora for still having Serbia as a program country, as one Slovak NGDO worker said. Others from this sector claimed that the narrowing down of the geographical targets is the consequence of "the dialogue of the governmental and non-governmental part of the society" (Beňáková, Mihálik, and Brezáni 2010: 148). In both cases, it was again an external actor that shaped the development policy.

What is perceived as Austria's national interest is closely tied to its external economic relations. These, among other things, explain the geographical focus of Austria's ODA. In contrast to, e.g., Sweden or Switzerland with their considerably higher levels of exports going to Africa, Latin America, and Asia, Austria's exports went to Southern and Eastern Europe. "[T]he predominantly small and medium-sized Austrian businesses apparently were not overly interested in overseas markets and thus failed to trigger appropriate subsidies in the guise of ODA" (Hödl 2013). Another factor was the lack of large transnational corporations that would seek overseas markets. This influenced the political elite to focus on the European states, and the media and the state-dependent NGDOs followed. Whereas the proclaimed regional focus reflected the general move to help the so-called Least Developed Countries (LDCs), especially those in Africa, the actual (financial) regional focus more or less reflected Austrian geopolitical interests (ibid., see also Lightfoot and Obrovsky 2016 for a similar argument). Thus, the Austrian Development Agency gives 45.35% (of around 6.22% of Austrian ODA) to LDCs (ADA 2017: 50); however, due to foreign student costs and, in the case of Turkey, also due to an Austrian school in Istanbul, the top three recipient countries of the bilateral ODA (i.e., of 44.1% of the Austrian ODA) in 2015 were Turkey, Bosnia and Herzegovina, and the Ukraine (Obrovsky 2016: 70).

There is a similar allocation of the Slovak ODA regarding student costs that put Serbia in second place on the Slovak list (PMVRO 2016: 13). As research for the years 2001–2008 shows, the main determining factor for the choice of recipients in the Visegrad Four countries, including Slovakia, is the recipient's regional proximity. In particular, the aid during this period went to the Western Balkans and the Commonwealth of Independent States (countries from the former Soviet Union). However, Slovakia was an outlier to a certain extent. Unlike the ODA of the Czech Republic, Hungary, and Poland, the Slovak ODA may have had a "poverty focus" (Szent-Iványi 2012: 81). Yet, even after a greater rise of ODA for African countries in 2012, the rise in ODA for them analyzed by Szent-Iványi was of a temporary nature, as has been known to the leading figures in the Slovak development apparatus. After a decade of the preference for the Western Balkans, today the Slovak ODA is focused mainly on the Eastern Partnership. The numbers show that the Ukraine, Serbia, Kenya and Moldova received the most Slovak ODA in 2015, with 60% of the ODA going to Europe and 22% going to Africa (ibid.: 12–13). In sum, both Austria and Slovakia focus, not on the poorest countries, but on those within their geographical proximity, which also happen to be those that their respective national interests focus on.

The East–West relationship within the field of development cooperation is visible also in the normative perspective on the regional focus of the ODA allocation. In the CEE research, the question of Europeanization was for a long time understood as based on the quantity of aid and on the regional focus (Lightfoot 2010; Vittek and Lightfoot 2009; Horký 2010; Gažovič and Profant 2015). Being European meant contributing to the norm of helping those most in need – in other words, eradicating poverty. The aim of a truly European country should thus be helping in an LDC. As already mentioned, Szent-Iványi has shown that the Visegrad countries focus mainly on the countries in their proximity, which do not belong among the poorest in the world. The Slovak officials could thus be criticized for not adhering to a European norm that has been constructed as positive and related to altruism – helping the poor.

As has been shown, Austria also defies the image of the EU as an entity that helps the poorest, as its aid reflects its geopolitical interest. In this sense the distinction between the old and new donors is problematic, as a donor who supposedly belongs among the old, i.e., experienced, donors does not follow the norm that the new donors are expected to follow. This is the case, not only with Austria, but, for example, also with Greece, which also sends its aid to its immediate neighbors (Horký 2012a: 73). A division of donors on the basis of the geographical location of the recipients could be yet another way to put donors into groups.

Still, in 2016, Lightfoot and Obrovsky perceived the decision to focus on the Western Balkan countries as "an important step into the right direction" (Lightfoot and Obrovsky 2016: 19), which shows how the norm has changed. However, their argument further supports the main argument of this book as in their text, Austria is represented not as an old donor, but as a "small country" that is supposed to "find [its] niches and deliver specific contributions focussed on small partner countries" (ibid.). So, why not propose another division between small and large countries?

Regarding other European norms, their analysis of the 20 years of Austrian development cooperation since Austria joined the EU allows them to speak of a shallow Europeanization in relation to Austrian development policy, emphasizing the low level of spending, tied aid, insufficient policy coherence and low budget support that put Austria "in with the Southern European states" (ibid.: 18).

A deviation from the norm of the poverty focus (which seems to be changing) also casts doubt on the norm itself. Is the focus really based on poverty, or is there simply a coincidence between poverty and the focus of the largest European donors? And could one really speak of a coincidence? The most traditional donors possibly send their aid to LDCs because of their poverty, but the LDCs are also within their geopolitical interests and are their former colonies as well. The Austrian and Slovak (and Greek) geopolitical interests simply lie elsewhere, and the poverty in the countries they give aid to is not as extreme as that in Sub-Saharan Africa.

Thus, the discourse of Europeanization possibly shows that Slovakia does not adhere to the European norm of poverty eradication, but at the same time the analysis of the social construction of this discourse shows that power relations might be at play. Former colonial countries are capable of setting a norm that suits their geopolitical interests. Those who do not follow the norm are not respected for following their geopolitical interests, but are criticized for not following the European norm; therefore, they need to be taught what it means to be European. The Austrian (as well as the Greek) case shows that there are old EU members who do not follow the norm just like the new donors. The distinction between new and old donors in the case of a regional focus is thus problematic, and a distinction on the basis of the geopolitical interests seems to be a better way to distinguish between the donors.

However, these arguments have one more twist – the discourses of effectiveness and complementarity and coordination of aid. These discourses legitimize the Slovak regional focus on the Eastern Partnership and the sectoral focus on the transition experience. Horký, writing for the Czech Republic in relation to the transition experience, claims that "the transition experience is a perfect tool for justifying the use of tied technical or political assistance for the promotion of political, security and commercial interests in the middle income countries of East and South Eastern Europe" (Horký 2012b: 28). Further research would be necessary to actually show that behind the discourse of complementarity and effectiveness lies the national interest or more particular interests, but the danger is clearly there.

My aim with regard to this particular issue, however, is not to focus here on the morality of the regional focus, but apart from pointing out the similarity between Austria and Slovakia in this regard, it is to suggest another avenue of research. How was it achieved that the utmost altruistic norm – poverty eradication – has been diluted by other norms that enable EU countries with their national interests focused on countries outside sub-Saharan Africa to engage in development cooperation in the region of their choice and not lose in the altruistic contest? An analysis of the evolution of these norms could show that the new member states may have a say in the EU development policy nowadays and are able to defend their interests against the interests of stronger players. One should not forget that the argument that altruism also needs to be effective is useful in this new discourse as well. The actors most often perceived as connected with the norm of altruism belong to the non-governmental sector. The next section compares these sectors in both of the examined countries.

The non-governmental sphere: too close for comfort

The development apparatuses in Austria and Slovakia have non-governmental sectors with similar characteristics. These include the functioning of the NGDOs, their relation to the government, and their relation to each other. The Slovak and Austrian NGDOs are in principle private and not participatory. The Slovak ones are smaller than the Austrian ones, often consisting of around ten employees, but the basic form in both countries is the same. The only organizations with a more massive membership that engage in charities or development cooperation are the Christian organizations. The fact that people do not participate in the NGDOs does not mean that this sector is weak. These NGDOs are close to being transaction actors that are characterized by "ties – enduring and temporary – among organized non-state actors and between them and political parties, power holders, and other institutions" (Petrova and Tarrow 2007: 79). Their being incapable or weak in mobilizing people does not mean that these NGDOs would be unable to realize their interests. They just use other means, which depend on the "political opportunity structure" and "resource access" (Císař 2008: 74–81). In both countries, the political opportunity structure and resource access are connected, as the resources come to a great extent (but not exclusively) from the national governments, and these governments also open the political opportunities for these NGDOs.

In Slovakia, for 30% of the NGDOs, grants from the state represent 30–40% of their budgets. In 22% of the NGDOs it is 50%, and in another 22% it is 80–90% (Brezáni 2013). The state funding is simply crucial for the Slovak NGDOs. People in Peril could serve as an example. According to their 2015 Annual Report this NGDO got 68.3% of its income from public resources (and 51.4% from the government) (PiP 2016). The Slovak NGDO sector is thus under state patronage.

An important element of the political opportunities structure is the openness of political institutions. In the Slovak case, one could speak of an interdependence of the government and the non-governmental sector (see, e.g., Interview No. 13 2013). On the one hand, the NGDOs are dependent on the financial resources from the government; on the other the Ministry of Foreign Affairs depends on the capacity of the NGDOs to carry out projects. The Ministry needs someone to do what it has committed itself to, but does not have its own capacities. According to the NGO workers, the NGOs have to provide expertise to the Ministry, because the workers there sometimes simply "do not know what is going on in reality."

Due to the lack of capacities the Ministry allows the NGDOs to help create necessary official documents. This cooperation is institutionally established in the Memorandum of Understanding between the NGDO Platform and the MFA. The Ministry, in the Memorandum, "recognizes the importance of the Platform," and according to the Memorandum, the Platform "is supposed to provide expertise, analyses and initiatives in the process of the creation of crucial strategic development policy documents […] in accordance with the need of the Slovak MFA" (MZV SR and PMVRO 2010). In exchange the Ministry is supposed to "help build NGDOs' capacities" through "financial support of capacities and institutional existence […] [and] financial support of development projects and programs of the NGDOs," co-financing of the projects of the EU and the support of volunteers (ibid.). The NGDOs are thus very specific actors, as the structure of political opportunities could hardly be more open for them.

However, due to this openness, they are losing one of the important functions of a transaction actor – an adversarial role toward the government. The NGDOs in Slovakia are thus more like the complementary organizations that are typical of Japan (Young 2000: 163; see also Profant 2015). They complement the state in one particular state policy.

Just as it is the case in Slovakia, the state and the NGDOs in Austria are interdependent. The relationship started together with the emergence of Austrian development aid. Already in the 1960s especially (but not exclusively), the Christian associations conducted development projects whereas the state "limited itself to choos[ing] the focus sectors and project partners in Austria" (Obrovsky 2006: 251). The NGDOs claimed the servicing role in carrying out the projects with the state securing financial and political support. "NGOs were funded by the state in a quite generous way concerning the autonomy of [the] NGOs concerned" (Jaklin, Wank, and Wolfram 2013: 5). This symbiotic relationship was implicitly included in the 1974 Foreign Assistance Act (ibid.). The NGDOs were perceived as having the necessary knowledge to execute the projects, and the state provided assistance to them with its diplomatic representations. Therefore, Obrovsky (2006: 252) writes that the administration of the development cooperation and politics were dependent on the information collected by the NGDOs.

At the same time, many NGDOs "were created by the government and depended entirely on public funding" (Hödl 2013). Raffer (1995: 46) described NGOs as "de facto state-run enterprises [which] are supposed to enable the state to have fewer posts and make it easier to run its official development aid without its own agency" (Raffer 1995: 46). Zauner even perceives NGOs as "an extended body of political authorities" (in Obrovsky 2006: 252); however, at the same time, he speaks of trust between the two as the relationship is based on mutual knowledge between the employees in both spheres.

Similar to the Slovak case, in this case the NGDOs' dependent position weakens their critical role. The Austrian state follows the logic of "he who pays the piper calls the tune" (Obrovsky 2006: 264), and this can lead to the NGDOs limiting themselves to carrying out orders and services demanded by the government (ibid.). If they were to really watch over the state, they would have to rely on their own financial resources. Unlike the charity NGDOs, which are not trying to change the social and political structures, those NGDOs that attempt to do so are getting into a conflict of interests between what Obrovsky (ibid.: 265) calls the Voice and the Servicing functions. This is then visible in the NGDOs' public works, as these are often "confronted with the demand to present the work of their principal in a positive light; for example, the editorial teams of relevant development journals note a greater pressure than elsewhere" (Maral-Hanak 2008: 115). In sum, the NGDOs in Slovakia and Austria, just like those in many other countries, are "too close for comfort" (Edwards and Hulme 1996; Banks, Hulme, and Edwards 2015). Their relation to the state has a negative impact on their public engagement against the state policies. At most they focus on safe issues such as insufficient funding for the NGDOs, the number of recipient countries, or their poverty level, and rarely publicly question state foreign policy.

Finally, the question of cooperation between the NGDOs shows yet another similarity between the Austrian and Slovak development apparatuses. According to Obrovsky, "there is no way [there can be a] cooperation between [Austrian] NGOs because there is a lot of competition […] if we are talking about funds"

(Obrovsky 2013). With the changes in the funding, "the NGOs started to see themselves as state contractors and therefore, competitors on a newly established 'aid market'" (Jaklin, Wank, and Wolfram 2013: 5). The financial cuts in the 1980s possibly resulted in the creation of the NGDO platform (today the *Globale Verantwortung*) that was supposed to represent their interests towards the state, but the NGDOs need to be visible even when alone. Even though they have their umbrella organization, for example, their educational and campaigning activities are part of their PR and not of the whole NGDO community. Moreover, the *Globale Verantwortung* is "only as strong as its members allow and [there are] much stronger members [...] for example Caritas, [or the] Red Cross" (ibid.). These NGDOs do not need to discuss their work with small NGDOs or the *Globale Verantwortung*. According to Schicho, there is no cooperation here in the sense of "[C]ould we do a project together?" (Schicho 2013).

The situation in Slovakia is similar. The system of funding creates a competitive environment between the Slovak NGDOs as they fight for the same money from one budget. Where one wins, another loses. NGDO workers are aware of the problem and, even though their relationships remain friendly, particular interests prevail. The reasons for the lack of cooperation include the protection of one's know-how in the field-work, local contacts, knowledge about particular locations, knowledge about how to write projects or about the project management, and/or knowledge about the transition experience, and also the reputations of particular NGDOs (Michálková 2013). There are possibilities that could make, for example, the cooperation in Kenya more effective, but "the NGOs do not use them fully" (Michálková 2013: 47). Michálková finds five factors that prevent cooperation: the grant system that turns the NGDOs into competitors, the amounts of funding for particular projects (200,000 euro for a project) that are too small to induce cooperation, the lack of contacts between the NGDOs, their lack of knowledge of each other's projects, and cooperation with stable partners abroad that discourages attempts to change anything (ibid.: 50–55).

In sum, just like the Austrian NGDOs, the Slovak NGDOs do projects mostly on their own. There is an interdependence between the state and the non-state sector in both states as well, and this interdependence may be related to a lack of NGDOs' criticism of the state. Given all the similarities in the NGO-state relations between Austria and Slovakia, one could ask again, what is the difference between old and new donors? The next section focuses on the states' as well as personal motivations in the Slovak and Austrian development apparatuses.

Motivations for development cooperation: altruism, egoism, and professional interest

Even if the "development" cooperation has been induced from the outside, once both of the examined countries give aid, various motivations influence its dispersion. These motivations are quite similar. I focus here on the state level motivations and the NGDO employees' motivations.

With regard to the former, an analysis of motivations for Austrian development aid from the beginning of the Second (Austrian) Republic in 1955 until 1995 by Hödl (2004) identified four motivational factors – anticommunism, foreign policy, economic calculations, and humanitarian motives (ibid.: 198). Eder and Krobath (1972: 13–23) offered a similar set of motivational factors for it. Especially, the government representatives (e.g., Chancellors Klaus and Kreisky) highlighted international solidarity as a reason for giving aid. A "general political interest" (ibid.: 16) and "the motive [connected to] political neutrality" (ibid.: 15) were important inducements to give aid as well. Austria, just like Slovakia, cannot be accused of having any neocolonial aspirations connected to particular former colonies and in this sense differs from other donors. Another motivation was – again just like in the Slovak case (see below) – the creation of a positive image for Austria.

Hödl (2004: 198–217, 234–266) conducted a diachronic analysis of the changing motivations and goals. In the 1950s, the main motivation was the political need to show that the "free world" offers a way to industrialization and welfare that differs from socialism. In the 1960s, the reasoning behind "development" aid moved between the national interest and the moral obligation. During this period, aid was conceived as part of the membership in the West, to which Austria wanted to belong. At the end of the 1960s, aid became an answer to the danger of the center-periphery confrontation and was supposed to relax this tension. The 1960s also saw a rise in the moral argumentation of the Christian mission and socialist solidarity. At the same time, these arguments were expressed together with the need to follow the national economic interest. Aid was perceived as possibly useful for Austrian companies and the Global South as a possible market for Austrian goods. Aid therefore became tied as an instrument to support exports. Kreisky even openly spoke of development aid as an anti-cyclical economic instrument to support the demand in times of crises (ibid.: 204). Aid was also supposed to secure access to natural resources and aimed at bringing more friends to Austria, as such a small country needed them.

In the 1970s, with détente the anticommunist arguments lost their importance, but in the economic realm now both donors and partners were supposed to profit. Eder and Krobath (1972: 9–12) in this sense spoke of "donor oriented goals" and "receiver oriented goals." In practice, however, the aid remained tied (Hödl 2004: 209). This decade was characterized by the rise of the Global South that resulted in the disappearing of the moral reasoning. The states of the Global South became self-conscious subjects and were not helpless objects anymore.

The general acceptance of development aid in the 1980s resulted in a quieting down of the debate about the reasons for giving. At the same time the turbulences in the North might have pushed these topics into the background as well. With the acceptance, the aid development apparatus professionalized itself, and the discussions were now directed to operative goals rather than big ideas about motivations.

In the 1990s, the menace of the conflict between the center and the periphery disappeared from the discourse, and the aid focused on local political stability.

New threats appeared in the 1990s, with environmental problems, drug trafficking, and migration. All these political issues were supposed to be solved through development aid. Yet, "the support of Austrian capital's interests [...] plays until now an important role" (Hödl 2006: 33).

The motives of the Slovak development cooperation have also been analyzed at the governmental level. The analyzed documents from 2003 to 2009 show that there are three types of motivations for it. One of them is the already mentioned obligation to engage in development cooperation induced from the outside. The Slovak government gives aid because it has to. There is a binding international commitment for it to do so.

Second, this commitment has been accepted by the Slovak governmental officials because they want Slovakia to become a member of the international community (Gažovič 2012: 40). Just like in the Austrian case, according to Gažovič (2012) and Bátora (2004), Slovak ODA serves as an instrument to constitute the identity of the country as a mature international actor that will then be perceived as such by other actors.

In the official documents, the instrumental interpretation of ODA as a policy that Slovakia conducts because it pays back prevailed (Gažovič 2012: 42). The motivation here is self-interest. ODA has also been represented as an instrument of foreign policy in this case (see also Beňáková 2010). A third representation of ODA – as an altruistic endeavor – was present in the official documents as well, but "to a significantly lesser extent" (Gažovič 2012: 43). Thus, there are both altruistic and egoistic motivations present in the Austrian and Slovak development cooperation. This is not surprising as one can find such a mix in other donors' motivations as well. The important similarity here is in the perception that aid serves as an instrument to achieve international recognition.

There is another type of motivation for giving aid that merits attention. Development workers have their own reasons for engaging in the development cooperation. A quantitative research from 1995 (Hemedinger 1995) shows similar results to an earlier study from 1978 from Scholta and Zapotocky (in ibid.). The researchers in both cases asked people who returned from working in development industries abroad about their motivations for doing the work. Their answers were dominated by concerns about "social justice" or "solidarity with the people in the Third World" as well as the aim to "get to know different cultures" or "countries" (ibid.: 45, 48). Quite important was also the desire "to do something meaningful." And still two other important reasons were the "joy from traveling" and "learning something for one's occupation" (ibid.). A qualitative – oral history – study (Hödl 2010) focused on "development" workers active during the 1960s and 1970s. The main motive then was to help and it was often based on Christian inspiration, or the love for one's neighbor (ibid.: 101). The subsequent gradual move away from religious motivations is shown by Hödl as well as Hemedinger (1995: 45–46). Another important motive in this time period, just like in the 1990s, was the desire to get to know foreign cultures in connection with "adventures" (Hödl 2010: 102). Political motives were less prominent and were usually related, e.g., to the workers' outrage over the problem of hunger and their disapproval of the injustice in the foreign countries. Meanwhile, material or career motivations were even rarer in this period than in the 1990s (ibid.).

In my own research I asked the respondents a rather open question – why they do what they do. Among a few of the respondents this resulted in a description of their previous engagements, such as studying a course on development (Interview No. 21 2013) or (in the case of one respondent) just being led to this kind of work through one's parents' life experiences and one's own experience with the people one met (Interview No. 28 2013). In one case it was the political orientation of the respondent: "I was too leftist to do anything else than development cooperation [...] Development cooperation wasn't [...] very important for the government [...] so leftist people like me found a job in development cooperation" (Interview No. 22 2013). The respondents represented themselves not as having motivations or agency, but their occupation was represented as a result of other forces than their own.

Other than that, three main types of motivations emerged from my research. The first can be called the "idealistic approach" (Interview No. 26 2013) at the "personal-moral [level]" (Interview No. 9 2013), which is based on the idea that "one really should be helping [in] some way" (Interview No. 13 2013, see also Interview No. 27). This type of motivation was used frequently by respondents from both countries, but more so by the Austrian respondents.

Second, not necessarily in opposition to the idealistic approach was the self-interest of the development workers. One Slovak respondent from Pontis explicitly rejected having "missionary ambitions or feelings that [he is] helping those people, those poor Africans" (Interview No. 7 2013). A respondent from Austroprojekt stated that, during his preparation course, "99% or 95% were people who wanted to help; they wanted to do good and I never wanted to help; I wanted to go there because it was my interest to go there" (Interview No. 16 2013). This respondent, just like many others, was interested in other cultures, other people and traveling (see also Interview No. 13, 14, 17, 23, 25, 27 2013).

There was a connection between the self-interest and the moral motivation akin to the impossibility of giving a selfless gift in some of the answers. One respondent is "moving forward through this; I mean, maybe it is a totally egoistic answer, but it immensely gives me a lot; I learn a lot from those people" (Interview No. 10 2013); another gets up in the morning and has a feeling that he is "doing something useful" (Interview No. 28 2014). Simply put, "the objective is very meaningful" (Interview No. 24 2014). The motivation thus incorporates the selfishness into selflessness as one helps oneself through helping others. This argument is then supported at yet another level of interaction in one's own society as one gets "obviously positive feedback: 'Wow, you are an aid worker!' " (Interview No. 27 2013).

One could find the above mentioned responses in both countries, but the third type of motivation – the professional motivation – was more prevalent among the Slovak respondents. For quite a few of them, development cooperation seems to be most of all a job rather than a "vocation," as one respondent from Austroprojekt put it (Interview No. 17 2013). The respondents do what they do because they have a "professional interest" (Interview No. 9 2013) in it, it is "very interesting work" (Interview No. 5 2013), and/or they gain "new experience with project management" (Interview No. 14 2013). One Austrian respondent also mentioned that it is a good job that enables him to "combine creativity, [and] journalism [...] to put [the creativity] into a film" (Interview No. 26 2013).

In sum, the difference between the Slovaks and Austrians regarding these three types of responses was not great. There was a smaller amount of the morally oriented responses among the Slovaks. Especially Pontis employees stressed only their professional interest, but such answers were to a smaller extent present also among the Austrian respondents. On the Austrian side, apart from one respondent from Austroprojekt, everyone claimed (in various ways) to have a moral motivation to help other people. Finally, an explicit egoism and an interest in cultural exchange and traveling were rarer and were occasionally complemented by a connection between moral and self-interested reasoning. Most of the answers belonged in more than one category. The differences between the two countries were thus not great.

Conclusion

The aim of this chapter was to compare some of the more important elements within the Slovak and Austrian development apparatuses. The comparison shows significant similarities between them and casts doubt on the division of donors into the old and new ones. Both of the analyzed donors had their development aid induced from the outside. In order to become part of the free world or simply the West after the Second World War, the Austrian government accepted international agreements that demanded Austrian participation in aid to the Global South. Outside inducement was the most important factor that led to the reemergence of the Slovak aid apparatus after the Cold War.

Such an origin leads to an unsurprising lack of commitment to aid, not only at the governmental level, but also at the level of the public. Austria is one of the worst performing old donors in financial terms and, in this regard, is closer to the much poorer new donors group. Just like the new donors, Austria also belongs among the followers of other old donors. In this regard, a leader-follower distinction between donors might be better than the old-new distinction. The popular support of development cooperation is higher in Austria than in Slovakia; however, relative questions in the surveys bring answers that indicate a much lower support for foreign aid, suggesting a possibility that factors other than an alleged donor maturity might be at play.

The regional focus of both countries shows that it need not be the norm of poverty eradication or the norms of complementarity and effectiveness, but national interests that drive the regional dispersion of ODA. Austrian exports are to a great extent directed to Southern and Eastern Europe, and so is a large part of the Austrian ODA. National interest might be at play also in the Slovak regional dispersion to similar countries. The distinction between old and new donors with regard to the regional ODA focus is problematic, and an analysis of other old donors could show that national interest usually prevails in ODA regardless of the age of the donor. The geographical location of recipients could be yet another way to put donors into different groups. Financially, both development apparatuses were strongly influenced by their states' joining of the EU, and the low salience of the aid question keeps the ODA levels rather stable unless unexpected events such as a debt cancellation occur.

There are also important similarities with regard to the non-governmental sphere in both countries. Small, private, non-participatory NGDOs dominate this sector as has been confirmed by research from other countries. The interdependence between the governments and NGDOs leads to the weakening of NGDOs' critical perspective toward their most important donor. The systems of funding in both countries also cause a lack of cooperation among the NGDOs.

Finally, the declared motivation in both countries, just like in many others, moves between altruistic motivation and self-interest. An interesting finding is that there is an interest in both countries in using development aid as a means to be accepted as an international actor. With regard to the workers employed in the development apparatus, the Slovaks are more motivated by their professional interest than the Austrians, who more often stressed ethical motivations.

To conclude, all these elements show strong similarities between the Austrian and Slovak apparatuses, and they cast doubt on the distinction based on the alleged age of the donor. The rest of the book shows further similarities, but also differences in the Austrian and Slovak development discourses.

Notes

1 [I]n order to facilitate a greater Austrian participation in aid to developing countries [...], it is agreed that counterpart funds may also be made available through the annual investment programs for such aid, including, for example, technical assistance, long term export financing, and investment and export credit guarantee programs.

(Abkommen zwischen der Republik Österreich und der Regierung der Vereinigten Staaten von Amerika über die ERP-Counterpart-Regelung samt Notenwechsel, in Hödl 2013)

2 These were, apart from the Convention on the Organisation for Economic Co-operation and Development (1961) and the ERP Counterpart Settlement Agreement (1961), the following: the Agreement of the International Monetary Fund (1949), the Agreement of the International Finance Corporation (1956), and the Agreement of the International Development Association (1961) (Hödl 2013).

3 The figure is based on the DAC's new type of aid classification (OECD 2009) and includes budget support, core contributions, pooled programs, and funds and project-type interventions. In all of these categories one can expect an element of ownership, unlike in the rest of the Austrian ODA.

4 Genuine aid excludes imputed student costs, refugee costs, debt relief, tied aid, and interests on loans (Concord 2013). Some of the criticism of inflated aid has been accepted by national governments as stricter rules were adopted for refugee costs by the DAC, and some of the donors stopped considering loans as ODA. The OECD seemed to have accepted some of the criticism by introducing a Country Programmable Aid figure similar to the Genuine Aid figure. Still, one should be aware of the civil

society interest in counting only the ODA that goes abroad, where there is a greater potential for NGDOs to compete over such money.

5 Here is the exact wording of the question asked by Eurobarometer: "In your opinion, is it very important, fairly important, not very important or not at all important to help people in developing countries?" (Eurobarometer 2016: 6).

Bibliography

ADA (2017): ODA Report 2015. Federal Ministry for Europe, Integration and Foreign Affairs, Directorate-General for Development Cooperation, www.entwicklung.at/fileadmin/user_upload/Dokumente/Publikationen/ODA-Berichte/Englisch/ODA_Report_2015.pdf.

Banks, Nicola, Hulme, David, and Edwards, Michael 2015: NGOs, States, and Donors Revisited: Still Too Close for Comfort? *World Development* 66, 707–718, doi:10.1016/j.worlddev.2014.09.028.

Bátora, Jozef 2004: Identita a štátny záujem v slovenskej zahraničnej politike. *Medzinárodné otázky* 8(2), 39–54.

Beňáková, Nora 2010: SlovakAid – an Unemployed Foreign Policy Tool. *International Issues and Slovak Foreign Policy Affairs* 19(3), 3–22.

Beňaková, Nora 2011: Ochota Slovákov pomáhať? Radšej sa ľutujú (Rozhovor Karola Sudora). sme.sk, www.sme.sk/c/6151200/nora-benakova-ochota-slovakov-pomahat-radsej-sa-lutuju.html.

Beňáková, Nora, Mihálik, Ján, and Brezáni, Peter 2010: Rozvojová spolupráca a Slovensko v roku 2010. In: Brezáni (ed.): *Ročenka zahraničnej politiky Slovenskej Republiky 2010*. Bratislava: Výskumné centrum SFPA, 147–165.

Brezáni, Peter 2013: On the path towards the better relations: Role of the Slovak CSOs in the development assistance and aid effectiveness. RC SFPA.

Brzica, Daneš 2002: Slovensko v medzinárodnom systéme rozvojovej spolupráce. *Rozvojová pomoc a spolupráca*. Bratislava: Slovenský inštitút medzinárodných štúdií, 107–120.

Carbone, Maurizio 2015: Development and foreign aid. In: Jørgensen, Knud Erik, Aarstad, Åsne Kalland, Drieskens, Edith, Laatikainen, Katie, and Tonra, Ben (eds.): *The Sage Handbook of European Foreign Policy*. Thousand Oaks: SAGE Publications, https://uk.sagepub.com/en-gb/eur/the-sage-handbook-of-european-foreign-policy/book241829.

Čaučík, Marián, Krátka, Zuzana, and Pastorová, Ľudmila 2007: Slovensko a rozvojová pomoc v roku 2006. In: Brezáni (ed.): *Ročenka zahraničnej politiky Slovenskej Republiky 2006*. Bratislava: Výskumné centrum SFPA, 127–134.

CGD (2018): Commitment to Development Index. *Center For Global Development*, www.cgdev.org/commitment-development-index-2018.

Císař, Ondřej 2008: *Politický aktivismus v České Republice*. Brno: Centrum pro studium demokracie a kultury.

Concord 2013: Concord AidWatch 2013. The Unique Role of the European Aid. The Fight Against Global Poverty, https://reliefweb.int/sites/reliefweb.int/files/resources/CONCORD_2013_AidWatch_Report_1.pdf.

Concord 2016: Concord AidWatch. Report 2016. https://concordeurope.org/wp-content/uploads/2016/10/CONCORD_AidWatch_Report_2016_web.pdf.

Darnton, Andrew 2009: The Public, DFID and Support for Development – A Rapid Review. AD Research and Analysis, https://celebrityanddevelopment.files.wordpress.com/2011/02/darnton-rapidreview_ad011209.pdf.

Eder, Rudolf and Krobath, Hermann 1972: *Die österreichische Entwicklungshilfe. Politik – Organisation – Leistungen.* Wien – Dar Es Salam: Österreichische Forschungsstiftung für Entwicklungshilfe.

Edwards, Michael and Hulme, David 1996: Too close for comfort? The impact of official aid on nongovernmental organizations. *World Development* 24(6), 961–973.

Eurobarometer 2011: Making a difference in the world: Europeans and the future of development aid. European Commission, ec.europa.eu/public_opinion/archives/ebs/ebs_375_en.pdf.

Eurobarometer 2016: The European Year for Development – Citizens' views on development, cooperation and aid. European commission, https://ec.europa.eu/europeaid/sites/devco/files/sp441-devco-report-final_en.pdf.

Eyben, Rosalind and Savage, Laura 2013: Emerging and Submerging Powers: Imagined Geographies in the New Development Partnership at the Busan Fourth High Level Forum. *Journal of Development Studies* 49(4), 457–469, doi:10.1080/00220388.2012.733372.

Fialová, Zuzana 2011: Application of the Istanbul Principles for CSO Development Effectiveness by Slovak NGOs (Analysis). The Slovak NGDO Platform, www.mvro.sk/sk/e-kniznica/category/2-publikacie?download=1085:application-of-the-istanbul-principles-for-cso-development-effectiveness&start=20.

Foucault, Michel 1982: The Subject and Power. *Michel Foucault: Beyond Structuralism and Hermeneutics*. Chicago: Harvester Wheatsheaf, 208–225.

Gažovič, Ondrej 2012: Slovak Aid – oficiálna rozvojová spolupráca ako nástroj konštituovania identity SR? *Mezinárodní vztahy* 47(1), 22–46.

Gažovič, Ondrej and Profant, Tomáš 2015: Slovakia: A Donor Against its Will? In: Horký-Hlucháň, Ondřej and Lightfoot, Simon (ed.): *Development Cooperation of the "New" EU Member States. Beyond Europeanization.* Basingstoke and New York: Palgrave Macmillan, 64–81.

Ghica, Luciana Alexandra 2013: Is it worth grouping the new EU donors? Prezentované na The future direction of central and eastern European development policy – Finding a common role in a post-MDG world, Vienna: Austrian Research Foundation for International Development.

Hemedinger, Fritz 1995: *Idealisten, Abenteuerer, Weltverbesserer? Einsatzmotive, – vorbereitung und - probleme österreichischer EntwicklungshelferInnen.* Frankfurt am Main: Brandes und Apsel.

Henson, Spencer, Lindstrom, Johanna, Haddad, Lawrence, and Mulmi, Rajendra 2010: Public Perceptions of International Development and Support for Aid in the UK: Results from a Qualitative Enquiry. Institute of Development Studies.

HoC IDC 2009: Aid Under Pressure: Support for Development Assistance in a Global Economic Downturn. Fourth Report of Session 2008–09 Volume I. House of Commons International Development Committee, www.publications.parliament.uk/pa/cm200809/cmselect/cmintdev/179/179i.pdf.

Hödl, Gerald 2004: *Österreich und die Dritte Welt. Aussen – und Entwicklungspolitik der Zweiten Republik bis zum EU-Beitritt 1995*. Wien: Promedia.

Hödl, Gerald 2006: In der Endlosschleife. Leitmotive der österreichischen Entwicklungszusammenarbeit. In: Gomes, Bea, Maral-Hanak, Irmi and Schicho, Walter (ed.): *Entwicklungszusammenarbeit. Akteure, Handlungsmuster und Interessen.* Wien: Mandelbaum, 25–41.

Hödl, Gerald 2010: "Es tut mir nich leid, dass ich's gemacht hab'." Eine "Oral history" der österreichischen Entwicklungshilfe. *Journal Für Entwicklungspolitik* (3), 95–118.

Hödl, Gerald 2013: Chronic underachievement. Austria's development aid in historical perspective. In: Olesen, Thorsten B. and Pharo, Helge (ed.): *Saints and Sinners. Official Development Aid and its Dynamics in a Historical and Comparative Perspective*. Oslo: Akademika, 255–278.

Horký, Ondřej 2010: *Česká rozvojová spolupráce. Diskurzy, praktiky, rozpory*. Praha: SLON.

Horký, Ondřej 2012a: The Impact of the Shallow Europeanisation of the "New" Member States on the EU's Actorness: What Coherence between Foreign and Development Policy? *The European Union and Global Development: An "Enlightened Superpower" in the Making?* Basingstoke: Palgrave Macmillan, 57–73.

Horký, Ondřej 2012b: The Transfer of the Central and Eastern European "Transition Experience" to the South: Myth or Reality? *Perspectives on European Politics and Society* 13 (1), 17–32.

Hudson, David and van Heerde-Hudson, Jennifer 2012: "A Mile Wide and an Inch Deep": Surveys of Public Attitudes Towards Development Aid. *International Journal of Development Education and Global Learning*, 4(1), 5–23.

Hulényi, Peter 2004: Päť otázok trilaterálnej spolupráce. *Medzinárodné otázky*, 13(4), 80–85.

Interview No. 5 2013: Interview with the respondent from the Pontis Foundation. 3.7.2013, personally in Bratislava.

Interview No. 7 2013: Interview with the respondent from the Pontis Foundation. 15.7.2013, personally in Bratislava.

Interview No. 9 2013: Interview with the respondent from PiP. 13.8.2013, personally in Bratislava.

Interview No. 10 2013: Interview with the respondent from PiP. 15.8.2013, personally in Bratislava.

Interview No. 13 2013: Interview with the respondent from SAIDC. 15.8.2013, personally in Bratislava.

Interview No. 14 2014: Interview with the respondent from SAIDC. 26.2.2014, personally in Bratislava.

Interview No. 16 2013: Interview with the respondent from Austroprojekt. 7.10.2013, personally in Vienna.

Interview No. 17 2013: Interview with the respondent from Austroprojekt. 6.10.2013, personally in Vienna.

Interview No. 21 2013: Interview with the respondent from ADA. 20.11.2013, personally in Vienna.

Interview No. 22 2013: Interview with the respondent from ADA. 20.11.2013, personally in Vienna.

Interview No. 23 2013: Interview with the respondent from ADA. 26.11.2013, personally in Vienna.

Interview No. 24 2014: Interview with the respondent from ADA. 11.2.2014, personally in Vienna.

Interview No. 25 2013: Interview with the respondent from CARE. 20.11.2013, personally in Vienna.

Interview No. 26 2013: Interview with the respondent from CARE. 26.11.2013, personally in Vienna.

Interview No. 27 2013: Interview with the respondent from CARE. 27.11.2013, over Skype.

Interview No. 28 2014: Interview with the respondent from CARE. 11.2.2014, personally in Vienna.

Jaklin, Ulrike, Wank, Lukas, and Wolfram, Marion 2013: Changes in funding of Austrian development NGOs. *Shabka*, www.shabka.org/2013/05/20/changes-in-funding-of-austrian-development-ngos/.

Lightfoot, Simon 2010: The Europeanisation of international development policies: the case of Central and Eastern European States. *Europe–Asia Studies* 62(2), 329–350.

Lightfoot, Simon and Szent-Iványi, Balázs 2014: Reluctant Donors? The Europeanization of International Development Policies in the New Member States. *JCMS: Journal of Common Market Studies* 52(6), 1257–1272, doi:10.1111/jcms.12141.

Lightfoot, Simon and Obrovsky, Michael 2016: Austrian development policy – from global to neighbourhood policy? *Austrian Journal of Political Science* 45(2), 11–21, doi:10.15203/ozp.1088.vol.45iss2.

Maral-Hanak, Irmi 2008: Entwicklung kommunizieren: Öffentlichkeits - und Bildungsarbeit. In: Gomes, Bea, Maral-Hanak, Irmi and Schicho, Walter (ed.): *Die Praxis der Entwicklungszusammenarbeit. Akteure, Interessen und Handlungsmuster*. Wien: Mandelbaum, 103–123.

Melegh, Attila 2006: *On the East–West Slope. Globalization, Nationalism, Racism and Discourse on Central and Eastern Europe*. Budapest and New York: Central European University Press.

Michálková, Katarína 2013: *Efektivita rozvojovej spolupráce slovenských mimovládnych organizácií v Keni* (Diplomová práca). UK FSEV ÚEŠMV, Bratislava.

MZV SR a PMVRO 2010: Memorandum o porozumení medzi Ministerstvom zahraničných vecí SR a Platformou mimovládnych rozvojových organizácií, mvro.sk/?mdocs-file=765.

Obrovsky, Michael 1993: Strukturanpassung. Zu den politischen und administrativen Rahmenbedingen der österreichischen Entwicklunszusammenarbeit. AGEZ, 79–95.

Obrovsky, Michael 2005: Austrian Aid Policy. In: Stokke, Olav/Hoebink, Paul (ed.): *Perspectives on European Development Cooperation. Policy and Performance of Individual Donor Countries and the EU*. London and New York: Routledge, 113–135.

Obrovsky, Michael 2006: "Von der Solidarität zur professionell verwalten Wohltätigkeit": Entwicklungspolitisische NGOs in Österreich auf Identitätsuche. In: Gomes, Bea/Maral-Hanak, Irmi/Schicho, Walter (ed.): *Entwicklungszusammenarbeit. Akteure, Handlungsmuster und Interessen*. Wien: Mandelbaum, 249–270.

Obrovsky, Michael 2013: Interview with Michael Obrovsky. 19.11.2013, personally in Vienna.

Obrovsky, Michael 2016: Die öffentliche Entwicklungszusammenarbeit – Official Development Assistance (ODA). *Österreichische Entwicklungspolitik 2016. Fluchtbedingte Migration – Herausforderung für die EZA*. Wien: Österreichische Forschungsstiftung für Internationale Entwicklung, 59–75.

Obrovsky, Michael and Raza, Werner 2012: Reflexionen zu einer Neustrukturierung der Entwicklungspolitik in Österreich. *Österreichische Entwicklungspolitik 2012. Die Zukunft der Österreichischen Entwicklungspolitik*. Wien: Österreichische Forschungsstiftung für Internationale Entwicklung, 15–22.

OECD 2009: Reporting Directives for the Creditor Reporting System. Addendum on Types of Aid. Development Assistance Committee, Organisation for Economic Co-operation and Development, www.oecd.org/dac/stats/44479737.pdf.

OECD 2011: Special Review of the Slovak Republic's Development Co-operation. OECD Development Assistance Committee, www.oecd.org/dac/peer-reviews/49512222.pdf.

Olša, jr., Jaroslav 2003: The Czech Republic: an emerging partner for ACP countries. *the Courier ACP–EU* 198 (May–June), 21–22.

ÖFSE 2016: 2016 Österreichische Entwicklingspolitik. Fluchtbedingte Migration – Herausforderung für die EZA. Österreichische Forschungsstiftung für Internationale Entwicklung, www.oefse.at/fileadmin/content/Downloads/Publikationen/Oepol/OEPOL 2016_web.pdf.

Pearson, Lester, Boyle, Edward, de Oliveira Campos, Roberto, Dillon, C. Douglas, Guth, Wilfried, Lewis, Arthur, Marjolin, Robert E., and Okita, Saburo 1969: Partners in Development (The Pearson Report). Pearson Commission on International Development.

Petrova, Tsveta and Tarrow, Sidney 2007: Transactional and Participatory Activism in the Emerging European Polity The Puzzle of East–Central Europe. *Comparative Political Studies* 40(1), 74–94.

PiP 2016: Annual Report 2015. People in Peril.

PIPA 2001: Americans on Foreign Aid and World Hunger: A Study of US Public Attitudes. Program on International Policy Attitudes, www.pipa.org/OnlineReports/ForeignAid/ForeignAid_Feb01/ForeignAid_Feb01_rpt.pdf.

PMVRO 2016: Slovenská rozvojová pomoc v roku 2015. Hodnotiaca správa Platformy mimovládnych a rozvojových organizácií, www.mvro.sk/old/attachments/article/292/AidWatch%202015.pdf.

Profant, Tomáš 2015: Slovenské mimovládne "rozvojové" organizácie ako politickí aktéri. *Sociológia* 47(1), 113–138.

Profant, Tomáš 2018: The Social Construction of Slovakia as a Donor and its Power Effects. *Europe–Asia Studies* 70(3), 365–387, doi:10.1080/09668136.2018.1453486.

Raffer, Kunibert 1995: Österreichs Entwicklungshilfe: Ein trauriges Kapitel. *Österreichisches Jahrbuch für Internationale Politik* 12. Wien: Böhlau, 21–49.

Schicho, Walter 2013: Interview with Walter Schicho. 18.11.2013, personally in Vienna.

Smillie, Ian 1999: Public Support and the Politics of Aid. *Development* 42(3), 71–76, doi:10.1057/palgrave.development.1110063.

Szent-Iványi, Balázs 2012: Aid Allocation of the Emerging Central and Eastern European donors. *Journal of International Relations and Development* 15(1), 65–89.

Szép, Attila 2004: Oficiálna rozvojová pomoc Európskej únie a Slovensko. *Medzinárodné otázky* 13(4), 3–22.

Tichý, Braňo 2015: Pomáhajme utečencom (aj) u nich doma. *Pravda.sk* 5.8.2015, http://nazory.pravda.sk/osa/clanok/362751-pomahajme-utecencom-aj-u-nich-doma/.

Unfried, Berthold and Himmelstoss, Evaed 2012: *Die eine Welt schaffen. Praktiken von "Internationale Solidarität" und "Internationale Entwicklung."* Wien: Akademische Verlagsanstalt.

Vittek, Martin and Lightfoot, Simon 2009: The Europeanization of Slovak development cooperation. *Contemporary European Studies* 4(1), 21–37.

Young, Dennis R. 2000: Alternative Models of Government-Nonprofit Sector Relations: Theoretical and International Perspectives. *Nonprofit and Voluntary Sector Quarterly* 29(1), 149–172.

3 Hierarchization of “us” over “them” and its disruptions

The question of the way the Other is represented has been present in development discourse at least since the Ethiopian famine in 1984. Already prior to that, Anouar Abdel-Malek (1963) and Edward Said (1979) pointed to the hierarchic representation of the Occident and the Orient. Later on, elements of the postcolonial critique entered the development discourse and were mainstreamed into the discourses of participation and partnership.

The very same rules of formation of development discourse that govern the relations between the Global North and the Global South govern also the relation between East and West. The fall of the Berlin Wall did not change the structure of the discourse and the difference between East and West is just a reflection of the difference between North and South. The aim of this chapter is to show that the East and the West as part of the North represent the South in a very similar way and the temporal (old–new) distinction between them is therefore misplaced. It is in the analysis of the colonial hierarchy that one can see the postcolonial crossroads most clearly. The East is the Global Self and the Global Other at the same time.

The comparison of the Slovak and Austrian actors shows that, whereas the Slovaks hierarchize more often and in a sharper way than the Austrians, they also represent the Other positively on many occasions. But the difference between them and the Austrians is one of degree and not of substance. The similarity between them is much greater than one might guess on the basis of the categories “old” and “new” donors. This chapter therefore questions the use of the temporal distinction. The results for both donors confirm the extant postcolonial research on traditional donors (e.g., Noxolo 2006; Dogra 2014; Ziai 2004; Eriksson Baaz 2005) and new donors (e.g., Profant 2010; Pavlicová 2012; Horký 2011).

In the following I introduce the continuity with the colonial hierarchy in the development discourse and the effects of this discursive hierarchy. After that I focus on the disruption of this hierarchy by the discourses of partnership and participation. The theoretical underpinnings of the development discourse are further explored in the following section on logocentrism, the general law of development and their disruptions. After that, the empirical account of hierarchization in the discourses of old and new donors ensues, focusing on “their” negative and “our” positive representations, one-way interactions between “us” and "them," "our" and "their" enunciations of expertise and gratefulness and, finally, a specific case of how power hierarchically operates in the partnership discourse in the representation of practice. The sections after that show disruptions of the hierarchic development discourse in the attempts to fight negative stereotypes and to represent "them" positively, and a particular example of an almost reversal of the traditional hierarchy between "us" and "them" in one interview. In the conclusion I contemplate the consequences of the current trend of representing the Other in a positive way that is present in the most compelling form in one text from CARE Austria (CARE 2012a) and in an interview with one respondent from this organization (Interview No. 25 2013).

The continuity with the colonial hierarchy in development discourse and its effects

One of the discussions about colonialism focused on the question of the relationship between more material and more discursive aspects of colonialism. Whereas direct violence was clearly necessary to secure the flow of wealth from the colonized to the colonizer, the economic plunder would not be possible without a discourse that in one way or another legitimized this plunder. One can therefore speak of "a profoundly symbiotic relationship between the discursive and material practices of imperialism" (JanMohamed 1985: 64). At the same time the colonial discourse had further effects on the identities at both ends of the colonization. In other words, various ways of representing racial or cultural differences were necessary for the creation of the whole colonial institutional setting, but as these representations gained influence in the metropole, they transformed not only the colonies, but also the metropole.

The Orientalist structure of the colonial discourse was based on clearly delimited dichotomies that resulted in the creation of a superior Self and an inferior Other. Such a structure is not natural, but socially constructed. History shows different kinds of relationships between different cultures and between populations with different skin colors. For example, there was the case of Christian Ethiopianism, which contained a love or preference for things Ethiopian (Nederveen Pieterse 1992: 25), the racial equality between ancient Egyptians and their darker neighbors, the Nehesi (Hund 2003: 8–10), and the racial hierarchy between the English Protestants and the Irish Catholics, who were of the same color (Allen 2012). But, even the colonial relationship in British India during its early years was not based on the strong hierarchies that one usually identifies with colonialism (Nandy 1983: 4–5).

Yet the construction of the Other as the negative, inferior reflection of the Self prevailed. If the black subject was considered lazy, the white subject was industrious; if the black was irrational, the white was rational; if the black was promiscuous, the white was sexually restrained. In sum, if the Other was barbaric or savage, the Self was civilized.

Already during colonialism the dichotomies were occasionally reversed, and the noble savage was romanticized. More importantly, the Other was represented as childlike and incapable of governance and therefore as in need of guidance, in need of the Self bringing order and civilization to the Other. There are still competing discourses on colonialism, and some advocate for its reinvigoration (e.g., Cooper 2002). However, I agree with the definition of colonialism "as the conquest and control of other people's land and goods" (Loomba 2010: 8). The main effect of colonial discourse was the legitimation of colonialism.

Still, it should be clear that, just like today, in the 19th century and before then, identities and discourses were never as clear-cut as Said's Orientalism may imply. Bhabha (2004) shows well how cultural encounters resulted in hybrid "Selves" and hybrid "Others." This is particularly important in relation to the effect of colonial discourse on the societies of the West.

Next to the main effect of representing the Self as superior, as the crown of humanity that contributed to the Self's greater self-esteem, to its "feelings of omnipotence and permanence" (Nandy 1983: 35), there were other pathologies related to colonizers' identities. Just as the "black man [is] slave to his inferiority [so is] the white man slave to his superiority" (Fanon 2008: 42). This superiority led to a devaluation of feminine values and promoted values such as "competition, achievement, control and productivity – new forms of institutionalized violence and ruthless social Darwinism" (Nandy 1983: 32). Nandy sees a connection between the behavior towards colonies on the one hand and the behavior towards women, sexual minorities, children, and poorer classes on the other. "[T]he ideology of colonialism produced a false sense of cultural homogeneity in Britain" (ibid.) and thereby enabled the dominance of a small elite excluding any cultural criticism in regard to the colonial margins.

It is important to keep in mind that, even though the colonial domination was brutal and repressive, at the same time it operated on a basis of consensus. The partial consent was necessary to enable colonial governance. Colonialism was for the subject "a product of one's own emasculation and defeat in legitimate power politics. For the rulers, colonial exploitation [...] was in harmony with superior forms of political and economic organization" (Nandy 1983: 10). The collaboration of the colonized on a long-term basis would not have been possible "unless they had some acceptance of the ideology of the system" (ibid.).

Eventually, the consent of the colonized fell apart, and the oppressed started to voice their demands in various, often violent, forms. These protests, together with other factors, led to the replacement of colonial discourse with development discourse and to the end of formal colonialism.

Colonization has been, in general, legitimized by the civilizing mission that was focused especially on cultural change. An overall cultural improvement was supposed to be the result of this change. Development or social well-being was not addressed directly until the later part of the 19th century. Martina Kopf (2009) suggests the Berlin Conference in 1884/1885 as one of the possible beginnings of colonial development. Article six of the General Act of the Berlin Conference bound the European powers to "care for the improvement of the conditions of [native tribes'] moral and material well-being" (in ibid.). Care for the well-being of the populations in the colonies was later mentioned in the doctrines of "constructive exploitation" and "constructive imperialism" at the end of the 19th century and further emphasized in the dual mandate and the *mise en valeur* approaches in the 1920s. The human side of development was in all these cases more rhetoric than reality, though, as development was constrained by the policy of colonial financial self-sufficiency (Hodge and Hödl 2014: 11). There was then a co-occurrence of the terms "civilization" and "development" in the same discursive formation during the 1920s and 1930s (Dufour 2014: 330). After this period the development discourse replaced the discourse of civilization.

The origins of this change are to be found in the new political context of the 1930s and 1940s. Colonialism was criticized, for example, by the members of the British Labour Party and the French Section of the Workers' International, the international community, philanthropic NGOs, and international organizations such as the International Labor Office (Hodge and Hödl 2014: 13). Perhaps most crucial of all was the fact that "Africans were increasingly unwilling to stay in the limited roles that colonial rulers had assigned to them" (ibid.: 13). Not only did they engage in strikes and damaged mines and important infrastructure such as railways or ports, but more importantly they rejected the Eurocentric hierarchic rhetoric of civilization and demanded more equal treatment (Dufour 2014: 331). Simply put, there was an "urgent need" (Foucault 1980: 195) for a new interpretive grid for the North–South relations.

Subsequently, the civilized-savage binary was replaced with the developed-underdeveloped binary that enables the countries to develop – to advance gradually towards the same state of progress (Dufour 2014: 322).

Even though the development discourse abandoned the colonial-type racism, it kept a hierarchy between what used to be races nonetheless. Populations in the North were discursively constructed as modern, enlightened, and developed and therefore superior to their Southern traditional, backwards, and underdeveloped counterparts. However, people in the South were attracted to the development discourse, whose basis is a possibility to engage in the development race between potential equals. At the same time, the populations in the North kept their position, as they were still constructed as modern, enlightened, technologically advanced, and, in general, culturally superior.

The hierarchic feature thus remains the most important continuity of the development discourse with its colonial predecessor. "The basic structure of both discourses is the division of the world into the progressive, dominating part and the backward, inferior part" (Ziai 2006: 39, my translation). The discourse keeps its Eurocentric character with the European nations at the top of the ladder of social evolution.

The effect of this hierarchization is then similar to that of the colonial discourse. Constructed as superior, the people in the North still enjoyed the feeling of being at the top of the evolutionary ladder. The pleasure of superiority thus continues to flow from South to North. Whereas this may seem obvious in the figure of the white man – e.g., the colonial official turned development expert who remains in possession of the truth – Heron illustrates this hierarchy through an inferior Northern Self – a female development worker. Her respondents (middle-class Canadian women who worked overseas as development workers) feel themselves to be always ranked below men in their home country. The narratives of gender transgression point to a different perception of these white women in the field than at home. They express the feelings of "increased confidence, [...] of personal strength, [...] of being valued, [...] affirmed, [...] useful, [...] respected, [...] unique, [...] appreciated, [...] known, [...] important, [...] and of simply feeling good about oneself" (Heron 2007: 113). There is thus a continuity in this psychological effect from colonial to development discourse.

Another effect of hierarchization is that it enables domination. It is the hierarchical divide that makes the development interventions possible. Only if the Other is constructed as inferior can the superior Self intervene to lift him or her from the problematic situation. Only if the Other is inferior can the superior expert come and use his or her knowledge in the Other's situation, because s/he knows what is good and what will benefit the Other. The trustee needs his or her inferior counterpart to whom s/he can be a trustee. The Other needs to be constructed as inferior; otherwise the trustee could not attempt to shape his or her life.

This basic feature of development discourse is crucial, not only for the North–South division, but also for the hierarchic division between East and West, and between old and new donors. The effect of hierarchization is very similar in this field. It does not make possible a development intervention, but a demand for a particular type of action, for the acceptance of particular types of norms. As the Other (new donors) is inferior to the Self (an old donor), the Self can come and teach the Other how to behave as a good donor. The difference between the hierarchy between donors on the one hand and the hierarchy between donors and partners on the other is in the sharpness of the hierarchy. New donors have a much greater field of action to disrupt the hierarchic power relation.

This domination in the North–South development discourse is the basis for the exercise of power over countries that offer their natural resources to the global market. As the hierarchization enables the division into developed and underdeveloped countries, the development plans are the logical consequence of this binary. These are then written according to the current trends within the development discourse promoting, e.g., the privatization of state companies, or orienting the country towards cash crops. The result is, in general, the material flow from South to North, from the "underdeveloped" to the "developed," yet this does not have to be the case. The development discourse in the past included strategies such as the import substitution industrialization or delinking that clearly went against the material interests of the North. In this sense, the discourse is ambivalent and includes contradictory positions, which are united by their more general rules of formation, but oppose each other as development theories (see Escobar 1995: 42).

One can find a similar problem in the profit outflow in the economies of the new donors. They are considered less developed in terms of GDP per capita, HDI or productivity of the work force. At the same time, the West invests in the

East and the profits flow from the "underdeveloped" East to the "developed" West (Chmelař et al. 2016). This has been criticized with the use of the very similar language of the dependency theory (Nölke and Vliegenthart 2009). Yet, at the same time, the discourse of development is ambivalent and includes positions which enable the rise of productivity or GDP growth in the countries of the East at the expense of Western (and other) investors. The rules of formation thus remain the same, yet they make it possible for the East to develop in the traditional sense of the word.

Overall, the effect of hierarchization is twofold. On one hand, it is psychological, as the developed Self may derive self-esteem and pleasure from its superior position. On the other, the effect is material. Hierarchization serves as a discursive basis for a flow of material goods going from South to North. At the same time, however, the hierarchic discourse of development enables strategies against exploitation.

Whereas the colonial discourse kept a clear distance in the human evolution between the colonizers and the colonized, the development discourse enabled the possibility of overcoming this distance. The discourses of partnership and participation then attempt to represent "us" and "them" as equal partners in a common endeavor. This discourse thus disrupts and occasionally reverses the colonial and development hierarchies. The Other has become active over the years, and his or her agency enables a variety of destabilizations of the discourse. The deliberate attempts to represent the Other in a positive way and to act as his or her partner have their origin in the critique of Orientalism and in the participation and partnership approaches.

Even though participation had already been preached during the colonial era (Hodge 2007: 187; Hickey and Mohan 2004: 6), it became prominent from the 1970s. At least two factors contributed to the emergence of participation and partnership as new approaches. The first is the failure of the previous decades in development policy (Crewe and Harrison 2002: 160). These failures occurred due "to the fact that the populations concerned were kept out of all the processes related to [development projects'] design, formulation and implementation" (Rahnema 1992: 117). Participation and partnership became the new missing element that only needed to be incorporated, and development would work. In this way, partnership was supposed to remedy the problems in the Structural Adjustment Programs. These were not problematic in their content, but in their form:

> There has [...] been some mild dissatisfaction with the way Structural Adjustment Programmes have been imposed by the World Bank and IMF [...] The main target of the criticism has not been the substance of the SAP reform. These are seen as necessary. The problem [...] is rather the mode of delivering the message.
>
> (Schori in Dahl 2001: 6)

Participation and partnership were thus a response to development failures.

The second factor that contributed to the emergence of the partnership discourses was the critique of Orientalism that made its way into the development apparatus. This critique gained prominence especially after the Ethiopian famine in 1984. According to several authors, the discourse of partnership has been an attempt to disavow paternalism and thus to respond to the critique of Eurocentrism in development aid and cooperation (Eriksson Baaz 2005: 153; Noxolo 2006: 257). The passive Other therefore needed to be replaced by an equal partner. Such a representation of the Other could not be criticized by the critics of Orientalism within development. Whereas the more drastic images of starving kids are less visible, the problem of representing the Other as a passive object of aid still persists (Kiesel and Bendix 2010), even if these representations occur in the discourse next to more positive images of the Other (Dogra 2014).

Moreover, placing the onus of agency on the shoulders of the Other fit well with the neoliberal individualizing discourse. Just like an individual with a neoliberal subjectivity becomes responsible for his or her failures, so does the active partner or the participating actor become responsible for what they do.[1] In this sense the new approach was in accordance with the dominant discourse of the 1980s. The representation of the Other as active then served the need to blame the Other for failures as s/he now became equally responsible.

Henrietta Lidchi (1999) shows the change in representation towards this positive imagery. She analyzed Oxfam images that "were/are very deliberate, highly motivated answers to the truth claims and immediacy of negative images" (ibid.: 99). One may refer to the aim to represent the Other as active and to represent need with dignity as "deliberate positivism" (Dogra 2014: 7, 131). Sixteen years after Lidchi's analysis, it is clear that the *deliberate* attempts to represent the Other in a positive way are still present; however, as I argue in my research, the positive perspective has become naturalized *to a certain extent*, and occasionally, it does not seem that the positive representation of the Other is a conscious policy.

Just as the Other from the Global South is represented in a positive way, yet remains inferior, one can find a positive representation of the Eastern Other as well. By becoming a donor, this demi-Orientalized Other (Wolf 1994) is elevated almost to the status of the Self, but not quite as it remains a new, inexperienced donor that is inferior to the old, experienced donor.

The idea of participation/partnership has been welcomed by the most ardent critics of development (Escobar 1984: 392; Cooke and Kothari 2001: 13; Crewe and Harrison 2002: 77). Indeed

> [i]f people were to decide themselves what 'development' means for them and how it should be reached, this would be a fundamental contradiction to some of the rules of formation (enunciative modalities, objects and concepts) and would constitute a clear break from the development discourse.
>
> (Ziai 2006: 48, my translation)

This is the crucial element that points to the incoherence within the development discourse brought about by the idea of participation and partnership (Ziai

2014: 9–10). Expert knowledge is replaced by the local perspective. The hierarchy is reversed – the expert becomes a mere helper to the local population.

The discourse of complementarity and coordination of donors offers a similar disruption of the development discourse as the new donors become respected on the basis of their particular expertise which is connected to their transition to liberal democracy. They are no longer the novices learning about how to do development from, e.g., Austria, Canada or the UNDP; they are now experts in a particular field, and in this field other donors should follow their lead.

However, many critics pointed out that a reversal of the hierarchy is not the case for the North and South, and in practice the question "who is in the driving seat?" (Crewe and Harrison 2002: 155) remains pertinent. Identities of development workers are still formed by the hierarchizing development discourse (Eriksson Baaz 2005), and the partnership discourse in its textual form represents the partners in an unequal way (Noxolo 2006).[2]

Moreover, the deliberate positivism often aims at merely representing the Other as the "worthy self" (Dahl 2001: 19) or as the "deserving Third World women" (Dogra 2014: 39). "To be worthy of assistance you have to be a person who does not willfully refrain from using his or her agency" (Dahl 2001: 19). The problem with the focus on agency is that one may, in a neoliberal fashion, then blame the Other for a failure of a project rather than structural constraints (Dahl 2001: 20). Such an emphasis on the agency of the Other also betrays a distrust of the Other and doubts that the Other would be active in general, similarly to the demand that all Muslims condemn attacks by Islamist terrorists. It is therefore necessary to closely analyze the positive discourse about the Other and focus on its effects. Simply put, even if deliberate positivism may be a step in the right direction with unforeseeable but potentially very positive outcomes in changing the identities of Northern subjects, a closer examination of deliberate positivism is necessary. My research shows the limits of the positive representations that keep the hierarchies in place even though they try to minimize them. At the same time, responsibility is often put on the shoulders of agents represented as active in the discourse. As the chapter on depoliticization shows, development discourse more often than not omits other agents and forces which might be considered equally if not more responsible for the problematic outcomes of the social relations between the North and the South.

The following section analyzes logocentric representations of "us" and "them" that echo the colonial discourse of civilization and then shows the instances of the explicit use of the general law of development in the discourse. After that, the section shows the disruptions of logocentrism and of the general law of development in the analyzed discourses. Overall, the aim here is to cast doubt on the monolithic image of Orientalism created by Said (1979). Hybridity (Bhabha 2004) is more apt to serve as an analytical category for the study of hierarchic relations between Self and Other.

Logocentrism, the general law of development and their disruptions

The basic structure of development discourse is logocentric. "This term describes a disposition to impose hierarchy when encountering familiar and uncritically accepted dichotomies between West and East, North and South, modern and traditional … " (Manzo 1991: 8). Occasionally, the logocentric representations in the Slovak development discourse resembled the substantive distinction between Self and Other of colonial discourse.

One of the crucial questions asked by Foucault was concerned with how it is possible that certain objects appear as objects. "Is it possible to lay down the rule to which their appearance was subject?" (Foucault 2002a: 45) First, he wants to map "the surfaces of their emergence" (ibid.), to show where they can emerge as certain objects. In his example, he asks how it is that anomalies and deviations appear as such.

The discourse of psychiatry is very similar to development discourse in the sense of allowing anomalies and deviations to emerge as objects. They are both part of a wider logocentric pattern inherent to Western metaphysics. Logocentrism is a system of thought which posits "first principles and ultimately *a* first principle, an ultimate ground or *logos* which lies outside the system of differences which constitutes meaning in language" (Apffel-Marglin 1990: 102). Where Apffel-Marglin sees logocentrism in the Western science as connected to the violent acts of the Indian state in the name of development, Manzo shows the basic structure of the development discourse. The same logocentric pattern governs also the relation between old and new donors, with the old being the ultimate ground for the new.

Logocentrism has been the basis of the colonial discourse as well. The difference between the two discourses is that in the development discourse the superior white male has been replaced by the equally superior developed country or region. The object of development is now defined in socio-geographical terms rather than biological ones (Ziai 2006: 37; see also Dufour 2014: 329). Keeping the same basis for the definition of the Other – logocentrism – required after the discrediting of biologically-determined racism that the surface of emergence becomes a field that deals with countries or regions rather than with races. If people are to be treated in a hierarchical way, this is acceptable only in terms of a culture that can be changed or a society or region that can be developed. The nodal point of the development discourse thus changes from the white man to the developed, industrial society (Ziai 2006: 34–37).

Despite this change, it is possible to identify instances of colonial difference in the interviews. The most striking answers came from one respondent from the Slovak Agency for International Development Cooperation (SAIDC). She considered Kenya to be

> a completely different world [… Slovakia] belongs to the European civilization, and we have a completely different history, a completely different

> development that pushed us where we are today, and Africa, especially sub-Saharan Africa, really is somewhere else on this level [...] we are in a completely different civilizational dimension.
>
> (Interview No. 15 2014)

This respondent also offered a historical reasoning for this state of affairs:

> the European civilization has been here, one might say, for several thousand years, and Africa was for a long time undiscovered; simply put, there were not those civilizing centers in sub-Saharan Africa. Therefore this [African] society was not developing in this direction for the same period of time as [the society] in Europe.
>
> (Ibid., for a similar hierarchization see also Interview No. 12 2013, Interview No. 13 2013 from SAIDC)

These stark differentiations of "us" and "them" make up the surface of emergence on which weaker hierarchizations emerge. They are analyzed in the next section.

Concerning the formation of concepts, Foucault asks if it would not be possible to find a law that "would account for the successive or simultaneous emergence of disparate concepts" (2002a: 62). What rules or schemes link particular statements and concepts to one another? (ibid.: 67) Among other things Foucault focuses on the dependence of statements, which can contain the dependence of a hypothesis on verification or the dependence of a general law on a particular application (ibid.: 63).

Objects such as the illiterate, the malnourished, overpopulation, a failed state, bad governance, and the like emerge as such through the grids of specification (see the next section). The scheme that puts them into perspective is the connection to the difference between the developed and the developing. The concepts are formed within this general, logocentric pattern. Terms such as illiterate or malnourished are put together to merge into categories such as "developing" or "underdeveloped" (previously "backwards"). The more concrete concepts make sense as they build upon the existing binary developed-developing and strengthen it in this way, bestowing it with an ever-thicker aura of scientific expertise.

One can see here the "dependence of statements" (ibid.: 63). The particular application of the intervention into a field such as literacy depends upon the "general law" (ibid.) of development. The hypothesis-verification dependence happens in a tautological manner running back and forth between the general lack of development and a particular, verifiable lack that causes and is also the result of the more general "underdevelopment." This is similar to the so-called vicious circle of poverty. The concepts are thus formed within this set of dependencies that exist among them in logical relationships (e.g., there is no development without education, or the populations in developing countries are, in general, uneducated). This general law should be, according to a structuralist approach, followed in any utterance within the development discourse; however, my analysis shows important disruptions in this pattern and confirms similar research of the traditional donors (e.g., Dogra 2014; Ziai 2014).

Almost all the analyzed texts implicitly or explicitly followed the general law. PR articles used the term development less often, as they focused on the particularities of development without the need to invoke the master frame that, however, was present on each of the websites that contained the analyzed articles even if not in the particular articles themselves. Still the texts occasionally spoke of, e.g., "the development of the Kasigau region" (Pontis 2010a). The PR texts were destined for the public and accorded with a specific image of this public. They were short (a few hundred words each), and often followed a narrative of "them" needing help and "us" coming to help them. The national strategies or programs were different – official – documents which followed the main tenets of the development discourse in different ways (see below). Apart from a few critical texts (see Chapter 5), though, the term development served as an embracive term that often stayed implicitly behind the analyzed texts and was not mentioned.

There were a few respondents who used the term development without any hesitation in relation to the poorest countries. Edita Bednárová from the Slovak NGDO People in Peril (PiP) explicitly called Kenya a "developing country" in one public interview (Bednárová 2009); so did two respondents from ADA (Interview No. 21 2013, Interview No. 22 2013).

An unconditional acceptance of development rankings occurred mainly with regard to the countries that were considered relatively developed by the respondents. For example, one said,

> Georgia is [...] a country at a relatively good level of development. It is a normally functioning country. When you come there, the traffic works, the water-supply works, and services work without any problems, but they also need help [...] it is maybe Slovakia 15 or 20 years ago [...] they now go through stuff that we solved in the 1990s, some of it successfully, some of it less successfully.
>
> (Interview No. 13)

This representation of the Other confirms findings from another research, in which a Swedish development worker claimed: "I have thought that I have ended up somewhere in the 1910s, 1920s or 1930s in Sweden" (Eriksson Baaz 2005: 39).

Also, Tunisia was considered to be "quite a developed country" by a respondent from Austroprojekt (Interview No. 17 2013). Overall, most of the texts, regardless of the country of origin, as well as several respondents, followed the general law of development and did not cast any doubt on the connection between the terms development and developing and their numerous incarnations in particular social spheres. It was possible to find the construction of the Self and the Other as absolutely different (Interview No. 13 2013, Interview No. 15

2015). The logocentric structure of the discourse is explicitly present in further hierarchies between "us" and "them"; however, it is a much weaker form of logocentrism that no longer differentiates in absolute terms. The general law of development is, *in my opinion*, implicitly present in the PR texts, as the term "development" was often used on the website next to the analyzed texts, making clear the context of more particular topics such as education, microfinance, or sustainable development.

Yet it is worth pointing to the attempts to reverse both the logocentric nature of the development discourse and its general law. One respondent from PiP partly reversed the logocentrism and, to a certain, extent engaged in the romanticization of the Other following the neopopulist post-development discourse that has been criticized by several critics (see, e.g., Kiely 1999; Nederveen Pieterse 2000). Thus, for example, whereas "they" take care of "their" elderly or orphans, "we" put our parents and grandparents into hospices and do not take care of orphans who are related to us (Interview No. 10 2013). A similar reasoning was to be found in relation to climate change in a response from a respondent from CARE Austria: "we are the main contributors [to climate change] and they are the ones who suffer the most [because of it], probably" (Interview No. 25 2013). Yet, a clear-cut romanticization that would completely reverse the Eurocentric logocentrism into a pure anti-Western logocentrism did not occur.

Another way to avoid logocentrism at the surface of an object's emergence is through "classical" (Barthes 1972: 101) or "universal humanism" (Dogra 2014: 95), which represents the whole of humanity as one big family, claiming that there is "a solid rock of a universal human nature" (Barthes 1972: 101). Universal humanism also creates a world of equals and opposes the "absolute difference" of the colonial discourse. People as members of one humanity have no space for a substantial difference. According to one respondent from Austroprojekt, Tanzania "is not so distinct from other countries," and the difference between Austria and Tanzania "seems to be very big [... but] the problems of mankind are always the same [...] what really matters is the human relations and [...] that's very similar" (Interview No. 16 2013, see also Interview No. 20 2013). Universality is here based on a shared human culture. This cultural similarity exists of itself.

If the previous respondent points to an unequivocal position toward the Other in which it is basically the same, a respondent from PiP demonstrates the hybridity in the development discourse. The Other can be the same and different at the same time. This respondent divided the Kenyan society into the poor, "extremely simple people, whom we cannot understand because they think in a completely different way," and "middle class [...] people, who have the same access to information as we do [...] and I do not see much difference between us and them except for the color of our skin" (Interview No. 8 2013). The us-them logocentric difference remains here, and only a part of the Other has been accepted to become "us" – the world's middle class.

The general law of development that accounts for the dependence of statements in the discourse (Foucault 2002a: 64) was present in most of the texts and interviews. However, apart from a few critical blogs (Fialová 2013; Achleitner 2012, 2013), some of the respondents problematized the connection between development and the (socially constructed) reality of the so-called developing countries. Simply put, they were at unease with the term "developing" when it was supposed to label their partners. The respondents themselves sometimes spoke about development, but I had to quite often ask them directly. What this could mean is that this is not the term they would automatically use when talking about the Other. In almost all such cases they resisted the term to various degrees.

The respondents from the Austrian Development Agency and CARE were closest to unconditionally accepting the development discourse in relation to the poorest countries. They replied to the direct question of whether Bangladesh is a "developing" country as follows: "Sure, it is listed as a developing country" (Interview No. 21 2013). According to another respondent "Burundi definitely fits that least developed country kind of category [...] people [there] are generally poor" (Interview No. 27 2013). It is clear already in these answers that the respondents felt compelled to qualify their responses with the official discourse instead of using only their authority to justify their claims. Even though these responses in no way disrupt the development discourse, the respondents' invocation of the official discourse to back their answers is significant.

The most common were answers casting a stronger doubt on the law-like nature of the general law of development. Thus Kenya, according to a respondent from Slovak NGDO the Pontis Foundation, is a developing country "because someone called it that way [...] if there is a GDP per capita definition and they belong to the [low income country] level then, according to this definition, it is a developing country" (Interview No. 7 2013).[3]

A respondent from CARE classified Ethiopia as a developing country after being asked a direct question about whether it is a developing country: "I would say, according to all the OECD statistics, 'yes', and this is what we are usually looking at" (Interview No. 28 2014).

Overall, whereas the state-level texts (and Austroprojekt's Plan of Operation) spoke of "developing countries" without any hesitation, the PR articles focused on more particular matters related to microfinance, sustainable development and education, but occasionally also hierarchized the Other in this way. However, apart from a few exceptions, quite a few respondents from both countries showed unease with the use of this hierarchization. Considering that this term might be the most explicit expression of the hierarchy, which the respondents often countered with deliberate positivism, this result need not be a great surprise. The hierarchy in the generalized terms developed and developing might be too close to the racist colonial discourse and therefore needs to be disavowed as something imposed from impersonal rankings.

Whereas there was not a difference between the Austrians and Slovaks in terms of disrupting the general law of development, the colonial type logocentrism of absolute difference was articulated by two Slovak respondents and was partly reversed or resisted by one Slovak respondent and several Austrian respondents. One could find similar results in analyses of traditional donors (see, e.g., Noxolo 2006; Ziai 2004). The next two sections show the hierarchic representations of "us" and "them" in the development discourse, which includes the hierarchy in the relation between the speaking Self and the Other, and the hierarchy in the representation of practice of the functioning of power in the partnership discourse. After that, descriptions of the particular disruptions of the hierarchic development discourse follow.

Hierarchic representation of "us" and "them" in development discourse

If the general law focuses on the connection between the master signifier and its incarnations in practice, another category from the archaeological method offers a conceptualization of the variety of objects in the discourse. In order to analyze the formation of objects, Foucault introduces "the grids of specifications" (Foucault 2002a: 46) – the systems that divide, contrast, relate, regroup, and classify objects of the discourse. One may subsume the various indicators within the development discourse under such grids. Escobar (1995: 41) uses this approach in order to analyze development discourse: "Development proceeded by creating 'abnormalities' (such as the 'illiterate,' the 'underdeveloped,' the 'malnourished,' 'small farmers,' or 'landless peasants'), which it would later treat and reform." These abnormalities constitute the grid that specifies the object. Objects have to become visible. One needs a particular specification through which objects can emerge as objects.

Within the dominant grid of specification, there is a clear tendency to evaluate "them" negatively and "us" positively in all the analyzed texts and interviews except for one text and one interview from CARE (CARE 2012a, Interview No. 25 2013). The rest of the corpus depicts "them" in a positive way to various degrees even though negative representations dominate. In general, the Slovaks used more stereotypes and stricter hierarchies than the Austrians, but the difference between the Austrians and Slovaks was one of degree and not of substance. Also the respondents in state agencies were hierarchizing more than those in the NGDOs.

The most common representations were "their" negative representations, though they were often complemented with "our" positive portrayals. The hierarchy between "us" and "them" is achieved also through a one-way interaction between "us" and "them."

The most hierarchic representation of Self and Other was brought about by the interview question about the similarities and differences between "us" and "them."

Two respondents offered a theoretical insight into how these representations come about. One from ADA explicitly stated what is generally the case: "my reference system is my own society [...] and then I *see* what is functioning in Austria [...] and what isn't functioning in a developmental state" (Interview No. 22 2013, my italics). The respondent also mentioned the example that, in

Uganda, Ethiopia, and Palestine, "basic services do not function very well [...] [for example,] high schools, social security, or the police" (ibid.). A respondent from CARE also clarified how discourses work:

> [In Uganda,] in terms of infrastructure, there is no public service. And in Austria the public service is more or less perfect [...] in Uganda [...] you don't know when the bus comes, but in Austria if it says 10:15, it will come at 10:15.
>
> (Interview No. 26 2013)

According to this respondent, "this is the most *visible* difference" (ibid., my italics).

The development discourse structures what the respondents *see* (as functioning in Austria) or what becomes the most *visible* difference. The discourse directs our attention to a certain object and not another. Escobar writes that "[a]s time went by, new problems were progressively and selectively incorporated" (Escobar 1995: 42). The problems would be specified, but this specification "did not seek so much to illuminate [a] possible solution as to give 'problems' a visible reality" (ibid.). This is the main argument made about development discourse – it makes a particular part of reality visible and not another. This very specific visibility has the power effect of hierarchizing cultures, but, as the next sections show, other visibilities exist, and they disrupt the development discourse (see also DuBois 1991).

There is a similar visibility created by the discourse of old and new donors as this particular visibility creates a hierarchy between these donors. But isn't this hierarchy real? Aren't the new donors or, more specifically, people working in their development apparatuses less experienced than development workers who worked for decades in Austria or the United Kingdom? How could the experience from the communist period be perceived today in a way that would enable criticism of the term new donors? From a poststructuralist perspective, this is the wrong question to be asked as it omits the issue of power from its assumptions. One should ask, how is it possible that the communist experience was disremembered? Drążkiewicz-Grodzicka (2013) shows that, in Poland, this was even done intentionally. It could still be said that the development practice during the communist era was problematic because it was too tied to political preferences (not to mention the racism present in this practice, as well as the following of the classical modernizing development paradigm during this period), but at least this would imply that we are not new donors who are supposed to be learning from the old ones in the West, but merely that we are old donors who made mistakes in the past. Very soon it would be clear that Western donors conducted development aid before 1989 in a very similar fashion. However, what happened was an immediate subordination to the overall hierarchy between East and West and an acceptance of the idea that the East is inferior in yet another social field – that of development aid. Postcommunist donors could also today think about the useful experience from the communist past, especially in the understanding of the global economy as one of the sources of domestic problems, not only at home, but also in the Global South. However, this is not the main point to discuss in this regard.

The aim of this book is to problematize the hierarchic relation between donors, the non-inclusion of past experience is a result of this relation, and the question of what could be useful from the Czechoslovak (or Polish or Roumanian) experience is secondary and problematic given the unequal power relation. This very inequality makes the question unfair.

In the rest of this section, I present an analysis of the hierarchy between "us" and "them" in the North–South dimension – "our" positive and "their" negative representations.

A Slovak respondent from People in Peril (PiP) represented "us" positively as having the tendency "to use time effectively for some kind of self-education; one reads something or socializes or does something real" and represented "them" negatively as being "used to just staring and sitting" (Interview No. 11 2013, see also Interviews No. 3, 9 2013 for similar representations of "us" and "them" in relation to nature). The usual array of negative representations further distinguished Kenya from Slovakia: "a lower level of literacy, a lower life expectancy, a higher mortality among mothers, etc." (Interview No. 3 2013).

A respondent from Austroprojekt considered Burkina Faso to be "much more autocratic" and "much more corrupt" in comparison to Austria (Interview No. 16 2013, see also Interview No. 28 2014 with a respondent from CARE for a similar representation).

State level strategies offered similar hierarchies. Whereas Slovakia relies on "its transformation experience in building independent state institutions, development of a market economy and meeting the principles of democracy" (MFEA 2014: 7), Austria's knowledge of organic agriculture was represented as being "in international demand" (BMEIA 2012: 24). In this representation, Austrians are experienced within sustainable forest management and have know-how in "technology, forest ecology and silviculture, policymaking, law enforcement and citizen participation" (ibid.: 25).

On the side of the Other in the case of the Austrian Three Year Program, there are "weak institutions and deficits in public administration, [...] [while] [p]olitical, socio-economic and ecological problems, recently exacerbated by security issues, [are persisting]" (ibid.: 34, 35). The Slovak Medium-Term Strategy uses similar representations in relation to "them" such as "increase of threats," "terrorism," "illegal migration," or "exhaustion of mineral resources" (MFEA 2014: 7).

Apart from being related to a lack of knowledge on the part of the Other (see below), the negative representations in ADA's (nonacademic) journal *Weltnachrichten* (World News) were also related to a lack in material substance. For example, it stated that "there is a lack of machines, but also of credit for investing" in Armenia (Zimmer 2013). There are also several positive representations of Austria in the journal, such as "a reliable partner" (Geosits and Gruber 2014), or a "competent adviser" (Gottfried Pessl in Weissel 2014). Simply put, "our" representation was often positive, and "theirs" negative.

But again isn't all of this true? Isn't there a shorter life expectancy in Kenya than in Europe? Isn't there a problem with deforestation in the Global South? Isn't Burkina Faso more autocratic than Austria? Isn't there a lack of machines and available credit in Armenia? And aren't the Austrian advisors competent? In more theoretical terms, isn't there anything real behind the development discourse?

Certainly, there is a very real materiality, which is "baptized as 'under-development'" (Escobar 1984: 389). This materiality is sad and problematic. The aim of postdevelopment, though, is not to deny it, but to conceptualize it in different ways (ibid.). One may answer each of the questions with a doubt. These doubts may problematize the perspective which claims that the Western type of development is worth following, and other doubts may question the location of the origin of what goes under the name "development problems." For example, is longevity as we see it in the hospices of the West really desirable? Who causes deforestation, people using firewood or profit-seeking corporations? And what kind of progress does the availability of credit bring? Asking these questions redirects the attention to different problems than the ones found in the current development discourse. The sad materiality remains, but a different perspective on this materiality may change the way we deal with it. Hence, the importance of this research.

With regard to "their" negative and "our" positive representations, there is not a great difference between the Slovaks and the Austrians. Apart from that, however, the Slovaks use language that criticizes "their" cognitive capacities more often than the Austrians.

Another way of creating a hierarchy between the Self and the Other is through the representation of interactions between "us" and "them." These could be equal, as one would imagine interactions among partners should be. However, the research shows that, in the given cases, either there is no interaction at all, or the interaction goes one way – from the more to the less powerful actors, as is often the case, for example, in the unequal teacher-student relationship.

In a closely analyzed article from Pontis (2010b) "we" mostly "teach ['our'] colleagues from Kenya," "instruct them," "train them," or even "'infect' them" (with enthusiasm for technologies). On the other hand, local teachers are represented in interactive social actions only in relation to their Kenyan colleagues, to whom they are able to transmit knowledge, or when they have a "presentation ready for parents." Whereas "we" interact with "them," "they" "interact" mostly with things, or "their" actions do not have an effect on the world. When "they" interact with people, "they" do so only among themselves and not with "us." "We" interact with "them" as "we" teach "them," but as "they" are just taught, "they" cannot really interact back. It seems that "they" have nothing to offer to "us," and there is no space in the development discourse for "them" to engage in an equal interaction.

A much less hierarchizing article from CARE (2012a) offered a similar pattern in which "their" interactive actions concern only "themselves" with one exception – when a local named Fanatesh "contacted CARE in order to get more training." There is no actual interaction from "their" side towards "us" apart from "them" wanting "our" knowledge. One can find the same pattern also in the PR articles from Slovak NGDO PiP.

The state level medium-term documents offered a more negative representation of "them" than the PR texts. In this representation, "they" mostly do not act at all in the sense of having an immediate effect on the world ("they" are discussed in terms of, e.g., "persisting poverty," "increase of threats," and "their" absolute number decreasing). When "they" act, it is in relation to the "growth of consumption" and "exhaustion of natural resources." The fragile states are active in being a challenge. "They" thus either act in the destruction of the environment, act in being a challenge, or do not have an effect on the world at all.

However, the "emerging nations" in ADA's Three-Year Program act as they play an important role in the global negotiations and are trading partners for the countries of the Global South. The position of emerging powers in the world economy is thus reflected in the discourse, and "they" are granted a powerful position in the hierarchy of actors (see Chapter 4). It should be noted here that this change of position need not be due to the deliberate positivism of the well-intentioned development workers, but may be a reflection of the new geopolitical position of these countries.

More importantly, even though the texts offer plenty of instances of deliberate positivism when the Other is on its own, as soon as the Other is represented in a relation to the Self, the hierarchy is kept, and there seems to be nothing that "they" can offer to "us" that would result in an actual partner-like interaction. Finally, the focus on "us" and "them" as speaking actors reveals another form of hierarchy.

Can the subaltern speak? Spivak's important question aroused a discussion on the agency of the subaltern. The unequivocal answer ("The subaltern cannot speak." Spivak 1994: 104) was criticized for its "deliberate deafness to the native voice" (Parry 1987: 39). Even if Spivak's argument was persuasive, there certainly are other (maybe less subaltern) voices that are heard and, more importantly, are capable of creating their own discourses (Loomba 2010: 196). In order to find out about these not so subaltern voices, it is necessary to engage in an empirical analysis. Foucault offers a useful operationalization of the questions concerned with the agency of the speaking subjects.

In relation to enunciative modalities he asks, "What is the 'institutional site' of those who speak?" It is from this institutional site that the "discourse derives its legitimate source" (Foucault 2002a: 56). Rather than asking who speaks, the question of the institutional site is much more important. The person could be replaced, but the site and the position remain.

> Only from this position meaningful statements within the discourse are possible. Statements from a different position and therefore not claiming this kind of knowledge are outside the discursive formation, and are judged to be useless from the perspective of this discourse.
>
> (Ziai 2014: 6)

The dominant subjects of the development discourse are academics at the universities and employees of the development organizations, either at the international level (e.g., the OECD or the World Bank), or at the national level, as in the organizations analyzed in this research. Their words are powerful because they come from these institutional sites. However, words of development experts are equally powerful when they are voiced at the local level.

There is one example that clearly shows the importance of the international organizations in development discourse. In the Austrian Three-Year Program, the semiotic actions (renditions) come from important global actors (the IMF, the WB, the UN, and the EU). They do not belong to the Austrian population or to the actors from the Global South. The only semiotic action that is attributable directly to Austria does not convey the meaning intended by the speaker, which is common for lower-status social actors (Leeuwen 2008: 62) and represents Austria as "merely" actively engaged in the international debate about SDGs. Thus, it is not just that the text hierarchizes the North above the South or the West above the East, but also Austria subordinates itself to the international organizations, who are the speaking actors.

However, it would be premature to generalize one such instance of hierarchization. The above mentioned organizations certainly are dominant, but "[t]he institutionalization of development took place at all levels" (Escobar 1995: 46), and these levels would include NGOs or community development organizations. The discourse relies on the myriad local centers of power (ibid., Dubois 1991), and in this sense the much less powerful actors are crucial for the circulation of knowledge.

Foucault therefore also asks, "who is speaking?" (ibid.: 55). "Who … is accorded the right to use this sort of language (language)?… What is the status of the individuals who – alone – have the right, sanctioned by law or tradition, juridically defined or spontaneously accepted, to proffer such a discourse?" (ibid.). Just as "[m]edical statements cannot come from anybody" (ibid.: 56), nor can development statements. It is therefore meaningful to analyze who are these speaking actors.

First, it is important to note who gets to be named, as those who are quoted are usually also nominated. Nomination of actors brings a similarity between the Austrian and Slovak texts. In both cases "we" are nominated more often than "they" are. However, there is an important exception. In the microfinance PR article from CARE (2012a), "they" are nominated in 27% of the cases of all actors, and "we" are not nominated at all. Here deliberate positivism is very strong.

Due to the quite large number of articles in ADA's magazine *Weltnachrichten*, I have decided to apply a more rigorous method and counted how often people from the Global South and Global North are quoted (or paraphrased) in them. Altogether, there were 90 instances of quoted and paraphrased persons or interviews. "We" were quoted or interviewed or "our" words were paraphrased more often (53%) than "them" or "their" words (39%).[4] If one were to exclude a special issue on ten years of ADA and discussions between ADA's employees in the journal, the representations of the Self and the Other would be almost equal. In any case, even these numbers show that the response to Foucault's question "who is speaking?" (Foucault 2002a: 55) is clearly both "us" and "them." "They" are not the silent subjects of Joseph Conrad's *Heart of Darkness* (Achebe 1977).

Further analysis of *Weltnachrichten* reveals that whereas "we" are always represented by elite figures from national bureaucracies,[5] international organizations,[6] or non-governmental organizations,[7] "they" are represented by both elite figures (63%)[8] and non-elite figures (34%) such as farmers or handicapped persons.[9] If one excludes interviews in *Weltnachrichten* and focuses only on articles using quotes, the representation of non-elite parts of the population among "them" prevails significantly (67% vs. 33%). In the Slovak texts, elites on both sides dominated the semiotic actions.

These findings point to an elitist approach in both apparatuses. I would argue here that the results of my analysis support the claim that the Slovak development cooperation is a top-down process (Profant 2018) as well as Hödl's argument that "throughout the past half a century most Austrians failed to embrace development aid as something valuable, as something that constituted a part of the country's identity" (Hödl 2013), and a similar claim made by Obrovsky – that the "Austrian development cooperation is not a part of the Austrian identity" (Obrovsky 2013). This is visible in the omission of non-elite Austrians in *Weltnachrichten*. Why are there no quotes from, e.g., the Austrian plumbers or masseurs if this endeavor is supposedly supported by the whole nation? Austrian aid seems to take place between the elites from the political sphere, the (coopted) non-governmental sphere, and the state bureaucracy. Ordinary citizens and their opinions are not part of the discourse in *Weltnachrichten*. The general structure of the development discourse, in which experts from the North deal with the object (i.e., the population) in the South, is thus to a great extent adhered to.

The most important question with regard to the position of the subject is: Who says what? The general pattern that is repeated in the texts from both countries reserves quotes that explain various phenomena for "us" and quotes that express gratefulness for "them." International organizations such as the World Bank ("us") or the UNDP ("us-them") were represented through rendition and almost always provided an expert claim – e.g., that 3.5 million people die from diarrhea per year (the WHO in Burtscher 2013). "Our" elite figures are also in the position of experts engaged in less exact explanations,[10] or in self-praise[11]; these elites are content with the results of "our" project[12] or represent the Other negatively.[13] One could also read about "our" aims such as "improving the living conditions in our partner countries" (Ledolter in Gutenbrunner 2014).

In the Slovak texts, "they" are quoted expressing their hope for what a Slovak project can achieve (Pontis 2012) and about the improvement that occurred after the cooperation with Pontis (ibid.), and "they" also demand further loans (PiP 2009). There are also instances of "them" expressing gratitude (PiP 2012c).

In the *Weltnachrichten* articles, both the less powerful and the elite figures engage in expressing satisfaction with the projects supported by ADA. "They" use expressions such as "amazing," "happy," "very happy," "extremely," or "proud," and claim, for example, that "it is amazing what a difference the extra information does make" (Ali in Rabitsch and Sötz 2013). "They" also compare the bad situation before the project and the good situation after the project: e.g., "the machines are mostly old, but here we can learn with a technology run by computers" (Aguirre in Traxler 2013a). To a much lesser extent (23%), "they" also engage in explaining particular phenomena; for example, Riham Kharroub (who is from Palestine, but is currently employed by ADA) is "responsible for the projects in Western Jordan" (Kharroub 2014). The non-elite people from the Global South who get to be quoted sometimes mix explaining something with an expression of content, as in "Fair Trade makes us independent from 'the Coyotes', the local middlemen" (Santos in Traxler 2013b). As speaking subjects in CARE's articles, "they" are half of the time represented by children or teenagers, thereby contributing to "their" infantilization (a phenomenon also found among the British NGDOs, see Dogra 2014).

To conclude, with regard to the institutional sites, the international level dominates the national (and local) level in the North and the South. It is plausible to claim that whatever the subalterns (here including the local men) say or do only becomes interpreted through the lenses of the dominant discourse. I am not in any way claiming that "their" enunciations are insincere, but merely that these fit the hierarchizing development discourse.

"We" provide expertise or explain how things work, praise ourselves in terms of how good "we" are and, less often, make clear what is problematic about the Other, and "we" also state "our" noble goal of helping "them." Meanwhile, "we" are rarely quoted expressing a positive opinion about "them."

"We" speak more often than "they" do, but "they" are not silent. On the contrary, "they" are quoted quite regularly. "We" are represented only by elite figures; "they" are represented by both elite and non-elite speakers. However, whereas "we" are experts explaining various phenomena, "they" are grateful subjects expressing "their" content with what "we" do. The hierarchy between "us" and "them" is thereby kept despite rare occasions of deliberate positivism. The power relation is thus clear in the representation of "us" and "them." The next section shows that the discourse of partnership contains relations of power as well.

Power in partnership: Austroprojekt's Plan of Operation

This section differs from the rest of the chapter since it does not focus so much on the representation of the hierarchies, as it tries to show how power remains crucial for the understanding of partnership. Turning away from the positive and negative representations of the Other, Austroprojekt's Plan of Operation puts the Other directly into the working of an allegedly equal partnership. Foucault's approach to power proves very useful for this analysis.

The whole Plan is very much oriented towards partnership and participation. The chapter on the organization of the program in particular shows a commitment to local ownership: "NDDP is a programme wholly owned and controlled by the District Councils" (ibid.: 67). However, this participatory approach comes with a dose of conditionality and is thus close to what Foucault (1982: 341) called "the conduct of conducts." Foucault understands the conduct of others' conducts as part of an exercise of power or a broad understanding of the term "government." "To govern, in this sense, is to structure the possible field of action of others" (ibid.).

The authors admit behavior based on a power difference on the Austrian side as the "Austrian-financed programmes have [...] at times tried to bypass local institutions" (ibid.: 16) in the past, but now "the district development should become integrated into existing administrative structures" (ibid.). Still, a clear instance of power – conditionality – is present a few sentences later: "Districts receive funding only once minimum conditions are met and are sanctioned if performance remains poor. Once district council performance increases and a documented improvement in service delivery becomes visible, donors can begin to channel funds" (ibid.: 17, see also 76–77).

Such a direct approach to the exertion of power is complemented with much finer means: "[Those] community based farmer motivators [who] together with extensionists help to *mobilise* communities will be identified" (ibid.: 58, my italics), "[l]ivestock keepers will *be encouraged* to construct and use dams" (ibid.: 63, my italics), "[f]orest owners (villages) will *be facilitated* to construct/develop water sources [sic]" and regarding conservation of water sources, as people "still don't understand [...] the effects of deforestation [...] *sensitisation* trainings [...] will be conducted" (ibid., my italics). Local elites are supposed to help in this conduct of conduct: here a "[h]uman resource" (ibid.: 43) is to be trained to gain skills through an "*attitude change*" (ibid.).

This conditionality and this governmentality are strengthened with strict control: "It is envisaged that the donor (and PORLAG) will be much stricter in monitoring performance of the district and together enforce corrective measures should this be required" (ibid.: 72). The Foucauldian Panopticon (Foucault 1995: 195–228) then comes full circle on the next page: "While district staff can collect data during field visits only, the communities, target groups and individuals can continuously monitor activities and, at a certain stage, write reports on their findings" (ibid.: 73). The main effect of the Panopticon (i.e., a transparent prison in which one can see all the cells from the watchtower) is "to induce in the inmate a state of conscious and permanent visibility that assures the automatic functioning of power" (Foucault 1995: 201). The Other performs the required tasks without the need for a coercive subject to be present.

It is thus possible to see here several forms of power. First, one could clearly see its first dimension in the conditionality (see Dahl 1957; Lukes 2004), as A directly requires from B that "minimum conditions are met." Already here the term "minimum" points at a degree of freedom, as this conditioning power merely structures "the possible field of action" (Foucault 1982: 221) instead of forcing the subjects to act in a certain way without possible deviation, which would belong to the category "violence" (ibid.: 220). This "conduct of conducts" becomes even clearer as the vocabulary used in the Plan of Operation softens, and instead of conditions it speaks of motivation, facilitation, encouraging, sensitization, and attitude change.

The disciplinary form of power is further supported by the monitoring that, on the one hand, strengthens the structuring of the possible field of action as it is the donor who is to enact it. Yet, at the same time, on the other hand, subjects (i.e., target groups and individuals) are supposed to exert self-control as if constantly monitored by the donor. The disciplinary mechanism also presupposes mutual control among local subjects. Its result is the creation of a disciplined, docile body and mind.

The Plan thus openly aims at what Foucault calls "police" and does so in both senses of the word: "The police govern not by law but by a specific, a permanent and a positive intervention in the behavior of individuals" (Foucault 2002b: 415). The crucial point here is that power is exercised through an intervention in the behavior. The changes are to be effected by transforming human conduct indirectly rather than directly through the use of violence or strict prescriptions. At the same time, "human happiness becomes the object of police" (ibid.: 413). The power is exercised through positive interventions. Their aim is human happiness, as "[h]appiness of individuals is a requirement for the survival and development of the state" (ibid.: 414). The pastoral power[14] changed from salvation to "health, well-being (that is sufficient wealth, standard of living), security, [and] protection against accidents" (Foucault 1982: 215). These are the categories through which power is exercised and through which subjects are governed.

But, just as Foucault considered certain power relations to be "positive, valuable, interesting, and so on" (Foucault 1988: 11–13), this type of governance within development cooperation could be acceptable. People can accept government, and this can be "truly" democratic (i.e., participatory). The importance of participation is highlighted throughout the document. It is thus "accepted that the way forward is to formulate district development planning based on village plans originating from the community" (NDC-Austroprojekt and Orgut 2002: 18). Participation (and lack thereof) is sometimes explicitly result-oriented, as "water schemes are often broken down because they were planned and implemented without target group participation" (ibid.: 62), rather than being valued in terms of its own democratic worth. Taking into account the interviews with the respondents, I consider this moral quality of participation to be simply implicit rather than lacking. The self-monitoring, on the one hand, adds to the exercise of the panoptical form of power as claimed above, but on the other hand it could secure more participation and less control from the donor's side. Even if this were not the case, this government could still be welcome on the side of the local people, and therefore acceptable to an outsider intellectual trying to fight micro-mechanisms of power. An anthropological research of the local governmentality would be necessary for one to take a clear normative stance here.

In sum, Austroprojekt's Plan of Operation is a good example of how power is supposed to operate in development. The structuring of the field of decision-making is to be achieved through conditionality instead of coercion. Minds are supposed to change through sensitization trainings, and subjects are expected to watch over each other and thereby secure discipline. Whereas it was possible to find plenty of negative representations of the Other, there was also a remarkable equality in terms of knowledge distribution between "us" and "them." "Partnership" is thus not an empty word for Austroprojekt. Yet, closer analysis reveals that power is clearly present in the development partnership. This is not unexpected, and there is nothing wrong with the presence of power in a partnership. The problem arises with its distribution among actors. Here, the Plan of Operation fails to achieve greater equality. Some attempts to achieve such equality are described in the next sections.

Disrupting the development hierarchy through deliberate positivism

Having identified the main elements of the grid of specifications in the development discourse, I focused in the previous sections mainly on the hierarchies within this grid. It is important to note that the grid could be different. Even if one adheres to states and nations as the units of analysis and keeps these normative methodological assumptions of the development discourse, one can still choose other grids of specifications. For example, one can speak of a position of an "alternative universalism" (Ziai 2007: 72), which differentiates societies according to criteria such as criminality, suicide rates, solidarity within the given society, hospitality towards foreigners, or respect towards the elderly (Ziai 2004: 142). Such criteria could turn the development rankings upside down. In this sense, it is important to politically intervene with empirical research and analyze the dominant perspective by stressing alternative representations inside and outside the discourse. As already mentioned, different criteria could also change the way donors are perceived. Instead of old and new donors, there could be (post)colonial donors and other donors, or good and bad donors, depending, for example, on their ranking in the Commitment to Development Index. Donors could also be divided on the basis of their geographical reach and there could be global donors as well as local donors.

The above mentioned examples from the respondents concerned with "our" contribution to climate change or the way "we" care for the elderly show that a potential for such an alternative universalism clearly exists, even if it is not dominant. One respondent from CARE Austria mentioned the freedom of the press and Gini indicators (that correlate) and pointed to the possibility to focus on other indicators than "industrialization" or "development" (Interview No. 26 2013). He thereby expressed an utterance from a discourse of alternative universalism

The following two sections focus on deliberate positivism and its attempts to disrupt the hierarchic development discourse, mostly through fighting negative stereotypes. This part includes a softening of "their" negative representations, "their" positive representations within the development discourse and outside of it, and representations of "us" as enablers of "their" progress. In all these cases, the hierarchic relation between "us" and "them" that is typical for colonial and development discourses is kept, but the strength of the hierarchy is minimized, and "they" are represented in a very positive light. Several respondents contextualized negative stereotypes and (tried to) refuse(d) to generalize and compare societies, and one respondent engaged very strongly in a deliberate positivism, countering, even reversing, the hierarchy between "us" and "them." This respondent's arguments are analyzed in a separate section.

Fighting "their" negative representations and stereotypes

Deliberate positivism in its weakest form was present through the attempts to soften negative stereotypes and through representing the Other through negative qualities rather than through more direct personalizations of negativity. In both cases the hierarchy between "us" and "them" was kept, but deliberate positivism was clearly present in these instances. Two Slovak respondents represented "them" negatively, but did so in a softer way. The negativity was there, but at the same time it was weakened or countered in various ways. I will first present more direct attempts to soften the negativity of "their" representation and then I will use van Leeuwen's approach to analyze texts and show how impersonalization enables both the negativity and its weakening at the same time.

One respondent from Slovak NGDO PiP combined positive and negative representations of "them" in a single description. The Other is ascribed positive values, but s/he is never good on his or her own or without an objection. There is always something problematic about the Other. For example, the respondent claimed that the stereotype of "them" being lazy "does not hold true" (Interview No. 9 2013), but considered "them" to be "industrious [...] out of necessity because there really does not exist anything like a social system [in the given society]" (ibid.). "They" were also considered "skillful" (ibid.), but this was manifested in "their" " 'cunningness' " (ibid.). In every assessment, the positive representation was compromised in one way or another.

The softening of negative stereotypes fits the policy of deliberate positivism, as the Other is represented in a positive way (as, e.g., "industrious"), but this positivity is corrupted ("industrious out of necessity") or the Other is first represented in a negative way and then reconsidered as not so bad. Importantly, deliberate positivism here achieves "their" more positive representation, but at the same time it fails to challenge the hierarchy between "us" and "them" in the development discourse.

The instances of impersonalization were in accordance with the hierarchy in the discourse. "We" were impersonalized mainly as NGDOs or as SAIDC, "the Slovak Republic," "developed states," or international organizations, but also once as "aging and stagnating countries" (BMEIA 2012: 9). Overall, "we" were represented in rather neutral or positive terms.

"They," on the other hand, were mostly represented in negative terms. "They" were negatively impersonalized as, e.g., "migration," "terrorism," "poverty," "developing countries," "fragile states," and "countries with a low income" (MFEA 2014) or as "a high population density, [...] high unemployment, a high HIV/AIDS ratio [...] and gender inequality caused by cultural traditions" (PiP

2009). "They" are thus represented as being too numerous, as being unemployed, as having AIDS, and as oppressing women. The problems are impersonal representations of people who are connected to or allegedly cause these problems. In this way, these impersonalizations add negative connotations to the local people, but at the same time the impersonalization decreases the strength of the negativity, as the text does not say that, e.g., Kenyans have too many children; it just says that there is a high density in a region. I will deal with the depoliticizing consequences of the omission of representing the causes of these problems in chapter four.

Here the main point is that these representations fit well with deliberate positivism and at the same time keep the need for an intervention of the Self. On the one hand, the problem remains on the side of the Other (e.g., migration or unemployment), but on the other the social actors who would embody this lack are backgrounded, as "they" are impersonalized into migration, unemployment, etc. Deliberate positivism thus serves the need to represent the Other in a less negative way and thereby weakens the hierarchy between "us" and "them." At the same time, though, the negativity is merely softened and does not disappear. The structure of the development discourse is thereby kept.

Another way to show a hierarchy between Self and Other and its disruption is through the modes of activation and passivation. In the Three-Year Program and in the Slovak Medium-Term Strategy, these show a hierarchic pattern as well. When "we" are passivated, it is in relation to actions that do not include the Other – "we" obey "our" own rules or interact with ourselves. "Their" activations and passivations are more varied. Two groups stand out from the Three-Year Program – the poor (e.g., the "marginalized") and "developing countries" on the one hand and emerging powers on the other.

The poor are mostly passivated as an actor with whom something is to be done when "they" are objectivated as poverty, which is to be reduced and overcome, when it is "our" concern to support women, or when "their" human security and basic needs should be taken into account. In turn, "they" are activated when they are described as being poor[15] or when representing a threat[16]. However, there are a few instances of optimism which represent "them" as active, as "they" are entering an active middle class or getting out of poverty.

The category "developing countries" is also more often passivated than activated. "They" are activated in not reaching the MDGs, but also as "they" doubled their GDP per capita during the last decade and "they" are (with "us") equal partners in global relations. "They" are passivated when countries with young populations are seen as having better prospects (than aging and stagnating countries), and when it is said that growth is indispensable in "developing" countries, natural catastrophes threaten sub-Saharan Africa, or "our" concern is to be actively engaged in LICs. Both people and the countries from the Global South are thus passivated when they are seen as an actor who needs something or when "we" are concerned with "them." "They" are active in the sense of not being successful in development, but there are also "their" positive active representations.

The category of "emerging powers" offers a different perspective. "They" are activated when "they" play an ever increasing role, when "they" are setting the pace, and when it is stated that Asia will even overcome the G7's economic performance. However, when "their" actions are related to "us," "they" are represented in the passive mode: "they" are called upon to take over "their" responsibility, Busan involves "them" as strategic donors, "we" see "them" as partners in creating the global development agenda, and "they" are a concern for "our" foreign and development policy. Thus, the activation of "emerging powers" is related to "their" growing importance; however, the passive mode is used when "we" become the active actor who calls upon "them" to execute an expected task – in this case being a donor.

This is a very important divergence from the usual binaries of the development discourse, and one only wonders how the discourse is going to change once these states stop being "emerging" (i.e., actors from whom one can demand something that the emerging actor is not used to because of being emerging). The last representation of "them" being a concern for "our" foreign policy (as well as the whole discourse demonizing China; see, e.g., Turner 2014) offers a hint.

One can see a parallel here with the new donors as their relationship with the traditional donors seems to be similar. New donors are also active on their own, but in relation to the traditional donors, they are usually portrayed as inferior, which might translate into their passivation within the discourse on donors. More research is necessary in this regard.

So far, deliberate positivism succeeded in the weakening of the hierarchy between "us" and "them," yet the hierarchy was kept nonetheless. This hierarchy is present in "their" more direct negative representation as well as in more implicit negative representations that are either in the form of a corruption of the positivity or in the form of a countering of the positivity. Thus, in these statements, deliberate positivism is clearly present, but fails to achieve an anti-hierarchic outcome.

Regarding the difference between the Slovak and the Austrian development discourse, it is noteworthy that, in one closely analyzed article from CARE (2012a), "they" are never referred to through negative abstractions. Here, the deliberate positivism goes one step further. Such a strong positivity is not to be found in the other articles.

At the same time, the Slovak respondents engaged in more direct attempts to weaken or counter their negative representations of the Other; however, these respondents did not fully reverse the negativity.

More successful attempts to represent "them" in a positive way included "their" anti-stereotypical portrayal. Slovak NGDO Pontis engaged in this form of deliberate positivism, explicitly stating the aim to fight stereotypes (Pontis n.a., Šimek 2010; see also Zorád 2011 for the refutation of the stereotype of laziness). However, the overall stereotypical framing left the laudable anti-Eurocentric task unfinished.

One can read that "Kenya is good in technology," in particular in using mobile banking (Pontis n.a.), or that "[t]he development of communication infrastructure in many African countries is in direct contradiction to their lagging behind in the construction of roads, distribution networks and the accessibility of drinking water" (Šimek 2010). Whereas the linear thinking of one development path that consists of improving infrastructure is decipherable here, "we" are supposed to lose "our" stereotypes because people in Kenya use mobile phones in domains in which "we" don't. Cheap technology is thus the "effective solution for Africa" (ibid.), and it could bring a "new technological revolution in Africa" (ibid.).

The stereotype of the backward African is overcome in the first step, as s/he is represented as capable of using the newest technologies in more efficient ways than the people in the West. But, it is confirmed in the next step, as these technologies are supposed to create the necessary investment opportunities. Africa is represented as lacking investment opportunities, and others need to invest here for development to begin. The ICTs are supposed to help investors understand "this continent in a more complex manner as maybe very risky and unstable, but at the moment hiding a huge potential" (ibid.).

Thus, there is one universal development way that contains several aspects such as roads, distribution networks, and technologies. In one of them Kenya is a leader, and in the rest this leadership is in direct contradiction to areas where it is not a leader, and the continent is risky and unstable. Therefore, what Kenya needs is the spread of these modern technologies (with the aid of NGOs such as the Pontis Foundation), disregarding here for a moment the fact that Kenya is a leader in one of those fields.

This praiseworthy effort to fight stereotypes reproduces too many problematic aspects of the development discourse. These aspects effectively negate the effort and, in my opinion, the disruption of the discourse is not thorough. Yet, it is crucial to note that deliberate positivism is clearly present here.

Still, "they" were also represented in a positive, anti-stereotypical way by a respondent from PiP as "not lazy" and "purposeful" (Interview No. 9 2013), and other respondents represented "them" as "working a double amount of working hours" (Bednárová 2009).

The most positive representations of the Other were to be found in CARE's article on microfinance (CARE 2012a; see also Plan UK, CARE International UK and Barclays 2013). "They" were represented as knowledgeable and decisive actors in a respectable way, namely in connection with their function as farmers, yet at the same time "they" were represented as poor (and thereby in need of our aid). Other positive representations of "them" include the statements about self-organizations of the saving groups, the small groups having their own ideas, decisions being taken by the women themselves after they get credit, the regular nature of "their" meetings (which makes them look more reliable), and the locals Wednesh, Belaynesh, and Fanatesh showing that solidarity works. All these representations have a twofold legitimating effect – they show "them" as powerful individuals and groups succeeding in "their" attempts to overcome poverty, yet "they" are still represented as in need of help. Both representations thus legitimize the development intervention by the Self. The Other needs it, but also deserves it. The difference between this article and the Slovak article (Šimek 2010) is in the extent of "their" negative representations, which are stronger in the Slovak text; however, the structure of both articles is the same.

There was one particular attempt to avoid hierarchization in an article from PiP that warrants attention. It concerns the sentence "In cooperation with the local people, we will set up forest tree nurseries and ponds." One needs to think of other ways of representing this social action to realize that this is not the most equal one. The sentence could have been said in a partly reversed way (but was not), e.g.: The kwetu[17] organization has decided to set up ponds and forest tree nurseries and we will assist them; or, in a more equal way (that was also not used), The kwetu organization in cooperation with us will set up forest tree nurseries and ponds. The "we" in "we will set up" in the original sentence most likely means "we" and "them" together, and one could consider this critique an instance of unnecessary nitpicking.

However, not only can one read the same formulas in "We organized together with the pupils an open day ... " (PiP 2012d) or "We will be, together with the high school students, setting up and cultivating school gardens ... " (PiP 2012b), and the above mentioned alternatives are never used, but there are also clearer instances of hierarchy, as in one of the article titles (PiP 2012a): "We are developing agriculture also on the East coast of Kenya." Here the Other is missing completely. Thus, while the attempt to equalize the "partners" is unmistakably there, I merely argue that it fails, and PiP still represents the Other as inferior, even if in a much milder way than the way colonizers did 100 years ago.

Another form of fighting the negative stereotypes was present when stereotypical representations were occasionally put into a context and explained in relation to or applied to both Self and Other at the same time. A respondent from CARE Austria explained the dependency created by aid in the following way: "they knew these international NGOs were coming, and they knew the government wasn't going to come in, so, you know, where else could they look?" (Interview No. 27 2013). She thereby effectively neutralized the negative representation and represented dependency as something normal or rational.

Eriksson Baaz (2005: 96–97) offers a similar neutralization of the negative stereotype of being late in Tanzania as opposed to being on time in Sweden. This need not be a question of cultural difference, but it could be explained by the different material and infrastructural conditions for punctuality in Sweden and Tanzania.

According to one respondent from Slovak NGO PiP, the "lack of a social system causes that there is a much greater fertility among mothers" (Interview No. 9 2013). Disregarding that the respondent represents fertility as a problem, my point here is that he explained the rationale behind it.[18]

Another form of deliberate positivism was in putting the Self and the Other in equal positions in the development ranking. The negative representation of the Other was complemented with the same negative representation of the Self. A respondent from CARE Austria thus said the following about Uganda: "I would say there is corruption [there], but there is corruption here as well" (Interview

No. 26 2013). The discourse is clearly disrupted, and just like in the case of SDGs and sustainability (see, e.g., Ziai 2016), the universalism of an anti-corruption perspective is kept, but the Self is not on the top of the ladder, it is one of the problematic actors.

Some respondents had problems with generalizations about whole societies and also with making comparative judgments. In accordance with the post-modern approach, they explicitly took the position of a non-hierarchic difference.

One respondent from ADA problematized the possibility of comparison: "[How do] you measure [difference between people]? It is difficult to make general judgments without really getting into depths" (Interview No. 21 2013). Yet, this did not prevent her from pointing at the housing situation, pollution, and corruption as problems in the same answer (ibid.). In response to a direct question, she claimed that one cannot compare Austrian and Bangladeshi culture (but she then tried to do so by discussing the wealth difference between the two countries). The respondent thus showed the incoherence of the discourse that translates into subjects' identities. The non-fixity of a discourse makes it impossible to fully fix identities (Laclau and Mouffe 2001: 111). On the one hand, yielding to the critique of Eurocentric essentialization, the respondent is reluctant to make general judgments and compare societies; on the other hand, as an expert who actually experienced the difference (and also maybe felt compelled to give an answer because she was asked the related question), she replies in accordance with the Eurocentric discourse. The development discourse is thus incoherent, offering contradictory and possibly hybrid identities to its subjects.

A respondent from SAIDC claimed the following in a similar vein: "I think that there are no universal values" (Interview No. 14 2014), and she stressed that "when we are talking about differences I don't mean, by saying that [Kenya and Slovakia] are different, that we are better or that they are better; I just point to the differences" (ibid.). The problem with this position is that the hierarchy between Kenya and Slovakia crawls back as the differences that one points to are based on social aspects in which Slovakia mostly fares better according to the statistics that measure them. This respondent, for example, claimed that "[b]oth [Kenya and South Sudan] have a low income … which means that both differ from Slovakia with regard to the economic indicators … " (ibid.).

In both cases we see the attempt to follow the deliberate positivism approach in avoiding any hierarchic comparison. However, both respondents use the hierarchic grid of specifications as a discursive resource and fall back to the hierarchic representation. The contextualization of stereotypes offers a more successful disruption of the development discourse as the negative portrayal of the Other is represented as rational. These instances were rather rare, however, and there is no difference between Austrians and Slovaks in this regard.

Within the framework of deliberate positivism, the Other was sometimes also represented in a positive way either within or outside the development discourse. One of the most common positive representation of "them" – "the friendliness of [the] people" (Zimmer 2013) – is closer to the touristic discourse than to the development discourse. SAIDC employees represented "them" as, e.g., "nice" (Interview No. 4 2013) or "very open, very likable [...] eloquent [...] they have a gift of gab" (Interview No. 14 2014). A respondent from Austroprojekt considered Tanzania to be "a good country," as the "people are very nice, very responsive, [...] very open, [...] easy to communicate [with]" (ibid.).

Another positive representation of "them" that is closer to the touristic discourse focused on the landscape and echoed the colonial discourses about the different climate and vegetation in the colonies. For example, one can read in the *Weltnachrichten* about "blooming slopes" (Thiard-Laforet 2013), and the nature in Albania is described as "untouched" (Rössler 2013).[19]

Further representations of this sort that were related to the richness of the local culture were present in the interviews. According to a respondent from CARE, "Uganda is a very rich country with a lot of different languages and therefore cultures [... it] is called the pearl of Africa touristic-wise" (Interview No. 26 2013). These representations are in accordance with deliberate positivism, yet do not disrupt the development discourse, as being nice and having a rich culture or blooming slopes is rather remotely related to development and in fact may contribute to the problematic exoticization of the Other that juxtaposes the rich culture or nature of the Other with the reason and rationality of the Self.

Other positive representations clearly belonged to the development discourse. The most common positive representation of "them" within the development discourse was related to "their" will to learn: a South Sudan member of CARE's team "wants only one thing: education" (Ansari 2014), and Astam Khan thinks that "school is the first step on the way back to normal life" for his daughter (CARE 2006a).

PiP also represented "them" as trying to learn: "Girls themselves ask for the agriculture class to be taught outside in the garden," says the teacher in a female school (PiP 2012b).

One of the basic elements of the Orientalist discourse is rationality. Whereas the Self is rational, the Other is irrational in this discourse. This distinction was crucial first for the colonial and later for the development discourse, but it served the need to divide the population inside Western societies as well. As van Leeuwen makes clear, "the greater the power of social actors, the more likely it is that cognitive, rather than affective, reactions will be attributed to them" (Leeuwen 2008: 58). Changes in development discourse that follow deliberate positivism keep the hierarchy between "us" and "them"; however, this is not the rational-irrational, cognitive-affective distinction, but the distinction is located at the level of knowledge. Actors are all capable of cognitive action, but "we" are in possession of knowledge and most of the time impart this knowledge to "them."

However, one PR text from CARE Austria and the more practical Austroprojekt Plan of Operation represent the Other at several instances as knowledgeable, thereby eliminating and at one point reversing the hierarchy of the development discourse. The distribution of cognitive reactions thus shows not only a clearly hierarchic difference between "us" and "them" and a disruption of the hierarchy, but also a difference between the Slovak and Austrian NGDOs.

In a closely analyzed article by Slovak NGDO Pontis (2010b), "they" are represented as either not knowing,[20] knowing little,[21] learning[22] or at most as "understanding … the fact that being able to master technologies is important for their future.…" On the other hand, the cognitive reactions attributed to "us" are mainly related to "our" experiences. In the case of another Slovak NGDO, PiP (2009), there are three cognitive reactions on the side of the local women, all related to learning about how to do business. The representation here thus reflects the hierarchic division of the development discourse. The Self is represented to a great extent as knowledgeable, and the Other to a great extent as not knowledgeable, yet capable of learning.

In the case of CARE's article on microfinance (CARE 2012a), which represents "them" in the most positive way, "they" are engaged in several cognitive social actions. The community *decides* to give goats to the poorest first, the women *decide* how to *invest* the money and "they" *know* how to overcome poverty. "They" are thus represented as decisive actors who know rather than learn. The structure of the development discourse is thereby challenged the most by CARE from among the analyzed actors. CARE's article on education (CARE 2006b) offers a stronger hierarchy that, however, also follows the policy of deliberate positivism, as "they" are represented as lacking knowledge, but also as having it and even teaching. "Our" teaching is without a clear agent in this article (unlike in an article from PiP), which backgrounds "our" superior role as knowledgeable actors. As the distinction needs to be kept to legitimize the action, though, "they" are once represented as not knowing about AIDS.

Austroprojekt offers the most equal relation between "us" and "them." In its Plan of Operation "they" are represented as engaged in "participatory rural appraisals," "participatory poverty assessments," "logical framework analysis," taking "study tours," "planning" or "identifying policies." Also, "they" together with "us" "focus" on poverty, engage in "monitoring" and "evaluation," "develop strategies," and "bring new ideas." In the same text, "we" together with the part of "them" identified as planners and implementers are represented as in need of an understanding of the "target group." This is different from the other texts, which never start from the assumption that "we" first need to understand "them" before "we" can engage in development.

Austroprojekt's Plan of Operation offers an interesting perspective that does not hierarchize so much between "us" and "them" as it does so within their "ranks." The personalized representations distinguish between different subgroups of "them." Here, "they" are represented as the "target population," "implementers," "district planners," or "technical advisors." The discourse here breaks the North–South power/knowledge division. What remains is the general power/knowledge division, but this is kept entirely within "their" own ranks. Not only are "they" the planners and the implementers here, as the participatory approach would have it, but "they" are even the experts – the technical advisors. However, the notion of trusteeship is kept with the distinction between the planners and the target population. Only, this time, the North–South divide is not included. Later sections of the Plan try to solve this problem with the participatory decision-making. As has been shown, however, "they" do not seem to be succeeding in this. Still, next to being occasionally represented as knowledgeable, "they" are also represented through respectable functions.

It should also be noted that sometimes "their" positive representation was the result of "our" engagement. In the BoC Report, "their" successes are at the same time "Banking on Change key achievements" (ibid.: 4). These include women's "increased ability to influence men's decision making by 33 per cent" (ibid.), the number of people reached (ibid.: 4, 6), and the amount they saved (ibid.: 4).

It was also not uncommon to find a representation of "their" progress that begins with a negative and ends with a positive representation. "We" were represented as the key part of that progress. In the article from Pontis, one can read that

> [b]efore the Slovaks came to Kenya, teachers at Rukanga did not know how to work with it [Power Point], however after only three days of the training, they were able to create their own presentation of a very good quality.
>
> (Pontis 2010b)

This pattern was also visible in the *Weltnachrichten* articles that included "their" lack of knowledge as the negative representation and "their" capacity to learn as the positive one. For example, in Southern Nepal "they" lack "the know-how to improve" the productivity of the soil (Thiard-Laforet 2013). Therefore, "we" teach "them." "They" are thereby represented positively as capable of learning. But the learning remains crucial. For example, in order to secure an actual use of new toilets, "measures to build public awareness and education in hygiene" are required (Burtscher 2013). The representation of Austrians as experts, e.g., as "specialists in biological and sustainable agricultural production" (Thiard-Laforet 2013), then complements "our" image as enablers of "their" progress.

"Our" role was occasionally emphasized in a stronger way in the interviews. The Self is portrayed as the enabler:

> That means that only when we create an opportunity for them, and show them a way, it is their choice whether they take it … it is not about us dictating what they are supposed to do, but it is about us showing them that there is another way.
>
> (Interview No. 3 2013)

A respondent from ADA focused even more on our role: "it's up to us to help the country to set up economic and social development" (Interview No. 23, 2014).

The importance of the actors can be judged by how visible they are in the text, but also by their mode of activation or passivation, the activity the actors are engaged in and their relationships to other actors. "Our" role of enablers is clearly visible from this perspective as well. The analysis shows deliberate positivism in "their" representation as being active in terms of positive actions. However, overall the hierarchy between "us" and "them" is still present in the discourse.

There is one final way to put one social actor above another and that is through the representation of his or her standing in a society. An actor can be just a number or a member of a specific group, s/he can be named, and sometimes even his or her academic titles can be mentioned. Simply put, there are many ways social actors can be represented, and some of these ways represent the actor as more important than others.

In the PR articles, "we" were mostly represented as active through "our" function, which elevates "us" in the eyes of the reader and as a group either through the pronoun "we" or through the NGDO's name. "We" were thus represented as high-status actors not distant from the reader.

"Their" representation was more varied. Both Slovak and Austrian NGDOs represented "them" not only through "their" functions such as "teachers," "families," "small farmers," or "members of saving groups," but they also genericized "them" as "local people," "women," "the poor," "village women," or "children." Those who are genericized can be considered to be the distant others and not "real people" with whom we "have to deal in our everyday lives" (Leeuwen 2008: 36). Occasionally, in Austrian PR articles, "they" were also aggregated, i.e., represented as statistics as in "1.2 billion from the group 14–24 years old" (CARE 2013), or as in "the number of illiterates" or "every tenth child" (CARE 2006b). Aggregation, i.e., quantification, dehumanizes "them" even more than genericization. The programmatic documents from state agencies offered similar results. In both of them, genericization (e.g., BMEIA 2012: 9; MFEA 2013: 13), and aggregation (e.g., BMEIA 2012: 10; MFEA 2013: 7) were sometimes used.

The hierarchic representation, as well as deliberate positivism, are thus clear here. Unlike "they," "we" are never represented as generic or aggregated actors. Yet, it is important to note that this is not "their" only representation, as "they" are sometimes represented as individuals and, less often, "they" are also functionalized, which increases their importance. Both the Slovaks and the Austrians engaged in these more positive representations. As the next section shows, it is possible to represent "them" in an even more positive way.

An example of deliberate positivism: an interview with a respondent from CARE

With one exception I so far refrained from quoting one respondent from CARE (Interview No. 25 2013), who took the logic of deliberate positivism furthest as she managed to suppress almost all negative representations of the Other for most of the interview.[23] It almost seems as if a new regime of truth emerged in which the Other in relation to the Self is not to be connoted negatively.

It is first necessary to mention her strong reluctance to characterize Ugandans: "When you come as a foreigner [...] you are not able to understand easily [...] the clan structure [... and] different structures with power" (ibid.). Thus "I don't know if I can really describe Uganda" (ibid.). "Ugandans would certainly be the best [people] to say how their country is" (ibid.). She was also reluctant to generalize, but then represented "them" positively in relation to education: "Uganda has various resources, which are really developed well. I think they have a good education; they have some very good educational institutes" (ibid.).

Then she offered a more complex portrayal of "their" poverty. Even though poverty in Latin America "is more visual [and] it concerns [many] more people" than in Europe, "it doesn't mean […] that people are not able to manage that" (ibid.). Moreover, with regard to the poverty,

> we sometimes get the feeling that it's true, and it's not true; people are struggling a lot and you will find really poor people […] but it's also a little bit distorted […] certainly these countries also have a lot of good things and a lot of good life.
>
> (Ibid.)

The development discourse is thus incoherent inside a single identity, and a more nuanced – hybrid – representation of the Other is necessary here.

Despite the respondent's reluctance to compare the Austrian and the Ugandan culture, there were three instances of a reversal of Eurocentrism in the interview:

> at the moment I deal with a certain group of people and it feels like "Oh the Austrians are so slow and they don't get anything done, and the Ugandans, they are so great […] if they want to do something, they get it done."
>
> (Ibid.)

This respondent also resisted hierarchization with regard to gender inequality to a much greater extent than with regard to poverty:

> you would say, "OK, patriarchy is a key structure, but that happens in Austria [too]" […]. You could say it is worse in Uganda and then say it's better in Europe, but if we look at certain things, it's maybe more covered in Europe; it's more sophisticated […]. We think that we are very democratic, […] but in the end how many women are there in the parliament at the moment? I don't know … Austria has a very low percentage, and Uganda is probably better.
>
> (Ibid.)

Finally, as already mentioned, in relation to sustainable development, this respondent turned this hierarchy upside down as well: "we are the main contributors [to climate change] and they are the ones who suffer the most [because of it], probably" (ibid.). In all these three cases, the Eurocentric hierarchic representation was reversed.

Overall, the deliberate positivism that this respondent took close to its extreme is visible in the whole corpus. Even though negative representations of the Other and positive representations of the Self dominate in the corpus, there are clear attempts to soften "their" negative representations, fight the stereotypes and contextualize them, and also the trend to represent "them" positively is undeniable. This approach is visible also in relation to the use of the term "developing country."

However, one may need to rethink here (and not only here) the term "deliberate." How deliberate were the positive representations? Is it correct to speak of an intentional effort to represent the Other in a positive way, or has this intention been internalized and naturalized into a new common sense at least among some of the development workers? Maybe a new discourse with different rules of formation is emerging.

A more structuralist approach would problematize the use of the term "deliberate" from the outset. Whereas there are clearly intentional efforts on the side of NGDOs and international organizations to represent the Other with dignity and to avoid stereotypes (e.g., in the Slovak and Austrian codices; PMVRO 2010, and Globale Verantwortung 2012), at the same time, these norms are becoming a part of actors' identities. According to these new norms, a good development worker pays attention to the way s/he represents the Other. As soon as this paying of attention becomes normalized, the term "deliberate" becomes redundant. What used to be deliberate becomes a norm that does not need to be laboriously promoted at conferences, NGDO networks, and IO meetings and in codices. The Northern development subject portrays the Other in a positive way because that has become the norm. The development discourse about the Other thus seems to be becoming much more positive.

As this research shows, the discourse is actually incoherent. My point here is to emphasize that enough time has passed since 1984 for sections of the development apparatus to have internalized the part of the discourse that contradicts the classical development paradigm (Ziai 2004) that was dominant at least until the 1980s.

Conclusion

There are three clear findings in my analysis. First, the texts and interviews hierarchize "us" over "them"; second, they also often include instances of deliberate positivism, and, third, the Slovaks use sharper hierarchies and hierarchize more often than the Austrians. In the next part of the conclusion, I will first focus on the commonalities and then on the differences between the two donors. Then, in the second part, I will offer a few ideas on the trend of deliberate positivism and connect it with the question of depoliticization.

Slovaks hierarchize more often and in a sharper way than Austrians

The main similarity between the two development apparatuses was the overall tendency to have the same grid of specification that represents "us" positively and "them" negatively following Orientalism in development discourse. There were some responses among the Slovak respondents that echo a colonial logocentrism stressing the absolute difference between civilizations; however, these were rare, and several respondents tried to counter this type of logocentrism. Most of the texts from both apparatuses followed the general law of development and did not question in any way the connection between the master signifier and its various specific incarnations in the discourse. However, several respondents disrupted this homogeneous image.

Apart from representing "them" negatively and "us" positively, the analysis showed that whereas "we" interact with "them," "they" do not interact back in the development discourse. Such a structure of (lack of) interaction was present also in otherwise much less hierarchic texts. The analysis of enunciations showed a hierarchy between "us" and "them" in both of the national development discourses. Whereas "we" are the experts explaining various phenomena, "they" are the grateful subjects expressing content with what "we" do. One could therefore argue that, even though the subalterns do not seem to be silent anymore, their utterances still become part of the dominant discourses.

In Austroprojekt's Plan of Operation, I also analyzed the representation of the partnership and the supposedly partner-like interaction between the Self and the Other. This analysis reveals how power operates, not only directly through clearly defined conditions, but also indirectly through the conduct of conducts that structures the possible field of action of the Other. Also, disciplinary mechanisms of self-monitoring contribute to the effective operations of power.

The discourse of partnership thus contains very clear instances of power relations that betray a hierarchy despite the rhetoric of equal partnership. However, just as one cannot rule out positive outcomes of the more practical mechanisms of power, so should one not rule out the possibility of positive results of a comparison between different cultures.

In the texts and interviews, negative stereotypes were occasionally softened, and occasionally (partly) countered with an (unsuccessful) anti-stereotypical representation. The stereotypes about "them" were occasionally also put into context and represented as rational behaviors. Sometimes "they" were represented in a positive way outside of the development discourse as friendly and likable, or "their" country was represented as attractive for tourists, but "they" were also positively represented inside of the development discourse as willing to learn and industrious. There were also instances of refusals to generalize cultures and compare them on the part of the respondents.

Unlike the texts, the respondents were in general reluctant to explicitly hierarchize the Self and the Other by using the embracive term "developing country." This might be due to the general negative connotation that the term ascribes to the Other, and impersonal rankings served the need to relieve one of the responsibility for the hierachization. Furthermore, texts from both countries often functionalize "them" as teachers, farmers, or families and thereby represent "them" as important actors.

Other representations offer more differences between Austria and Slovakia. The logocentric nature of the development discourse was most visible in the interviews with the respondents from SAIDC. But some of the Austrian respondents (and one respondent from Slovakia), on the other hand, countered the logocentric surface of the object's emergence.

The excesses in colonial stereotypes were striking at this surface. One Slovak respondent spoke of Africa as undiscovered for a long time and without the civilizing centers that enabled development in Europe. Such a strong, colonial-like hierarchization was not present in any of the texts or interviews on the Austrian side.

As already stated, all the closely analyzed texts include some of "their" positive representations. These are present in the strongest way in one article from CARE. Whereas, in the Slovak texts, "they" are mostly represented as willing to learn and learning and sometimes as having learned something, in CARE's article, "they" are represented as actors who know rather than learn. However, in the second closely analyzed article from CARE, "they" are also represented as learning and not as knowing. Thus, the difference between the Slovak and the Austrian discourse is not entirely clear-cut.

A further difference between Slovak NGDOs PiP and Pontis on the one hand and CARE Austria on the other can be seen in the strength of "their" positive representation. Whereas PiP tones down "their" negative representations related to environmental destruction by not naming the responsible actors and often represents "them" by an impersonal reference to a (negative) quality such as poverty, CARE almost always personalizes social actors and uses a range of positive connotations (e.g., leading personalities, "them" having their own ideas, or "them" taking their own decisions). Simply put, CARE represents "them" as much stronger personalities than PiP and Pontis.

The interviews offer a greater similarity between the two national development apparatuses, as almost all of the respondents connoted "them" both negatively and positively. One respondent from Austria stood out from the pattern, as she represented "them" in a positive way to a much greater extent and thought that, for example, there are very good educational institutes in Uganda. Furthermore, the Austrians were slightly more critical towards the Global North than the Slovaks. Even though in both countries several respondents admitted to corruption and environmentally problematic practices in their country of origin, more Austrians did so, and unlike the Slovaks, some Austrians admitted to unequal gender relations in Austria.

Overall, in terms of the Slovak-Austrian new-old distinction, the results show that there is no substantial difference between the two donors – both of them mostly hierarchize, and both of them also weaken or disrupt the hierarchizations. Both actors thus follow the development discourse with its incoherencies. Given the new donors' past as international donors, the question of whether it is legitimate to use the temporal differentiation arises. Is it the power relation created by the old-new distinction that demands that the new accept the norms of the old as legitimate? An argument could be made that my results show precisely the novice-teacher difference. In this view the Slovaks are just not there yet – they need to learn to speak the anti-racist language, and after that it will be possible to let them enjoy a truly full membership in the donors' club. I would argue that neither Slovaks, nor the Austrians, speak the anti-racist language. Nor is it the case for other Western donors, as the existing literature shows. All the donors reflect the incoherent nature of the discourse, and they all engage in the hierarchic Eurocentric representation. The question then remains: if Slovaks have their past of international aid, and if they do not substantially differ in their relation to the Other from other Western donors, on what basis can they still be called a new donor? The following chapters contribute to the argument by problematizing the difference in politicization and legitimization of development. They cast further doubt on the postcolonial difference between East and West embodied in the new-old donor distinction.

In terms of what both of the analyzed discourses have in common, they hierarchize "us" over "them," but also include instances of deliberate positivism. This research thereby confirms the more nuanced findings from the field of critical development studies. Where Escobar found hierarchic representations three decades ago and was criticized for his monolithic or unitary depiction of development discourse (e.g., by Cooper and Packard 1997: 10), other authors find more varied representations. Kiesel and Bendix (2010) show that the Other on German posters is active to a certain extent, with this activity being enabled by the development worker. Wilson (2012) puts the positive representation of the Other as, e.g., a hyperindustrious entrepreneur into the racial context of the colonial era, finding striking similarities with the current neocolonial period. Dogra (2014) analyzes images of the deserving Third World woman and notes that the context of these representations turns women's struggle for survival into a question of efficiency rather than exploitation. Dahl (2001), in a similar vein, criticizes the neoliberal representation of the worthy Other. Clearly, the positive representations do not reverse the power inequality between Self and Other and these representations are problematic in terms of depoliticization (see Chapter 4).

As much as the findings of all these authors are pertinent, I see a greater potential in the discursive change that all these authors implicitly or explicitly acknowledge. Lidchi's (1999) important insight about the positive representation of the Other together with the official promotion of participation and partnership can lead to a much more serious incoherence of the discourse (Ziai 2014) than the one we are currently observing. This may have a crucial impact on development workers' identities. Where Heron (2007), Goudge (2003) and Eriksson Baaz (2005) see a clear line between the rational Self and the irrational, corrupted or dangerous Other, Hödl (2010) finds narratives about equal, cordial encounters.

My findings show that, even though the hierarchy in the discourse dominates, the overall picture is certainly not unequivocal. Moreover, the softening or countering of the Orientalist hierarchy in the development discourse occasionally goes hand in hand with more politicized criticism. However, as the above-mentioned authors show, there are limits to this politicization.

Deliberate positivism and its limits

If the already mentioned most positive text (from CARE) and the interview that was most positive about the Other represent the current trend in the way the Other is represented, it might be useful to rethink the postcolonial critique of hierarchization. Absurd attempts not to hierarchize the Other that I heard about from various NGDO workers (personal communication) show that this critique of Eurocentrism has its limits.

The aim of the postcolonial approach is not only to seek a less hierarchic representation of the Other in development cooperation, but it also involves "reorientation towards the perspectives of knowledges [...] developed outside the west" (Young 2003: 6). In other words, the aim is to let the subaltern speak and achieve a more varied representation of the world. However, this approach does not aim at a complete erasure of hierarchic representations. As the text from CARE shows, this is probably impossible and, I would argue, also undesirable. There is nothing wrong with representing a useful hierarchy (or a useful unequal relationship) as a hierarchy, e.g., the relationship between a teacher and a student, as also Foucault (1988: 11–13) claimed. Attempts to refrain completely from hierarchic representations lead, in the case of one NGDO worker who deals with volunteers, to the problem of explaining during a preparatory weekend the differences that await the volunteers in Kenya. She asked the following question during our discussion: "Is this about creating a new terminology that nobody understands?" (personal communication).

As much as this example is telling, it does not mean that, for example, the most positive text about the Other from CARE is not problematic. It is problematic as part of a hierarchic discourse. It is this discourse that needs to change. An exchange of ideas and experience is perfectly fine as long as it does not go only one way and is not based on persisting unequal relations of power. Recent anti-racist videos show the limits of the critique of hierarchization (Jefferess 2013). These videos (e.g., "Who Wants to Be a Volunteer?") mock colonial stereotypes, but do not go any further. The development apparatus is nowadays very much capable of producing representations that do not include colonial stereotypes and keep hierarchization to a minimum. As much as this is laudable and actually can have an unforeseeable impact in terms of Northern identities, there is a danger of not going further and not asking how it is possible that "they" are almost always represented as inferior in relation to "us" in the development discourse, even if this is done within the language of equal partnership.

Postcolonialism is also concerned "with developing the driving ideas of a political practice morally committed to transforming the conditions of exploitation and poverty" (Young 2003: 6). This moral commitment leads to the conclusion that an analysis of Othering may soon be obsolete, and we may begin to analyze questions such as: Is it not strange that "we" are always helping "them," but "they" are never helping "us," even though "they" are in no way inherently inferior, and therefore there is no reason for "them" to be *always* lagging behind? This leads to the problem of depoliticization. The next chapter addresses this issue.

Notes

1 Several empirical studies show how microfinance promotes individualized entrepreneurial subjective modalities (Rankin 2001; Brigg 2001; Fernando 2006; Karim 2011); however, such aims are not always achieved (Rankin 2001; Karim 2011; Lazar 2004).
2 Hödl (2010) finds more equal and cordial relationships between the Northern Self and the Southern Other in interviews with Austrian development workers than Eriksson Baaz.
3 However, this respondent criticized the GDP definition for being "too simplifying" (ibid.) and was not content with the fact that countries get written off because they are called developing. She also had "a problem with the judgment, with dividing countries into developing and developed" (ibid.).
4 The missing 8% belongs to the categories "us-them" and "unclear."
5 For example, Robert Zeiner, Director Programs and Projects International, ADA.
6 For example, Hedwig Riegler, President of the Working Group for Statistics, DAC OECD.
7 For example, Annelis Vilim, Director of AG Globale Verantwortung.
8 For example, Mimoza Dhembi, Head of the Budget Department, Ministry of Finance, Albania.
9 For example, Noor Jelle, a farmer from Kenya, or Christina Petkovic from Macedonia.
10 E.g.: "One who cannot read and write remains caught in the poverty trap," Ulrike Schelander, Director of CARE Austria in CARE 2005.
11 Sometimes our self-praise gains noteworthy proportions: In one article from PiP, a male teacher from Kenya reports on the girls' desires to study in the school garden, thus supporting PiP's claim that "our concept of an ecological garden is *the best* solution for the adaptation to the climate change in sub-Saharan Africa and the way to food security" (PiP 2012b, my italics).
12 E.g.: "95% of CARE saving associations endure after we pull out of a project" (Wagner-Hager in CARE 2011).
13 E.g.: "It is a vicious circle. Children are taken out of school and get themselves children whom they can barely feed and therefore they get married early" (Wagner-Hager in CARE 2012b).
14 By pastoral power Foucault denotes the relation Christianity introduced between spiritual leaders and those who are to be led on their way to salvation. It focuses on the mind of an individual and guides him or her throughout their entire life, demanding the innermost secrets to be revealed. "This form of power is salvation oriented (as opposed to political power). It is oblative (as opposed to the principle of sovereignty); it is individualizing (as opposed to legal power) … " (Foucault 1982: 214).
15 For example, "they" live below the poverty line with low incomes and are in a poverty trap.
16 For example, "they" are not stopping at "our" frontiers and are also represented by growing migration and terrorism.
17 Kwetu means home in Swahili.
18 However, this was followed by an application of the development linearity, as the interviewee saw a similarity between "them" now and "us" before the First World War, when "we" also used to have families with 10–15 children: "thus I think that they will catch up with us as that economic development unfolds" (ibid.).
19 Note the recent law imposing a moratorium on issuing forest clearing permits in Albania due to serious deforestation of the country (news24 2016).
20 "Before the Slovaks came to Kenya, teachers at Rukanga did not know how to work with it … ."
21 "They already had the basics of working on a PC."

22 "In the 5 days of the training we have learned a lot … ."
23 Her negative representation of "them" was present only with regard to microfinance as she spoke about CARE's practical role after a direct question: "What is your role in it?"

Bibliography

Abdel-Malek, Anouar 1963: Orientalism in Crisis. *Diogenes* 11(44), 103–140.

Achebe, Chinua 1977: An Image of Africa. *Massachusetts Review* 18(4), 782–794.

Achleitner, Wolfgang 2012: Das Entwicklungskonzept in der Krise: Zivilisatorische Kritik aus Lateinamerika. *INTERNATIONAL – Zeitschrift für internationale Politik* 3(2012), 8–11.

Achleitner, Wolfgang 2013: Das Weltsozialforum in Tunis: Kleinbauern gegen Naturvermarktung. *INTERNATIONAL – Zeitschrift für internationale Politik* 2(2013), 4–7.

Allen, Theodore W. 2012: *The Invention of the White Race*. London and New York: Verso.

Ansari, Aimee 2014: Südsudan: Hoffnung für die Zukunft. CARE, www.care.at/news/news/suedsudan-hoffnung-fuer-die-zukunft/.

Apffel-Marglin, Frédérique 1990: Smallpox in two systems of knowledge. In: Marglin, Stephen A. and Marglin, Fredérique Apffel (ed.): *Dominating Knowledge. Development, Culture, and Resistance*. Oxford and New York: Oxford University Press, 102–144.

Barthes, Roland 1972: *Mythologies*. New York: The Noonday Press.

Bednárová, Edita 2009: Keňa (rozhovor viedla MR, SŠ). karierabezhranic.sk, www.karierabezhranic.sk/karierny-svet/zahranicie/afrika/kena/.

Bhabha, Homi 2004: *Location of Culture*. London and New York: Routledge.

BMEIA 2012: Three-Year Programme on Austrian Development Policy 2013–2015. Federal Ministry for European and International Affairs, Directorate-General for Development Cooperation, www.entwicklung.at/fileadmin/user_upload/Dokumente/Publikationen/3_JP/Englisch/2013-2015_3-YP.pdf.

Brigg, Morgan 2001: Empowering NGOs: The Microcredit Movement Through Foucault's Notion of Dispositif. *Alternatives: Global, Local, Political* 26(3), 233–258.

Burtscher, Robert 2013: Sauberes Wasser allein genügt nicht. *Weltnachrichten. Information der österreichischen Entwicklungszusammenarbeit* 1(2013), 3–4.

CARE 2005: CARE: Analphabetismus ist weiblich. CARE, www.care.at/news/presseaussendungen/care-analphabetismus-ist-weiblich/.

CARE 2006a: CARE eröffnet erste Schulen nach Erdbeben im Allai-Tal. CARE, www.care.at/news/presseaussendungen/care-eroeffnet-erste-schulen-nach-erdbeben-im-allai-tal/.

CARE 2006b: CARE: AIDS bewirkt Bildungsmissstände. CARE, www.care.at/news/presseaussendungen/care-aids-bewirkt-bildungsmissstaende/.

CARE 2011: Frauen und Geld: Mit Mikrokrediten und Kleinspargruppen aus der Armut. CARE, www.care.at/news/presseaussendungen/frauen-und-geld-mit-mikrokrediten-und-kleinspargruppen-aus-der-armut/.

CARE 2012a: Ein Dorf zieht an einem Strang. CARE, www.care.at/news/news/ein-dorf-zieht-an-einem-strang/.

CARE 2012b: CARE zum 1. Internationalen Tag des Mädchens am 11. Oktober: CARE, www.care.at/news/presseaussendungen/care-eroeffnet-erste-schulen-nach-erdbeben-im-allai-tal/.

CARE 2013: Bankensektor ignoriert 2,7 Milliarden potenzielle KundInnen. CARE, www.care.at/news/presseaussendungen/bankensektor-ignoriert-ueber-2-milliarden-potenzielle-kundinnen/.

Chmelař, Aleš, Pícl, Michal, Bittner, Jan, Volčík, Stanislav, and Nechuta, Aleš 2016: Analýza odlivu zisků: Důsledky pro českou ekonomiku a návrhy opatření. Příspěvek k debatě o udržitelnosti českého hospodářského modelu. Oddělení strategií a trendů EU Sekce pro Evropské záležitosti & Odbor analýz a informací Úřadu vlády České republiky, www.vlada.cz/cz/urad-vlady/vydavatelstvi/vydane-publikace/analyza-odlivu-zisku-dusledky-pro-ceskou-ekonomiku-a-navrhy-opatreni-155656/.

Cooke, Bill and Kothari, Uma 2001: The Case for Participation as Tyranny. In: Cooke, Bill and Kothari, Uma (ed.): *Participation: The New Tyranny?* London and New York: Zed Books, 1–15.

Cooper, Robert 2002: The new liberal imperialism. *Guardian*, 7.4.2002, www.theguardian.com/world/2002/apr/07/1.

Cooper, Frederick and Packard, Randall 1997: Introduction. In: Cooper, Frederick and Packard, Randall (ed.): *International development and the social sciences: essays on the history and politics of knowledge*. Berkeley, Los Angeles and London: University of California Press, 1–41.

Crewe, Emma and Harrison, Elizabeth 2002: *Whose Development? An Ethnography of Aid*. London and New York: Zed Books.

Dahl, Gudrun 2001: Responsibility and Partnership in Swedish Aid Discourse. Nordiska Afrikainstitutet, http://mercury.ethz.ch/serviceengine/Files/ISN/102625/ipublicationdocument_singledocument/9506b4a3-6e3e-42a1-a16c-d89d232059f4/en/9.pdf.

Dahl, Robert 1957: The Concept of Power. *Behavioral Science* 2(3), 201–215.

Dogra, Nandita 2014: *Representations of Global Poverty. Aid, Development and International NGOs*. London and New York: I.B. Tauris.

Drążkiewicz-Grodzicka, Elżbieta 2013: From Recipient to Donor: The Case of Polish Developmental Cooperation. *Human Organization* 72(1), 65–75.

DuBois, Marc 1991: The governance of the third world: A Foucauldian perspective on power relations in development. *Alternatives: Global, Local, Political* 16(1), 1–30.

Dufour, Françoise 2014: The Notion of 'Development' in French Colonial Discourses: Changes in Discursive Practices and Their Social Implications. In: Hodge, Joseph Morgan, Hödl, Gerald, and Kopf, Martina (ed.): *Developing Africa. Concepts and Practices in Twentieth Century Colonialism*. Manchester: Manchester University Press, 322–340.

Eriksson Baaz, Maria 2005: *The Paternalism of Partnership: a Postcolonial Reading of Identity in Development Aid*. London: Zed Books.

Escobar, Arturo 1984: Discourse and Power in Development: Michel Foucault and the Relevance of his Work to the Third World. *Alternatives: Global, Local, Political* 10(3), 377–400.

Escobar, Arturo 1995: *Encountering Development. The Making and Unmaking of the Third World*. Princeton: Princeton University Press.

Fanon, Frantz 2008: *Black Skin, White Masks*. New York: Grove Press.

Fernando, Jude L. 2006: Introduction. Microcredit and empowerment of women: blurring the boundary between development and capitalism. In: Fernando, Jude L. (ed.): *Microfinance. Perils and Prospects*. Oxon and New York: Routledge, 1–42.

Fialová, Zuzana 2013: Koho alebo čo vlastne rozvíjame? *SME*, 15.3.2013.

Foucault, Michel 1980: *Power/Knowledge: Selected Interviews and Other Writings 1972–1977. ed. Colin Gordon*. New York: Pantheon Books.

Foucault, Michel 1982: The Subject and Power. *Michel Foucault: Beyond Structuralism and Hermeneutics*. Chicago: Harvester Wheatsheaf, 208–225.

Foucault, Michel 1988: Power, Moral Values, and the Intellectual (interview with Michael Bess). *History of the Present* 4(Spring), 1–2, 11–13.

Foucault, Michel 1995: *Discipline and Punish. The Birth of the Prison*. New York and Toronto: Random House.

Foucault, Michel 2002a: *Archaeology of Knowledge*. London: Routledge.

Foucault, Michel 2002b: The Political Technology of Individuals. *Power. Essential Works of Foucault 1954–1984* 3. London: Penguin Books, 403–417.

Geosits, Christian and Gruber, Claudia 2014: Auf dem Weg zur Wissensgesellschaft. *Weltnachrichten. Information der österreichischen Entwicklungszusammenarbeit* 3(2014), 20.

Globale Verantwortung 2012: Leitfaden zur Umsetzung des CONCORD-Code of Conduct zum Umgang mit Bildern und Botschaften 2006, www.globaleverantwortung.at/images/doku/coc_leitfaden_endversion.pdf.

Goudge, Paulette 2003: *The Whiteness of Power: Racism in Third World Development and Aid*. London: Lawrence And Wishart.

Gutenbrunner, Manuela 2014: Zehn Jahre ADA – ein Grund zum Feiern? *Weltnachrichten. Information der österreichischen Entwicklungszusammenarbeit* 2(2014), 3–4.

Heron, Barbara 2007: *Desire for Development. Whiteness, Gender, and the Helping Imperative*. Waterloo: Wilfrid Laurier Univ. Press.

Hickey, Samuel and Mohan, Giles 2004: Towards Participation as Transformation: Critical Themes and Challenges. In: Hickey, Samuel and Mohan, Giles (ed.): *Participation. From Tyranny to Transformation?* London: Zed Books, 3–24.

Hodge, Joseph Morgan 2007: *Triumph of the Expert. Agrarian Doctrines of Development and the Legacies of British Colonialism*. Athens: Ohio University Press.

Hodge, Joseph Morgan and Hödl, Gerald 2014: Introduction. In: Hodge, Joseph Morgan, Hödl, Gerald, and Kopf, Martina (ed.): *Developing Africa. Concepts and Practices in Twentieth Century Colonialism*. Manchester: Manchester University Press, 1–34.

Hödl, Gerald 2010: "Es tut mir nich leid, dass ich's gemacht hab'." Eine "Oral history" der österreichischen Entwicklungshilfe. *Journal Für Entwicklungspolitik* 3, 95–118.

Hödl, Gerald 2013: Chronic underachievement. Austria's development aid in historical perspective. In: Olesen, Thorsten B. and Pharo, Helge (ed.): *Saints and Sinners. Official Development Aid and its Dynamics in a Historical and Comparative Perspective*. Oslo: Akademika, 255–278.

Horký, Ondřej 2011: Depoliticization, instrumentalization and legitimacy of Czech development cooperation: A case of imposed altruism? *Éthique et économique/Ethics and Economics* 8(1), 120–132.

Hund, Wulf D. 2003: Inclusion and Exclusion: Dimensions of Racism. *Wiener Zeitschrift zur Geschichte der Neuzeit* 3(1), 6–19.

Interview No. 3 2013: Interview with the respondent from the Pontis Foundation. 25.6.2013, personally in Bratislava.

Interview No. 4 2013: Interview with the respondent from the Pontis Foundation. 26.6.2013, personally in Bratislava.

Interview No. 7 2013: Interview with the respondent from the Pontis Foundation. 15.7.2013, personally in Bratislava.

Interview No. 8 2013: Interview with the respondent from PiP. 15.7.2013, personally in Bratislava.

Interview No. 9 2013: Interview with the respondent from PiP. 13.8.2013, personally in Bratislava.

Interview No. 10 2013: Interview with the respondent from PiP. 15.8.2013, personally in Bratislava.

Interview No. 11 2013: Interview with the respondent from PiP. 19.8.2013, personally in Bratislava.

Interview No. 12 2013: Interview with the respondent from SAIDC. 8.8.2013, personally in Bratislava.

Interview No. 13 2013: Interview with the respondent from SAIDC. 15.8.2013, personally in Bratislava.

Interview No. 14 2014: Interview with the respondent from SAIDC. 26.2.2014, personally in Bratislava.

Interview No. 15 2014: Interview with the respondent from SAIDC. 11.6.2014, personally in Bratislava.

Interview No. 16 2013: Interview with the respondent from Austroprojekt. 7.10.2013, personally in Vienna.

Interview No. 17 2013: Interview with the respondent from Austroprojekt. 6.10.2013, personally in Vienna.

Interview No. 20 2013: Interview with the respondent from ADA. 19.11.2013, personally in Vienna.

Interview No. 21 2013: Interview with the respondent from ADA. 20.11.2013, personally in Vienna.

Interview No. 22 2013: Interview with the respondent from ADA. 20.11.2013, personally in Vienna.

Interview No. 23 2013: Interview with the respondent from ADA. 26.11.2013, personally in Vienna.

Interview No. 25 2013: Interview with the respondent from CARE. 20.11.2013, personally in Vienna.

Interview No. 26 2013: Interview with the respondent from CARE. 26.11.2013, personally in Vienna.

Interview No. 27 2013: Interview with the respondent from CARE. 27.11.2013, over Skype.

Interview No. 28 2014: Interview with the respondent from CARE. 11.2.2014, personally in Vienna.

JanMohamed, Abdul R. 1985: The Economy of Manichean Allegory: The Function of Racial Difference in Colonialist Literature. *Critical Inquiry* 12(1), 59–87.

Jefferess, David 2013: Humanitarian Relations: Emotion and the Limit of Critique. *Critical Literacy: Theories and Practices* 7(1), 73–83.

Karim, Lamia 2011: *Microfinance and its Discontents. Women in Debt in Bangladesh.* Minneapolis and London: University of Minnesota Press.

Kharroub, Riham 2014: Wenn Arbeit an Grenzen stößt. *Weltnachrichten. Information der österreichischen Entwicklungszusammenarbeit* 2(2014), 27.

Kiely, Ray 1999: The Last Refuge of the Noble Savage? A Critical Assessment of Post-Development Theory. *The European Journal of Development Research* 11(1), 30–55.

Kiesel, Timo and Bendix, Daniel 2010: White Charity: Eine postkoloniale rassismuskritische Analyze der entwicklungspolitischen Plakatwerbung in Deutschland. *Peripherie: Zeitschrift für Politik und Ökonomie in der Dritten Welt* 120, 482–495.

Kopf, Martina 2009: Vom Kolonialbeamten zum Entwicklungshelfer. *Südwind. Magazin für internationale Politik, Kultur und Entwicklung*, 11, www.suedwind-magazin.at/vom-kolonialbeamten-zum-entwicklungshelfer.

Laclau, Ernesto and Mouffe, Chantal 2001: *Hegemony and Socialist Strategy. Towards a Radical Democratic Politics*. London and New York: Verso.

Lazar, Sian 2004: Education for Credit: Development as Citizenship Project in Bolivia. *Critique of Anthropology* 24(3), 301–319, <doi:10.1177/0308275X04045423>.

Leeuwen, Theo van 2008: *Discourse and Practice. New Tools for Critical Discourse Analysis*. Oxford: Oxford University Press.

Lidchi, Henrietta 1999: Finding the right image. British development NGOs and the regulation of imagery. In: Skelton, Tracey and Allen, Tim (ed.): *Culture and Global Change*. London and New York: Routledge, 87–101.

Loomba, Ania 2010: *Colonialism/Postcolonialism*. London and New York: Routledge.

Lukes, Steven 2004: *Power. A Radical View*. London: Macmillan.

Manzo, Kate 1991: Modernist discourse and the crisis of development theory. *Studies in Comparative International Development* 26(2), 3–36.

MFEA 2013: Medium-Term Strategy for Development Cooperation of the Slovak Republic for 2014–2018. Ministry of Foreign and European Affairs of the Slovak Republic, https://issuu.com/slovakaid/docs/strednodoba_strategia_oda_sr_2014-2_83963017c1b288.

MFEA 2014: Správa o oficiálnej rozvojovej pomoci Slovenskej republiky za rok 2013, www.slovakaid.sk/sites/default/files/informacia_o_oda_za_rok_2013.pdf.

Nandy, Ashis 1983: *The Intimate Enemy. Loss and Recovery of Self under Colonialism*. Delhi: Oxford University Press.

NDC-Austroprojekt and Orgut 2002: Plan of Operation for Ngorngoro District Development Programme. Phase 1. Ngorngoro District Council and Austroprojekt and Orgut Consortium.

Nederveen Pieterse, Jan 1992: *White on Black. Images of Africa and Blacks in Western Popular Culture*. New Haven and London: Yale University Press.

Nederveen Pieterse, Jan 2000: After Post-Development. *Third World Quarterly* 21(2), 175–191.

news24 2016: Albania bans cutting down trees for 10 years. *News24*, 2.5.2016 www.news24.com/Green/News/albania-bans-cutting-down-trees-for-10-years-20160205.

Noxolo, Patricia 2006: Claims: A Postcolonial Geographical Critique of "Partnership" in Britain's Development Discourse. *Singapore Journal of Tropical Geography* 27(3), 254–269.

Nölke, Andreas and Vliegenthart, Arjan 2009: Enlarging the Varieties of Capitalism: The Emergence of Dependent Market Economies in East Central Europe. *World Politics* 61(4), 670–702, doi:10.1017/S0043887109990098.

Obrovsky, Michael 2013: Interview with Michael Obrovsky. 19.11.2013, personally in Vienna.

Parry, Benita 1987: Problems in Current Theories of Colonial Discourse. Oxford Literary Review, 9(1), 27–58, doi:10.3366/olr.1987.002

Pavlicová, Vendula 2012: Stereotypical Images of the Global South in the Media: The Role of the Development Actors. In: Tůmová, Jana (ed.): *Crucial Problems of International Relations through the Eyes of Young Scholars "Actors and Actorness in International Relations: State and Their Discontents."* Praha: Nakladatelství Oeconomica, 97–110.

PiP 2009: Podpora podnikania vidieckych žien v západnej Keni (2008–2009). People in Peril, https://clovekvohrozeni.sk/podpora-podnikania-vidieckych-zien-v-zapadnej-keni-2008-2009/.

PiP 2012a: Poľnohospodárstvo rozvíjame aj na východnom pobreží Kene. People in Peril, https://clovekvohrozeni.sk/polnohospodarstvo-rozvijame-aj-na-vychodnom-pobrezi-kene/.

PiP 2012b: Už ďalšie štyri školy majú výživnejšiu stravu. People in Peril, https://clovekvohrozeni.sk/uz-dalsie-styri-skoly-maju-vyzivnejsiu-stravu/.

PiP 2012c: Slováci na Veľkú noc priniesli deťom v Keni radosť. People in Peril, https://clovekvohrozeni.sk/slovaci-na-velku-noc-priniesli-detom-v-keni-radost/.

PiP 2012d: Ďalšia kenská škola je hrdá na svoju školskú záhradu. People in Peril, https://clovekvohrozeni.sk/v-keni-na-strednej-skole-ngenia-sme-otvarali-novu-skolsku-zahradu/.

PMVRO 2010: Kódex používania obrazového materiálu a podávania správ. Platforma mimovládnych rozvojových organizácií, www.mvro.sk/sk/kodexy/kodex/uplne-znenie-kodexu.

Pontis n.a.: Kenya. Pontis Foundation, www.nadaciapontis.sk/we-help-in-kenya-en.

Pontis 2010a: pontis preparatory trip to kenya brought new computer laboratory to regional high school. Pontis Foundation, www.nadaciapontis.sk/article/pontis-preparatory-trip-to-kenya-brought-new-computer-laboratory-to-regional-high-school/275.

Pontis 2010b: slovak teachers taught their colleagues from kenya how to use information technologies. Pontis Foundation, www.nadaciapontis.sk/article/slovak-teachers-taught-their-colleagues-from-kenya-how-to-use-information-technologies/277?lang=en_US.

Pontis 2012: new computer labs connecting slovak and kenyan students. Pontis Foundation, www.nadaciapontis.sk/article/new-computer-labs-connecting-slovak-and-kenyan-students/281.

Profant, Tomáš 2010: Fair Trade z pohľadu postrozvojového prístupu. *Mezinárodní vztahy* 45(2), 71–98.

Profant, Tomáš 2018: The Social Construction of Slovakia as a Donor and its Power Effects. *Europe–Asia Studies* 70(3), 365–387, doi:10.1080/09668136.2018.1453486.

Rabitsch, Waltraud 2013: Entwicklung neu (über)denken. *Weltnachrichten. Information der österreichischen Entwicklungszusammenarbeit* 4(2013), 3–4.

Rabitsch, Waltraud and Sötz, Elisabeth 2013: Nachhaltig zusammenarbeiten. *Weltnachrichten. Information der österreichischen Entwicklungszusammenarbeit* 4(2013), 10–11.

Rahnema, Majid 1992: Participation. In: Sachs, Wolfgang (ed.): *The Development Dictionary. A Guide to Knowledge as Power.* London and New Jersey: Zed Books, 116–131.

Rankin, Katharine N. 2001: Governing Development: Neoliberalism, Microcredit, and Rational Economic Woman. *Economy and Society* 30(1), 18–37.

Rössler, Daniel 2013: Auf neuen Pfaden. *Weltnachrichten. Information der österreichischen Entwicklungszusammenarbeit*, 1(2013), 18.

Said, Edward 1979: *Orientalism*. New York: Vintage Books.

Šimek, Jakub 2010: Informačné technológie a ich prínos pre rozvoj v Keni. In: Aleksanyan, Tigran (ed.): *Perspektívy podnikania v Afrike – pondikanie v Angole, Keni a Líbyi.* Bratislava: Národná agentúra pre rozvoj malého a stredného podnikania, 25–32.

Spivak, Gayatri Charkravorty 1994: Can the Subaltern Speak? In: Williams, Patrick and Chrisman, Laura (ed.): *Colonial Discourse and Post-colonial Theory: A Reader*. New York: Columbia University Press, 66–111.

Thiard-Laforet, Susanne 2013: Die reichen Gaben Demeters. *Weltnachrichten. Information der österreichischen Entwicklungszusammenarbeit* 4(2013), 12.

Traxler, Gottfried 2013a: Fachkräfte "Made in Mexiko." *Weltnachrichten. Information der österreichischen Entwicklungszusammenarbeit* 2(2013), 18.

Traxler, Gottfried 2013b: Starker Kaffee von starken Menschen. *Weltnachrichten. Information der österreichischen Entwicklungszusammenarbeit* 3(2013), 21.

Turner, Oliver 2014: *American Images of China: Identity, Power, Policy*. London and New York: Routledge.

Weissel, Nikolaus 2014: Zehn Jahre Wirtschaftspartnerschaften. *Weltnachrichten. Information der österreichischen Entwicklungszusammenarbeit*, 2(2014), 26.

Wilson, Kalpana 2012: *Race, Racism and Development: Interrogating History, Discourse and Practice*. London and New York: Zed Books.

Wolf, Larry 1994: *Inventing Eastern Europe: The Map of Civilization on the Mind of the Enlightenment*. Stanford: Stanford University Press.

Young, Robert, J. C. 2003: *Postcolonialism. A Very Short Introduction*. Oxford and New York: Oxford University Press.

Ziai, Aram 2004: *Entwicklung als Ideologie? Das klassische Entwicklungsparadigma und die Post-Development Kritik zur Analyze des Entwicklungsdiskurses*. Hambrug: Deutsches Übersee-Institut.

Ziai, Aram 2006: *Zwischen Global Governance und Post-Development: Entwicklungspolitik aus diskursanalytischer Perspektive*. Münster: Westfälisches Dampfboot.

Ziai, Aram 2007: The Meaning of "Development": A critical Perspective. *Journal Für Entwicklungspolitik* 2, 67–79.

Ziai, Aram 2014: Progressing towards incoherence: Development discourse since the 1980s. *Momentum Quarterly: Zeiotschrift für sozialen Fortschritt* 3(1), 3–14.

Ziai, Aram 2016: *Development Discourse and Global History: From Colonialism to the Sustainable Development Goals*. Oxon and New York: Routledge.

Zimmer, Gunther 2013: Balance schaffen. Interview by Manuela Gutenbrunner. *Weltnachrichten. Information der österreichischen Entwicklungszusammenarbeit* 2(2013), 16–17.

Zorád, Lukáš 2011: Keňania chcú pracovať, no nevedia ako, hovorí rozvojový pracovník (rozhovor viedol Matúš Krčmárik). www.sme.sk, www.sme.sk/c/6077830/kenania-chcu-pracovat-no-nevedia-ako-hovori-rozvojovy-pracovnik.html.

4 (De)Politicization of unequal power relations in development discourse

The problem of depoliticization has been introduced by Marx already in 1844 in his book *On the Jewish Question* (Marx 2012). One might go further into the past and argue that "[d]epoliticization is the oldest task of politics" and that "[p]olitics is the art of suppressing the political" (Rancière 1995: 19, 11). The problem of removing conflicting issues from the political field has been dealt with by a number of scholars (Bourdieu 2002; Crouch 2004; Flinders and Buller 2006; Foucault 2002: 403–417; Mouffe 2005; Pettit 2004; Rancière 1999; Rose 2004; Simmel 2009; Wilson and Swyngedouw 2014a; Žižek 1999). In connection with depoliticization, one could speak about a small sub-field of political science that stretches out to various social issues such as law (Shihata 1986), environment (Swyngedouw 2011), economy (Swanson 2008), or development cooperation. It is possible to encounter depoliticization in all these and many other fields (for a list of relevant sources see Flinders and Buller 2006: 294).

Within development studies, the number of authors engaging with the problem of depoliticization is growing (Brockington 2014; Dogra 2014; Easterly 2013; Erkkilä and Piironen 2009, 2014; Feldman 2003; Ferguson 1994; Harris 2001; Hout 2012; Hout and Robinson 2009; Jaeger 2007; Kamat 2014; Kapoor 2012; Li 2007; Löwenheim 2008; Manji 1998; White 1996, 2006). There is also a scholarly interest in studying how development politicizes unequal power relations (Ferguson 2006; Van Ausdal 2001; Williams 2004). All these authors employ the concept of depoliticization or related concepts (e.g., the post-political); however, more often than not, they do so without a closer operationalization of the term (for an example, see Flinders and Buller 2006). Whereas overarching definitions of depoliticization are found in the work of these scholars, a more nuanced understanding of various forms of depoliticization is still missing.

The first aim of this chapter is to provide such a nuanced understanding – to operationalize the concept of depoliticization. This task is complemented with the aim to operationalize the concept of politicization as there are different forms of politicization in the corpus. The second aim will be to compare the extents to which the Slovak and Austrian texts analyzed in the study and the respondents in the related interviews depoliticize and the extents to which they politicize unequal power relations. There is a clear difference between the texts and the interviews in this regard that is worth noting. Both the Austrian and Slovak development apparatuses mostly depoliticize unequal power relations and potential conflicts. The analyzed texts, apart from a few articles from the "critical development" genre, almost always depoliticize unequal relations. There are differences between the Slovaks and Austrians in this respect as the Austrians politicize unequal power relations more often and in a stronger way, however several Slovaks do so as well and this difference between the Slovaks and Austrians is thus one of degree and not of substance.

In order to begin with the operationalization, it is necessary first to define what exactly the terms "the political," "politics," "police," "politicization," and "depoliticization" mean.

The political, politics, police, politicization, and depoliticization

One needs to begin with the terms "politics," "police," and "the political" in order to be able to define the term depoliticization. I will follow the basic definition from Carl Schmitt (2007), according to whom the political presupposes a friend-enemy distinction (ibid.: 26). There is always a potential conflict between the two sides that may result in a war as the most extreme form of their fight (ibid.: 33). War is not the aim or the content of politics, but is always present as a real possibility. "The high points of politics are simultaneously the moments in which the enemy is, in concrete clarity, recognized as the enemy" (ibid.: 67). At such moments, politics is closest to the political.

One should not conflate the political with other spheres such as religion, morality, economics, or nationalism (which can be a problematic distinction in itself; see, e.g., Latour 1993). The political is not one such sphere, but is embodied in each of them (see also Wilson and Swyngedouw 2014b: 10). Every sphere of human conduct can become political, but need not. As soon as there is a conflict in a particular sphere of life, this sphere becomes political. Thus, religious wars are political wars at the same time, and a class is not just an economic, but also a political, category (Schmitt 2007: 37). The political "does not describe its own substance, but only the intensity of an association or dissociation of human beings whose motives can be religious, national [...] economic, or of another kind" (ibid.: 38).

The political is thus an abstract notion of an absolute conflict. Such a conflict remains a mere possibility that can never fully materialize, as the conflict itself always contains a particular content (e.g., gender, race, etc.). It is thus not possible to reach the political, as the political is always there as an ideal that enemies strive to reach in order to politicize the issues at hand, but at the same time they cannot reach it, as this would mean creating an impossibly pure conflict without a content.

As such, the political is a useful concept that enables us to define the terms politics, police (or management, or administration), politicization, and depoliticization (see Figure 4.1). Politics is the space in which groups strive to reach the

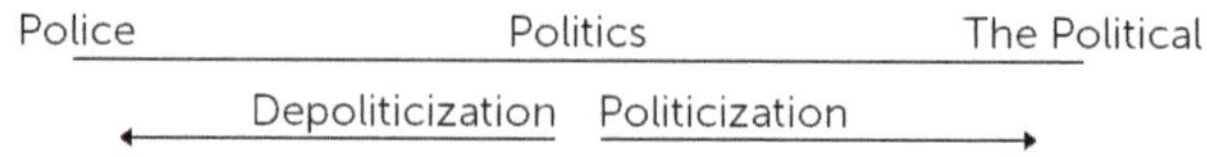

Figure 4.1 Depoliticization.

political, but also the space in which political issues become depoliticized. Politics can be defined as the political at one extreme, and at the other extreme as police. The politics is thus "the meeting ground" between the political and the police (Rancière in Wilson and Swyngedouw 2014b: 12).

Currently, the practice of politics to a great extent overlaps with the practice of police. Today, one can understand politics as "technocratic mechanisms and consensual procedures that operate within an unquestioned framework of representative democracy, free market economics, and cosmopolitan liberalism" (ibid.: 6). Such a perspective on politics, however, does not do justice to the potential of the repoliticization that may occur in the political process. Politics is "the set of practices through which an order is created" (Mouffe in ibid.). It is the contingent construction of hegemony (ibid). Both the practice of depoliticization and the practice of politicization are political actions. They occur within the realm of politics and denote actors' possibilities. They can push either towards the political or towards the non-political police that suppresses or disavows the political in political issues.

Police denotes the type of politics that is devoid of the political. The friend-enemy antagonism is not visible within the realm of police that operates on an allegedly consensual basis. Police denotes "specific techniques by which a government in the framework of the state was able to govern people as individuals significantly useful for the world" (Foucault 2002: 410). Governance here lacks the friend-enemy conflict and is conducted through particular institutions that reproduce a given social hierarchy. The political antagonism is suppressed or disavowed through these institutions, and the relationship between the antagonistic parties is represented as consensual. Therefore a mere administration is required for the governance (or the policing) of the social realm.

These three terms enable numerous further specifications of depoliticizing and politicizing practices that constitute a crucial political practice and enable further political engagements to take place or disable them from taking place. Politicization is a political practice of including the friend-enemy element in a particular case. It is a preparatory stage for the conflict between enemies (i.e., for the political) to take place. Depoliticization then denotes (political) attempts to suppress or disavow conflicting issues with clearly defined or potential enemies (see the image). The reason for focusing on the problem of depoliticization then is that it constitutes a social wrong that should be rectified. In order to do so, one first needs to identify instances of depoliticization – hence my research. Depoliticization of unequal power relations is further problematic as it normalizes a state of inequality that is not useful for or accepted by the weaker side of the relationship. It is for these reasons that one should engage in analyzing depoliticization and in repoliticizing depoliticized but highly political issues.

The dominant depoliticizing discourse is occasionally disrupted by instances of politicization, but sometimes it is difficult to determine the strength of the politicization or whether one can even speak of politicization in the given case, and sometimes even politicization can be depoliticizing.

In what follows, my overarching aim will be to show that depoliticizations and politicizations are important parts of development discourses in Austria and Slovakia. One can find explicit depoliticization in the rhetoric of an important donor – China, whose dominant claim is that its aid is dispersed purely on a non-political basis (see, e.g., Mawdsley 2012). Research shows, however, that there are political interventions coming from this donor. Thus, a finding about any kind of (de)politicizing practice is in itself important, as such a finding becomes a political intervention by pointing at such (de)politicizing practices. Further, I will try to show how these depoliticizations and politicizations are achieved. Reaching this aim can enable those who produce the development discourse to change their depoliticizing practices. It also serves the aim of political science to better understand our social world. Finally, I will engage in comparing the Slovak and Austrian (de)politicizing practices to answer the main research question of this book.

The following part analyzes the instances of depoliticization and the part after that focuses on forms of potential or actual politicization.

Forms of depoliticization

Depoliticization is achieved through various ways. One of them is a spatial delimitation that includes local reasons for poverty, local instruments to solve the problem of poverty such as access to market, microfinance, or education, and local legitimation of development projects. These forms of depoliticization include more abstract assumptions such as that the market is inherently benign. Finally, depoliticization can be based on technological solutions, on the omission of agents, and on a particular temporal focus, and an explicit invocation of a consensus among potentially conflicting actors within development cooperation.

Spatial depoliticization

Spatial depoliticization is the main form of depoliticization in development cooperation policy. This policy, especially if performed by NGOs, is most often focused on the local level and, as such, depoliticizes struggles at other political levels. Aiming at changes at the level of a village or a community can disregard interferences into these spatial units from the regional, state, and international or global political levels. Political struggles between actors at different levels are usually unequal, and the focus on one particular level can lead to an omission of these struggles and thereby to their depoliticization.

Before proceeding further, it is necessary to note that, whereas the NGOs and state agencies that I analyzed are mainly (but not exclusively) concerned with the local, the rest of the development apparatus is also concerned with the national and the global level. More importantly, the development discourse in no way prohibits the politicization of these two levels. There have been clear attempts to politicize the global connections between North and South through dependency, unequal exchange, and world-system theories, the New International Economic Order (NIEO), and the Dag Hammarskjöld report (see, e.g., Rist 2008). Most recently, global education, the Sustainable Development Goals, and policy coherence also offered space for politicization of Northern consumption patterns as well as Northern policies towards the Global South. Attempts to engage with politics at the global and national level also include the concepts of global governance and good governance. However, research shows that both good and global governance discourses have depoliticizing effects (see, e.g., Abrahamsen 2000; Erkkilä and Piironen 2009, 2014; Hout and Robinson 2009; Jaeger 2007; Löwenheim 2008). The same may apply to the practice of policy coherence (Adelle and Jordan 2014; Ziai 2007; Carbone 2008; Matthews 2008) and to global education (Andreotti 2014; Danielzik, Kiesel and Bendix 2013).

I would therefore argue that the currently dominant efforts to include the international and the national level in the development discourse fail to politicize the potential conflicts at these levels, and between these and other levels. Thus the argument that there is a division of labor between NGOs that engage at the local level and other actors, who engage at the national and international level, is problematic, and it is worth pointing at the various instances of spatial depoliticization among the Slovak and Austrian actors.

The development apparatus thus seems to be a multifocal anti-politics machine and could be understood as a dispersed form of institutional depoliticization (Flinders and Buller 2006: 298). Its highly political task – to reduce poverty, or to improve people's living conditions (i.e., development) – is entrusted to explicitly apolitical IOs, NGOs, or the private sector, all of which engage where the alleged lack of development is occurring.

This institutional depoliticization contains a discursive element that puts development actors into a position from which locally (or nationally) delimited intervention becomes the logical solution. Thus, the World Bank produces a particular discourse in order to become useful as a development organization, as an organization that can engage in a development project. The World Bank creates a particular image of a country, in which, among other things, the people of Lesotho are represented as subsistence farmers and not as miners who regularly migrate to South Africa (Ferguson 1994: 71). Lesotho itself is represented as a national economy that "is rich or poor according to the natural resources that lie within its boundaries" (ibid.: 62) and not due to the relation with its neighbor. Ferguson mentions several other important elements of the World Bank's discourse on Lesotho, but here it is crucial to note that, in order to be able to engage in a development project, the World Bank does not represent political changes in South Africa as relevant for the development of Lesotho.

> The World Bank mission to Lesotho is in no position to formulate programs for changing or controlling the South African mining industry, and it has no disposition to involve itself in the political challenges to the South African system of labor control known as *apartheid*.
>
> (Ibid.: 71)

Promoting political challenges would mean overstepping the apolitical institutional role that development actors are supposed to fulfill.

In short, the reasons for poverty in Lesotho need to be depicted as confined within the borders of Lesotho. Such a portrayal is common in development discourse. Apart from local reasons, the spatial depoliticization includes various local instruments (access to an inherently benign market, microfinance, and education) as the solution to the local reasons for poverty. Another spatial depoliticization contains the local legitimization of the involvement of the development apparatus.

Just as the World Bank does not deal with political conflicts in South Africa when devising development programs for Lesotho, so do the analyzed texts and respondents find the reasons for poverty mostly at the local level and not at the international level.

The first part of Austroprojekt's Plan of Operation for the Ngorongoro District Development Programme shows in a succinct way the main problems in Ngorongoro. But, all of the descriptions of the problems exclude political issues. The plan follows Burkina Faso's National Poverty Eradication Strategy in listing the causes of Ngorongoro's poverty. These include: "[a] dependency syndrome among the poor, rapid population growth, a poor transportation system, an insufficient number of extension workers, etc." (NDC-Austroprojekt and Orgut 2002: 8, see also ibid.: 13, 22).

In this and a few other instances, the reasons for the local problems are located in Tanzania. There is no mentioned connection to other places. The visibility of the local area is made to fit the requirement of the project. As the project is local, the problems, as well as the solutions to them, also need to be made local. To make a connection to the Global North would disrupt the visibility of the problems being located in the South. What Thomas Pogge (2002: 15) calls "explanatory nationalism" and Ulrich Beck (2003: 453) "methodological nationalism" here deserves the term methodological localism or regionalism. Its effect is the protection of activities occurring at a different spatial level, but materially connected to the local level, from scrutiny.

The Slovak respondents from Pontis, SAIDC, and PiP also to a great extent ignored the political problems related to spatial units beyond the national state, such as the unequal trade relations or the colonial legacy. A respondent from Pontis spoke about the following in relation to the reasons for poverty: a lack of resources, the low level of wealth of individuals or their parents, an insufficient or irregular income, a low level of savings, drug abuse, the local culture, too many kids in families, a low level of education, and an insufficient social and health infrastructure (Interview No. 7 2013, see also Interview No. 3 2013, Interview No. 5 2013).

This respondent thereby engaged in the discursive practice of poverty disaggregation. Poverty is here elaborated "through details of its components or related dimensions" (Dogra 2014: 85). These components are represented as the causes of the poverty, which

> gives the impression that substantial information is being provided, but obscures the fact that the "information" is tautological and circulatory. The information at best merely splits up the manifest symptoms of a complex issue to show them as various "causes."
>
> (Ibid.)

Thus, e.g., "a low level of wealth of individuals or their parents" or "insufficient income" (Interview No. 7 2013) are definitional traits of poverty, but at the same time the lack of income (i.e., capital) leads to or reproduces poverty. However, the origins of this lack are not explained by the respondent. In such cases, poverty is simply disaggregated into numerous components that lack explanatory power and exclude political conflicts.

Other local reasons for poverty are informed by hierarchic representations of the Self and the Other. For example, in the Slovak Medium-Term Strategy, one can read that due to the growing demands on the standard of living in the "developing countries [...] there is a growth of food and energy consumption, [and an] exhaustion of natural resources ... " (MFEA 2013: 5). One can also read in *Weltnachrichten* about the "prognosticated growth of population and the enormous use of resources [that] put the world in front of a great challenge" (Burtscher 2013). These are instances of the depoliticization that is common to the sustainable development discourse. Instead of focusing on the consumption where it occurs the most, the first text foregrounds the growing consumption in the Global South, and the second one reproduces the Malthusian discourse and does not focus on those responsible for the use of resources, but points to the prognosticated population growth. As Escobar (1996: 330) claims, the blame is shifted "away from the large industrial polluters in [the] North and South and the predatory way of life fostered by capitalism and development to poor peasants and 'backward' practices such as slash-and-burn agriculture." Thus, one side of the political conflict over resources is omitted, and the conflict disappears and thereby becomes depoliticized. The problem of resource exhaustion is present; however, it is present not as a political conflict, but as a problem of the Other in the Global South.

Overall, the reasons for poverty are often located at the local level. Respondents and texts from both of the examined national discourses depoliticize by localizing the reasons for poverty. Both old and new donors engage in the same kinds of discursive operations related to depoliticization.

Spatial depoliticization is, in general, related to particular issues on which the local projects focus. Local reasons for poverty lead to the use of local instruments. As a development agency needs a discourse that "provides a place for the agency to plug itself in" (Ferguson 1994: 69), the discourse contains a variety of very concrete problems. The solution to these problems is to be found in a local intervention. The texts and the interviews I analyzed focused on various topics related mostly to the local or national level (e.g., the lack of education, the lack of access to financial services and other markets). These realms are constructed in such a way that a project focusing on the local level seems like a logical solution to the problems presented in such spatial terms.

The wide array of these topics or elements makes it seem that the development apparatus is focusing on all the possible realms of life and therefore cannot be accused of actually omitting significant parts of development. The simultaneous focus on healthcare, education, infrastructure, economy, governance, etc. represents development cooperation as targeting all the possible elements of development at the same time. An NGO should just choose where to engage (e.g., healthcare), other NGOs will engage in other topics (e.g., education), and this complex approach will lead to development.

Relating this point to the previous one, I claim that all these topics remain at the local level and have a depoliticizing effect through their sheer amount. I focused on three topics in the texts – environmental projects, educational projects, and microfinance projects. All of them were connected to a local level and omitted relations of power at all levels (including the local) except for that of the households. Further topics that focus on the local level (including the national) and were included in the corpus were concerned with the lack of IT, the lack of market access, the lack of knowledge, the need for capacity building, the lack of natural resources, corruption, good governance, etc. They all make it seem as if all that necessarily had to be targeted was already targeted. Moreover, the projects are often legitimized by the local consent through the discourses of partnership and participation.

It is possible to imagine a counterargument from particular NGO workers. They could claim that they simply do their job in one specific field and they cannot focus on everything. Everyone does his or her part, and together they make development happen. My argument here is that the amount of the various topics in which one can be active makes it look as if they exhausted all the possible fields of action. However, by engaging only in the abovementioned spaces of intervention, more political topics (at various levels) are left unaddressed. This approach depoliticizes political conflicts as it disregards political issues.

The general focus on the local level can be found most clearly in the sectoral priorities of state agencies. SAIDC's priorities include education, healthcare, good governance, and building of civil society, agriculture and forestry, water and sanitation, energy, and support of the market environment development (MFEA 2013: 10–11). As is clear from the list, these (including good governance, see below) are all non-political, technical issues suitable for the type of development Ferguson writes about.

In particular, for example, an agricultural project is probably not meant to focus on political issues, and in the case of South Sudan this is mentioned explicitly. The focus in this case is on "implementation of new techniques and methods" (ibid.: 14). The problem is not that new agricultural techniques and methods would not be useful, but that none of the abovementioned priorities are directed to political problems.

Local issues are addressed by local projects administered with practical institutional instruments such as the ones from the Slovak Medium-Term Strategy. These include block grants, small grant schemes, micro-grants, supplies of goods and services, and support of start-ups (ibid.: 21–24). One would have to analyze them to actually find out what these tools were used for. Nevertheless, a project can politicize (see, e.g., Van Ausdal 2001) and, for example, a microgrant could be used by an NGO to organize people to protest against the IMF conditionalities. But I *assume* that this is rarely the case, and these micro-tools are *probably* more often used for micro-issues of immediate relevance to the recipients.

The tendency towards depoliticization can be perceived in the interviews with respondents from the Slovak NGDO PiP as they are putting the NGOs' "small work" (Interview No. 8 2013) before the larger issues. Thus, to reach development,

> one needs money […] to build some capacities, to build some governance, to build schooling […] one shows them some new methods, e.g., how to better farm organically […] they will not manage without some kind of a microloan […] and then there is, of course, the building of some kind of infrastructure provided by the state.
>
> (Interview No. 9 2013, see also Interview No. 10 2013, Interview No. 11 2013, Interview No. 5 2013)

Two respondents from CARE Austria mainly spoke about projects during the interviews with them (Interview No. 27 2013, Interview No. 28 2013). Despite the fact that one of them promoted a holistic approach as opposed to a sectoral one, he also focused on projects and communities (Interview No. 27 2013).

There were also instances of politicization in the examined materials, especially in the interviews (see below); however, local instruments to reach development were dominant in both of the analyzed discourses. The three main particular forms of spatial depoliticization through local instruments were access to market (which was related to an inherently benign perception of the market), microfinance, and depoliticization through education.

One of the most common ways of focusing on the local level is by pointing at the lack of access to the market in the given case. This is often represented as one of the crucial reasons for poverty. The market is here represented as an inherently benign force that only needs to be accessed in order for development to take off.

Ferguson's account of the discursive construction of Lesotho shows the importance of the lack of access to the market in the World Bank's overall argument. Its discourse describes Lesotho as unable to produce a saleable surplus "due to the absence of opportunities for selling agricultural goods" (Ferguson 1994: 57). One of the problems of development is isolation. "If Lesotho is undeveloped because it has been an unpenetrated backwater […] then developing it requires connecting it with the rest of the world" (ibid.: 56–57). The building of roads to secure the connection to the market is crucial.

Ferguson also shows the evidence contradicting the World Bank discourse: "Basotho [the people of Lesotho] have been marketing crops and livestocks [...] since the 1840s, and those with surpluses to sell have always known how to go about selling them" (ibid.: 57). The problem is thus not the failure to introduce markets, "yet it is regularly assumed in the 'development' literature that the reason people are not selling crops or livestock is simply that they have never had the opportunity to do so" (ibid.). The access to market thus remains a problem despite the evidence.

The Austrian Three-Year Program follows the development discourse in this regard and includes the following guiding principle: "Subsistence of farming enterprises through improved productivity and market access" (ibid.: 25). The *Weltnachrichten* make a similar, more general claim: in Terai, Nepal, the problem is "the access to [the] international market" (Thiard-Laforet 2013, see also BMEIA 2012: 24, NDC-Austroprojekt and Orgut 2002: 25). All that seems to be necessary for development is access to the market.

There are more particular ways to secure an access to market. According to one respondent from Slovak NGDO Pontis, in order to reach development "it is important to create the possibilities and opportunities for the people, because that is what the country lacks the most" (Interview No. 3 2013). She offers an example of a community of basket weavers – old women – who do not know how to distribute their goods, while in Rukanga everyone already has these baskets. This led to a group of students making a Facebook site for them where they advertise all their goods in order to reach potential customers (ibid.). It need not be only the internet that would bring access to the job market, as the physical infrastructure should do this as well. For example, new public transport possibilities in Tirana make it easier for women to accept a job (Thiard-Laforet 2013). It seems as if a job was waiting for a woman in Tirana to take a bus and go to work, or as if there was an unsatisfied demand out there for baskets waiting for weavers to connect with potential clients. The argument is the same – all that is missing is the connection. The political economy and the power relations behind the job market in Tirana or the world market for products such as baskets are not problematized.

As the development discourse focuses on access to market it avoids at the same time any discussion about the market itself. If an access to market is desired, it remains implicit that the market is desired as well. The market is thereby depoliticized as a neutral space that offers opportunities for its participants and can secure development by the virtue of its functioning. In this way the functioning of the market is represented as inherently benign. With such a "*depoliticized*, that is, essentialist" (Swanson 2008: 57) notion, any political involvement in what is represented as "the economy" is perceived as interfering with the smooth operation of the so-called economic laws (ibid.; see also Teivainen 2002). Instead of politicizing the economy by representing it as a place of (potential) conflicts, as a place that is constituted by "numerous 'economic,' 'political,' 'cultural,' and 'natural' process[es] surrounding [these conflicts]" (Swanson 2008: 59), "the economy" is represented as self-regulating, as separate from the rest of society with its own laws, types of behavior, motivations, and forms of thinking (ibid.: 63). Its benign character thus goes without saying.

Such a perspective was clearly present in both of the national discourses. For example, one can read in the Austrian Three-Year Program that the Austrian "private sector involvement in developing countries [...] is a win–win situation" (BMEIA 2012: 27). Not only can Austrian companies "contribute greatly to training and job creation," but they also "gain access to new markets and opportunities" (ibid.). On the other hand, "foreign investments mean opportunities for developing countries" (ibid.). Just like in the case of microfinance (see below), the market is represented as advantageous for all its participants.

Several respondents also saw trade and the market mainly as a positive or potentially positive force. According to one respondent from PiP, "the market is something that should be used, because it is a thing that exists and works" (Interview No. 11 2013, see also Interviews No. 8, 9 2013, Interview No. 28 2014).

The inherently benign quality of the market gives it an impersonal authority that is usually reserved for state laws. In a text from PiP it is simply presumed that, for doing business, it is "important to separate private from the company's finances" (PiP 2009). This is what the women learned at the training, together with the basics of effective planning, setting business goals, and the necessity of saving. The content of the seminars is strongly influenced here by the perspective that the participants can succeed in the market if only they learn what is necessary. The possibility that the market makes it impossible for everyone to succeed or that particular actors are better positioned to compete in a market is excluded.

It is important to note that two respondents from Pontis were reluctant to elaborate upon the question about the role of the market in development, as they simply "[did] not know" (Interview No. 3 2013; Interview No. 5 2013). It seems that trade is not an important issue in this organization. Here, depoliticization is achieved through ignorance. The market and its unequal power relations are simply ignored. Both of these respondents also uncritically mentioned the theory of comparative advantages that has been criticized in the academic literature through, e.g., the Prebisch-Singer thesis.

Negative effects of the market were implicitly accepted in relation to microfinance and sustainable development by the respondents. Some of the respondents turned away from the free market dogma here and argued in favor of distorting the market.

A respondent from CARE offered the following argument:

> you distort the market, of course [...] but in the beginning when [...] they go through a reconstruction phase [...] offering something below what the loan shark is offering; [it] might not necessarily be a bad thing, but it should be for a limited time [only].
>
> (Interview No. 28 2014; see also Interview No. 27, 2013)

The loans from PiP were subsidized and given under much more favorable conditions than those from the local sources, and "that is why people liked [PiP] so much" (ibid.). I asked the respondent, who "definitely [prefers a] free market" (Interview No. 11 2013), whether she thinks that it would be correct to borrow at rates that are lower than the market rates. She answered: "Definitely in the first step, because there were many talented women who could not afford the actual rates" (ibid., see also Interview No. 9 2013). She thus contradicted her previous answer.

It seems as if the experience with the way the financial market functions for the poorest slightly adjusted the opinions of the respondents. They thought that, in general, the free trade works fine, but in this particular case it might be better to distort it, but only "in the first step." After that, the local people should again borrow at market rates. Distortion of the market was also represented as necessary in relation to sustainable development (Interview No. 9 2013).

However, it needs to be acknowledged that a regulated access to a market may lead to a particular type of what is called development. South Korea and Taiwan are typical examples of this. The rules of the global trade do not make it impossible for a government to succeed in its "developmental" efforts (disregarding here the likely necessity of authoritarian measures). However, I would argue that these same rules make it impossible for every government to succeed. At the same time, the environmental limits prevent world-wide development of this type as well. Thus, whereas access to market can lead to development for some countries or people, it is impossible for everyone to "develop." Therefore, this access is a political issue, and the NGOs and state agencies depoliticize this issue by representing the access as something that only brings about development. The focus on the access to market that one can encounter in the Austrian, as well as in the Slovak, discourse replaces possible focuses on more political causes of poverty. The argument about an access to market often includes access to financial services.

The way the microfinance discourse depoliticizes by focusing on the local level is analogous to the way the access to market is represented in the development discourse in general. Access to loans (i.e., the financial market) is most often represented as capable of securing a substantial change in the microfinance discourse.

Microfinance is then based on the idea that "the interests of multinational corporations are compatible with the interests of the poor" (Karim 2011: xx). Johnathan Murdoch (2000: 617) calls it "the win–win proposition: microfinance institutions that follow the principles of good banking will also be those that alleviate the most poverty." The companies are represented in the microfinance discourse as a benign force that brings about the right form of development (see also Fernando 2006b: 166). There simply does not seem to be a conflict between the interest of the lenders and that of the borrowers – both are supposed to gain from microfinance. This is made explicit in the Banking on Change report co-authored by CARE Austria, which states that "[t]he [Banking on Change] initiative [...] busts the myth that banks have no interest in meeting poor customers' needs" (Plan UK, CARE International UK and Barclays 2013: 1), and that "financial services providers [...] cater to the needs of poor people" (ibid.: 5).

This basic assumption is only implicitly present in the analyzed texts and interviews. One can infer the basic win–win assumption from the overall positive framing of the poor getting access to *any kind* of microloans and the positive framing of microfinance as a general practice in the analyzed texts, both of which are to be found in the analyzed texts and interviews. Those who offer loans are, in general, not problematized.[1]

Thus one can read that "the smallest credit" can mean "a way to economic independence" (Schelander in CARE 2006a; see also Daniels in CARE 2013b). If only there was an access to the formal financial market for the poor "millions of people could find [a] way out of poverty" (CARE 2013a; see also Plan UK, CARE International UK and Barclays 2013: 5, 9, 23, 24).

Even though CARE follows a different model than private companies offering microloans, it praises microfinance in general, thereby legitimizing the corporate lending practices. The same applies to Slovak NGDO PiP. This win–win assumption is related to a perception of the market as benign in general.

Another form of depoliticization in microfinance was related to education and individualization. The "saving culture" element is crucial for the microfinance discourse. Respondents from CARE also stressed the importance of the knowledge and skills CARE brings: "financial literacy [...] self-esteem, confidence building" (Interview No. 25 2013). According to another respondent, VSLA projects are successful "primarily because [they're] just focused, from the CARE perspective, on training and sharing knowledge, and then from the community perspective it's about their own ability to manage their resources" (Interview No. 27 2013). This "own ability" is crucial in individualizing poverty. The discourse represents the poor as capable of improving their lot on their own.

The problem is that "an accompanying effect of this individualisation of poverty is its depoliticisation: as [the] poor are made responsible for their poverty, redistributive approaches to poverty alleviation tend to be ignored" (Brigg 2001: 248). According to Rankin (2001), small farmers with social rights are replaced by female clients who are free to compete at the market and at the same time are responsible for their families. Lazar (2004: 314) complements this view by arguing that, even if microfinance meetings lead to the creation of collective organizations, these "are on the whole extremely depoliticized when compared with others, such as the trade unions of street traders." In this view, the way to fight poverty is not by changing the unequal relations, but by offering the poor a place in a supposedly equal competition. When they fail, they are to be blamed, and the structural problems remain intact. In other words: "When poor women are constructed as responsible clients in this way, the onus for development falls squarely on their shoulders" (Rankin 2001: 29). Poverty is then not the result of failed policies of the state, but since the market is allegedly a neutral arbiter between equal actors, poverty is the result of wrong choices made by the poor. These choices can be rectified by training in financial literacy or confidence building.

All the success stories found in the analyzed texts contribute to the individualization of poverty. They represent individuals as capable of succeeding with the aid of microloans and microfinance projects. For example, one borrower claims: "I always dreamed about having my own saloon […] now I believe that I can do it and take my life into my own hands" (CARE 2013b; for a similar story from CARE see Qorban 2005). The problematic untold part of this story is that a potential or actual failure can then be the result of the actions made by those who do not figure in the PR materials.

Thus, the way out of poverty begins with an "access to saving services" and goes through "asset building and […] sound money management" (Plan UK, CARE International UK and Barclays 2013: 13). Finally, "with better financial management skills, even people with very small and unpredictable incomes are able to put themselves in a position where they can invest more in their families and their income-generating activities" (ibid.: 14). The individual strategy for saving in order to invest or saving for a rainy day is represented as sound money management, something that everyone can engage in. The only problem seems to be the lack of skills. How unpredictable income comes about is not relevant in the microfinance discourse. It is, for example, here that political economy could enter the discourse, but does not.

Finally, from a broader perspective, a positive representation of microfinance creates an image in which financial globalization is a positive force reaching every poor person on the planet. Financial liberalization is legitimized through an alleged success of microfinance. The practices based on the microfinance discourse treat all female borrowers as clients. This is what Fernando calls "clientification of gender" (ibid.: 27) and it is similar to the effects the image of homo oeconomicus had for neoclassical economics. As the women are constructed as homo oeconomicus (even if at the same time they are constrained by their kin obligations), the general neoliberal reforms of the state gain legitimacy (ibid.). Any demands by social movements or unions can be dismissed on the basis of the existence of the rational woman who empowers herself through the market rather than more collective mechanisms.

The spread of neoliberalism, financial globalization, and financial sector liberalization is, within the win–win scenario, considered as "a prerequisite for poverty reduction [that] serves to legitimate this outcome" (Weber 2002: 136). Since microfinance is supposed to lead to poverty reduction, it is necessary to pursue financial liberalization, which will enable actors offering microfinance to work. The discourse not only contains this assumption, but at the same time it also contains the confirmation of this assumption. All the research papers and scientific articles that focus on the repayment rates seem to prove that microfinance is good.

In this way, "[m]icrofinance functions as a catalyst for financial sector liberalisation" (Weber 2002: 135). It facilitates this liberalization, and through microfinance, financial globalization can reach the local level. Therefore, Bateman (2010: 165) can claim that "[m]icrofinance is 'local neoliberalism'." As actors are assumed to be rational and reachable at the lowest income strata, capital can penetrate into the most intimate spheres of people's lives. Microfinance enables this local reach of global finance. It thus "facilitates and entrenches neoliberal forms of governance" (Weber 2006: 55).

In sum, there are three ways in which microfinance contributes to depoliticization of unequal power relations. First, the win–win formula constructs the dominant microfinance actors as contributing to development or poverty reduction and not as those who exploit the poor. Second, individualization makes the poor responsible for their own development or poverty. The responsibility of other actors is excluded from the discourse. Third, the microfinance discourse connects local and global practices of financial liberalization and thereby legitimizes the global ones. The problems connected to financial globalization are thereby depoliticized. These forms of depoliticization were, in general, problematized neither in the Slovak nor the Austrian discourse. The depoliticizing discourse of microfinance is the same for both old and new donors. Only one respondent from CARE Austria, who was more experienced with microfinance, offered a somewhat critical perspective of it (see below).

The last form of spatial depoliticization is based on education. Bowles and Gintis (1976, see also 2002) argued that the most important function of education in US society is depoliticization. According to them, "[e]ducation plays a major role in hiding or justifying the exploitative nature of the U.S. Economy" (ibid.: 13). Their argument is based on quantitative evidence that shows the persistent inequality in American society and the inability of education to alter this inequality. The problem with the education system, then, is that it

> legitimates economic inequality by providing an open, objective, and ostensibly meritocratic mechanism for assigning individuals to unequal economic positions. The educational system fosters and reinforces the belief that economic success depends essentially on the possession of technical and cognitive skills....
>
> (Ibid.: 103)

A similar pattern is decipherable in the education discourse within development. Spitzl shows that, in this case, almost as if by magic, education becomes the "central instrument for changing the world and for the reduction of poverty" (Spitzl 2011: 66). Thus, the leading metaphor in the education discourse is the "key" (ibid.). Education becomes "the key that gives access to the twenty-first century" (UNESCO 1996), "the key to bridging the widening gulf between rich and poor" (World Education Forum 2000), or "the key to unlocking the cage of human misery" (Annan 2003; these three quotes are from Spitzl 2011: 66).

There is a clear pattern of ascribing to education a large, if not the largest, role in the process of development. This allows the dominant actors to turn attention away from unequal power relations in the global, as well as the local, setting and focus people's attention on educational aspirations. The discourse is powerful because it makes people desire education as their "passport" to a better life, or to a better life for their children. By focusing on education or other "ways to development," structural problems remain hidden and are not problematized.

There was almost a complete agreement with the basic tenet of the educational discourse in the analyzed texts and interviews. For example, the texts said that "education is [...] a leverage for development" (Findl and Gruber 2014) or that "education is the fastest way to escape from poverty" (Pontis 2010a; see also Geosits and Gruber 2014; BMEIA 2012: 29; CARE 2006b).

The role of formal education in development was considered "huge" (Interview No. 7 2013), "one of the greatest" (Interview No. 5 2013) and "crucial" (Interview No. 3 2013) by respondents from Pontis. In CARE, all four respondents followed the discourse of education in development and claimed that "[education] is one of the core factors of development" (Interview No. 25 2013) or that "education is really the way out of poverty" (Interview No. 27 2013; see also Interview No. 28 2014; Interview No. 26 2013).

Apart from a more general perspective on the relation between education and development, there were more particular positive representations of education that depoliticized unequal power relations. One can, for example, read in the *Weltnachrichten* that "[t]he higher the level of education, the more awareness is there in the whole extended family about the danger of infection" of the Ebola virus (Findl and Gruber 2014). Such information may be correct, but at the same time the article ignores and thereby depoliticizes the impact of political and trade relations on the healthcare budgets of some of the sub-Saharan countries by not mentioning these relations (see, e.g., Perez 2014).

There was a particular connection between education and economic opportunities. It was stated that there is a "need to promote initiative and entrepreneurial thinking" (BMEIA 2012: 22). According to a respondent from PiP, "[e]specially the role of the market is important, but for that role we need a quality education that will raise people in this direction [i.e., creating one's own job rather than waiting to be employed by someone else]" (Interview No. 8 2013). Education supposedly "improves job chances of the future professionals and can sustainably increase the competitiveness of a country" (Rössler 2014b; see also BMEIA 2012: 27).

The market is here represented as an opportunity, and people only need to be educated and willing to become active entrepreneurs. Similarly to the microfinance discourse, this approach individualizes poverty. More importantly, the same perspective is applied to the national level. A country needs a good educational system in order to be competitive in the world economy. In both cases, one needs to argue in a nuanced way, as empirical experience shows that education and entrepreneurship can indeed lead to a (monetary) success in life (Causa and Johansson 2010) and to (a Western-type) development (Amsden 1989; Wade 1990; Kim 1997; Nelson and Pack 1999). As already stated, the problem is that this is not possible for everyone. Not every American can fulfill his or her American dream. At the national level, not every country can be like South Korea. Not only is it environmentally impossible, but increasing one's competitiveness in the global race means decreasing the competitiveness of someone else. The inequality in the global race is thereby naturalized and depoliticized, and so are the unequal starting positions of the countries. Texts and respondents from both Austria and Slovakia engaged in this depoliticization. The belief in education is even more striking when one considers that, in both countries, the number of educated people increases, but inequality rises as well. The depoliticizing education discourse is present in both donors regardless of their age or level of development.

Finally, it is not just that local reasons for poverty lead to local solutions, but also local legitimation serves the need of the development discourse to legitimize the practice of development. There are two particular types of legitimization that are frequently used in the development discourse – the authority of the local population and the authority of partnership. A social practice can be legitimate not because, for example, an expert says so or on the basis of a moral tale, but because the local community or the local government demands such a practice. Such legitimations are normatively anchored in the participatory and partnership approaches. Even though these approaches may lead to a politicization of local power struggles (see below), they also focus on the local community and thereby contribute to spatial depoliticization.

There were two instances of local legitimation. On a general level, the state agencies and respondents supported the participatory or the partnership approach (MFEA 2013: 5; BMEIA 2012: 32). The importance of the participation and partnership approaches was also visible in the frequent use of the terms "participatory" and "participation," which are used more than 70 times in Austroprojekt's 110-page Plan of Operation, and the terms "partner" and "partnership," which are used 15 times in the same text. Local legitimation also appears in PR texts. For example, "Fanatesh [contacted] CARE in order to get more education" (CARE 2012; see also PiP 2012b). CARE's action was thus legitimized by a recipient of its aid.

In relation to credit, the local demand became crucial. Not only anecdotal evidence, but also "research increasingly shows that poor people do want to access a range of financial products" (Plan UK, CARE International UK and Barclays 2013: 17; Interview No. 9 2013). The preference for subsidized loans coming from the locals legitimizes the local project.

The lack of politicization here is in omitting to mention that those who demand the loan have very few other possibilities, and their decision is not entirely free, but their field of decision-making is structured by the situation in which they find themselves to be. In Žižek's (2008) conceptualization, one can speak of an objective or a systemic violence that is invisible at first sight. The formulations used in the Report and the quotes in the PR articles disregard this structural issue.

Some of the respondents also supported the participatory approach. A respondent from ADA thought that "the most important reason [for achieving development] is that the people want to develop themselves, and they create the vision of what their development should look like. And then we can support them" (Interview No. 23 2014; see also Interviews No. 24, 28 2014; Interview

No. 3, 16 2013). It should also be mentioned that the participatory approach was more prevalent among the Austrian than among the Slovak respondents.

Overall, the spatial forms of depoliticization include the focus on local problems, local solutions to these problems, and local legitimization of these solutions. These problems include an access to an inherently benign market and the proposed solutions include microfinance and education. In all these cases, the focus on the local leads to a spatial depoliticization in which actors from both new and old donors' apparatuses engage. The next section analyzes further forms of depoliticization – through technological solutions, omission of agents, different temporal frameworks, and an explicit consensus invocation.

Depoliticization through technological solutions, omissions of agents, an explicit consensus invocation, and temporal depoliticzation

The main element of depoliticization is the practice of "rendering technical" (Li 2007: 7). This has already been elaborated upon in the previous sections. Here, the crucial point is that rendering *technical* focuses on issues related to technology. As "experts are trained to frame problems in technical terms" (ibid.), they engage not only in various non-political matters such as access to financial services or education, but also emphasize the need for *technological* solutions. The development industry is based on various assumptions, including the perspective "that technology alone solves poverty" (Crewe and Harrison 2002: 23). Whereas Crewe and Harrison "do not claim that no link between poverty and technology exists" (ibid.: 33), their analysis of the Intermediate Technology project for the distribution of stoves in a community shows that, in the development discourse, "it goes without saying that technology improves people's incomes and access to resources" (ibid.: 32), and the implication of the Intermediate Technology perspective is that "poverty is caused by technological gaps and is solved primarily by technological improvements" (ibid.: 33).

Such a rendering *technological* was also present in the analyzed interviews. One respondent from Slovak NGDO PiP claimed that this NGDO contributes to the eradication of poverty "on a small scale [...] that is, the bottom-up way" (ibid.). He offered an example – "collecting rain water" (ibid.). This showed not only the preference for spatially delimited solutions, but also the preference for technological solutions. For another respondent, the role of technology is "certainly important" because, for example, cell phones "can help those farmers in finding out about the current seed prices" (Interview No. 11 2013, see also Interview No. 9 2013).

Technological solutions are equally present if not more prevalent in the sustainable development discourse in the form of technological optimism. The mainstream sustainable development discourse takes the form of ecological modernization (Adams 2009: 117–170). In this dominant discourse strand, sustainability is to be achieved through a regulation of markets and through technological changes.

Such technological optimism is present in the blog of PiP employee Lukáš Zorád and also in other PiP texts. This author writes about energy-saving ovens that will decrease the consumption of wood (PiP 2011; Zorád 2013). The importance of technology (using light to scare lions, bio-digesting toilets that reduce the consumption of coal and wood, and mobile banking) is also invoked in his blog entry on the TED Talks in Nairobi (Zorád 2012; see also PiP 2012c). Other technological solutions to environmental problems coming from PiP respondents included recycling, wind power plants, solar collectors, hydroelectric power plants, biogas, soft technologies such as a trickle irrigation system (Interview No. 8 2013), electromobiles, carbon filters, and clay ovens (Interview No. 9 2013).

The most important technology is the collection and storage of rainwater for later use (PiP 2012a; Zorád 2011a, 2011b, 2011d). "There is enough water for everyone; the point is how we use it" (Zorád 2011d). One can, of course, only agree that storing rainwater might be useful under the current circumstances. The problem is whether this is "the point" that is to be made about a drought. The lack of political ecology is most visible here as social, political, and economic questions are crucial to the issue of drought (Adams 2009: 202–241). Technology might be useful, but it denies politics its place in people's lives. The material misery in Kenya is reduced to a technological problem of special toilets and ovens that reduce the consumption of wood, of mobile banking that connects people, of the internet, which brings the missing information to the people, and, finally, of rain water storing facilities that prevent droughts and famines from taking place. The unequal power relations on the local, regional, national, and international level are put aside. "We" never appear in the discourse as those who might be in one way or another partly responsible for the material misery in Kenya, but are represented as the generous helpers with the "best solution[s]" (PiP 2012a).

Another form of depoliticization can be related to the time in which politics occurs. There are three types of such temporal depoliticization. One is focused on the past, another on the present period, and the third one on the future. The first depoliticization is concerned with the basic question about the reason why some countries are developed and some are not (see, e.g., Landes 1999; Blaut 1993; Weber 2005; Diamond 1997; Pomeranz 2000; Rodney 1981). Without trying to answer this question here, there might be a middle ground that includes a political space of conflict between the West and the Rest. Even if one claims that the origin of the difference in wealth or development is not based on any kind of conflict, but is due to climate or cultural traits, there is overwhelming evidence that shows that the difference was at least in part sustained by the oppression of the Rest by the West. I am thus arguing that even such a moderate position includes a political element in responding to the question of reasons for poverty. This political element, however, can be depoliticized if one focuses on issues going back in time.

Three respondents from SAIDC mentioned natural conditions as one of the conditions for reaching development (Interview No. 12 2013; Interview No. 13 2013; Interview No. 15 2014). More particularly, they spoke about natural resources, climate, the geographical landscape, and the position of the country.

Even though a respondent from PiP, in replying to the question about the reasons for poverty, started with some historical predisposition, "what in Africa could be colonialism" (Interview No. 11 2013), she also mentioned climate and that "in the case of Africa [...] in general more kids [means] more poverty" (ibid.). The follow-up question about the climate brought a clear answer from the realm of environmental determinism:

> In general, if you notice, the closer the nations are to the North Pole, the more relentless they are; they know how to plan better [...] down at the equator [...] you sow when it rains and so it goes; you don't need to plan.... (Ibid.)

Another form of temporal depoliticization focuses on the present and represents the current state of things as functioning well. Some of the respondents engaged in such representations. They portrayed the current measure to achieve sustainability as working with little need to add anything to that. One respondent from PiP responded to the question about the necessary measures to achieve sustainability by focusing on the need to educate the local people and motivate "them" "through the market [...] to plant the forest" (Interview No. 11 2013). Only after a direct question about possible measures in Europe did she reply that "we already have something here that is going on. We have carbon trading [...] environmental standards [...] related to raw materials mining, so I do not know what else to add [...] what can be done is already happening" (ibid., see also Interview No. 8 2013). Whereas the Other is represented as responsible for environmental problems, the Self is portrayed as engaged in protecting the environment and as doing all that is necessary.

Third, the development discourse contains a strong belief that people can improve their situation and that there is a better future awaiting us if we engage in development. Whereas, in the past, this belief in the future was related to the progress from the traditional society to a modern society, nowadays the future contains merely the escape from poverty (see also Ferguson 2006: 186–187). This belief is related to the belief in technology mentioned in the previous section. As the market allegedly fosters creativity in people, this secures technological improvement through inventions, and therefore we do not have to worry about current problems. The invisible hand of the market will become aware of different kinds of problems and deal with them. For example, the lack of oil or climate change will be managed through engines using a different kind of fuel.

It is not only technology that should solve the problems of the future. Education is another way to secure a better future that replaces attempts to deal with the present and its political issues here and now. In an article from Pontis that belongs to the education discourse, teachers understand the importance of the ability "to master technologies... for their future" (Pontis 2010b), and the local people "view information technologies and the ability to work with them as a means to securing a better future for themselves" (ibid., see also CARE 2014a). The only quality of information technologies in both cases is that of securing a better future. No other factors are connected to the mastering of ICT. ICT is related only to the better future. An abstraction on such a high and distant level as that of "a better future" also allows one to avoid and overcome any possible objection from a more particular and current perspective that would criticize ICT. One could, for example, contemplate how ICT changes everyday practices, but this is not the case.[2] Whereas this last type of temporal depoliticization is to be found also in the Austrian discourse, the satisfaction with the present and the environmental determinism which depoliticizes from the past were much more prevalent among the Slovak respondents.

Another very common way of depoliticizing potential and existing conflicts is by not representing the agents responsible for social processes. Without agents, these processes seem natural, or more specifically they are seen as results of unconscious forces or natural processes (Leeuwen 2008: 66). There is simply no agency to which one could ascribe the origins of these processes. The potentially innocuous literary style that dominates the official development language can sometimes have important depoliticizing effects. In a globalist discourse (Fairclough 2007: 8), globalization is driven by the idea of free market capitalism, and it is governed by rules. Globalization is thereby represented as a process without agents even though the globalist strategy "is very clearly the strategy of certain powerful agents" (ibid.: 9, see also 37–38, Fairclough 2003: 144). One could legitimately ask who is behind the idea of globalization (understood as the liberalization of the world trade), or who adopts the rules of globalization.[3]

One can read in the *Weltnachrichten* that globalization simply "determines our lives" (Hartmeyer 2012). According to a respondent from ADA, globalization is "unavoidable," and it is relevant how we "adapt to globalization" (Interview No. 23). But, there is almost nothing in the analyzed texts about the powerful agents who influence the processes that determine our lives (for an exception, see below).

Globalization was also partly replaced by the global economic crisis in the corpus. The actors behind this force were mentioned neither in the *Weltnachrichten* (Gutenbrunner 2014; Rössler 2014a), nor in the state medium-term documents (BMEIA 2012; MFEA 2013). For example, the Austrian Three-Year Program states, "Despite the economic and financial crisis, Austria is seeking to meet the Monterrey targets" (BMEIA 2012: 11; see also MFEA 2013: 5). This protects the actors behind the crisis and naturalizes this man-made phenomenon. The causes of the crisis are thus ignored and thereby depoliticized. The origin of the crisis moves from the world of politics (e.g., the capacity of the corporate lobby to influence governmental decisions) to the world of naturally-occurring events. The crisis (rather than social actors) is also the explanation behind the decline in the Slovak ODA level.

Another example of an unattributable force is negative social phenomena. Social inequality and unemployment "increase the risk of the formation of new centers of tension and conflicts" (MFEA 2013: 5). The omission here goes one step further. The usual explanans (e.g., unemployment or social inequality) here take the position of the explanandum, creating a meta-depoliticization of the economic crisis.

A similar perspective can be found in relation to climate change. The actors in climate change are often not named. CO_2 becomes a fetish in the environmental discourse. People in sustainable development "are not constituted as heterogeneous political subjects, but as universal victims" (Swyngedouw 2011: 268). There is thus an absence of conflicts about possible socio-ecological configurations in the democratic debate. It becomes unclear what terms like climate change or sustainability actually mean or whom they symbolize.

As CO_2 becomes the foe that needs to be dealt with, the problems "are not the result of the 'system', of unevenly distributed power relations, of the networks of control and influence, of rampant injustices, or of a fatal flaw inscribed in the system, but are blamed on an outsider" (ibid.: 269). This again leads to not naming those responsible for the greenhouse gas emissions.

Such omissions of the actors responsible for climate change were used on several occasions in the *Weltnachrichten* (Geosits and Gruber 2014; Rabitsch 2013; Rabitsch and Sötz 2013). In the Austrian Three-Year Program, one can read that the "CO_2 emissions threaten [...] the world climate" (BMEIA 2012: 10). Who emits the CO_2 is not mentioned.

In a similar way, in Austroprojekt's Plan of Operation hunting, charcoal burning, logging and seasonal burnings that destroy a forest are represented as simply happening. We do not know who is destroying the forest. On the one hand, this omission of agents could protect the poor from being stigmatized, but on the other, there could be other, more powerful actors involved in the destruction of the forest. There could be various transnational as well as more powerful local forces. All of this remains hidden if the actors behind these actions are not mentioned.

Another type of omission of political causes is related to a description of a problematic state of things. For example, the Slovak teachers from Bošany who participated in a project organized by Pontis do not regret taking part in the mission "[d]espite the not ideal accommodation" (Pontis 2010b). The reader does not get the information about how the "not ideal accommodation" in Rukanga came about. We learn nothing about the political processes such as (neo)colonialism, the local corruption, and other historical processes without which the current form of the accommodation would probably look a lot different (Profant 2018b).

Overall, depoliticization through the omission of agents is present in the development discourse in both Austria and Slovakia. The authors of the texts fail to mention the actors responsible for the recent economic crisis, for climate change, and for "underdevelopment," and also for other negative representations of the Other such as those related to AIDS, unemployment, human trafficking, deforestation, or accommodation.

Finally, political conflicts between actors can also be depoliticized through a portrayal of these actors as not having antagonistic interests. Such a "one world" (Sachs 1992a) or "universal humanism" (Dogra 2014: 95–124) discourse represents the whole of humanity (or a smaller group of people) as one group with no internal struggles. This is probably most visible in the discourse on climate change: "We are all potential victims. 'THE' Environment and 'THE' people, Humanity as a whole […] are invoked and called into being" (Swyngedouw 2011: 268). In this approach, "autonomy easily becomes an anti-social value, and diversity turns into an obstacle to collective action" (Sachs 1992a: 108). The world becomes perceived as a single homogenous space in which cooperation becomes an imperative. The manufacturing of such human unity was made easier by an image of the Earth taken from space – in it, the Earth appears as a "small and fragile ball shining blue against the dark of outer space" (Sachs 1992b: 26). This image enabled the discourse to speak of our planet (ibid.). All the conflicts between people were erased by a "we" representing the whole human race.

The Foreword to the Slovak Medium-Term Strategy sets the depoliticizing tone of the whole document with the necessity of cooperation: "No-one can solve the problems of this world alone" (BMEIA 2012: 5). "[A] future without global partnership is inconceivable" (ibid.: 7). In order for development to take place, people need to cooperate on a global scale. This is clarified in relation to a more particular issue – agriculture – as, in this sector, "a number of actors, such as the private sector, local authorities, scientific institutes or NGOs, play a special role" (ibid.: 24). They give advice, exchange knowledge, support technology transfer, or raise productivity, but nowhere can one read about their conflicts. It seems that it is expected of everyone to cooperate.

A blog entry from a PiP employee, Lukáš Zorád, on South Sudan takes this logic to the local place: "We all want the same […] It is necessary to cooperate" (Zorád 2011c). He goes on by saying that the local priest is doing his job, and Zorád is doing his – motivating teachers who can spark up the interest of young people – while others are trying to empower communities economically, and yet others press the local authorities in politics, but "[w]e are all connected by one goal: to empower a socially healthy [and] economically self-reliant society in a healthy environment" (ibid.). Zorád believes "that we are all inhabitants of one planet, one ecosystem that we share together and that is our common home" (ibid.). The one world discourse (Sachs 1992b) is moving at two levels here. It introduces a general commonality of people that on the local level is translated into a commonality of all those who are trying to improve things.

The category "we" here includes development actors together with the local teacher and the local priest. The category "Other" includes "the young people with big potential" (ibid.) and "local authorities and politics" (ibid.). "We" act, and "they" are those who are acted upon. There does not seem to be any conflict between "us," as "we" all aim at the same thing, and this peaceful cooperation moves to the barely mentioned "Other." The young people want the same thing, but they just need knowledge and to have their interest sparked up, and the same applies to the local authorities, who only need to be "pressed upon." Only here does a potential conflict appear. Maybe the local authorities have different interests. In Zorád's discourse, though, all the relations of power are put aside, as there is a common goal. There is no place for a conflict, which would disrupt the harmonious image in his discourse.

A similar argument related to a clash over water resources led ADA's then managing director to invoke the one world discourse, in which "closer cooperation is necessary. We all together need to take care that [water] resources [on] our planet remain clean and not dry" (Öppinger-Walchshofer 2013; see also CARE 2012).

Another strategy to create the myth of a global human community was to construct human nature as the crucial commonality of all people in the world.

> First the difference between human morphologies is asserted, exoticism is insistently stressed, the infinite variations of the species, the diversity in skins, skulls and customs are made manifest [...]. Then, from this pluralism, a type of unity is magically produced: man is born, works, laughs and dies everywhere in the same way.
>
> (Barthes 1972: 100)

This approach shows "that underneath there is but one human nature and a common human essence" (Dogra 2014: 96). This has already been mentioned in Chapter 4 as an instance of a non-hierarchic representation of the Self and the Other. Respondents from Austroprojekt spoke about the people in Tunisia as "function[ing] like ourselves" (Interview No. 17 2013), about the difference between Austria and Tanzania in terms of "the problems of mankind [being] always the same" (Interview No. 16 2013) and a respondent from ADA spoke about Austria and Nicaragua "becoming more and more similar" (Interview No. 20 2013). By essentializing people into representatives of a single human race, the discourse of universal humanism ignores the historical conditions that greatly vary for these members of one humanity. Barthes (1972: 102) distinguishes labor as a "historical fact" from birth and death as facts of nature (ibid.: 101) due to "its modes, its motivations, its ends and its benefits, which matter to such an extent that it will never be fair to confuse in a purely gestural identity the colonial and the Western worker" (ibid.: 102). The difference between people in terms of power, in terms of potentially conflicting interests, and in terms of potentially conflicting identities is depoliticized as people are represented as very much the same through the discourse of universal humanism.

In sum, the depoliticization through an explicit consensus invocation was achieved in the Austrian and Slovak discourses through the representation of people as a single group with little or no conflicts vis-à-vis the environment or the common effort to achieve development, or through cooperation being emphasized when conflicts were mentioned. There were, however, instances of a stronger politicization of conflicting interests in the interviews (especially in the Austrian ones), and I will focus on these in the next chapter.

* * *

It should be clear by now that both the Austrian and the Slovak development apparatus depoliticize unequal power relations and potential or existing conflicts between various actors. The first aim of this part of the chapter was to show the various ways in which this depoliticization is achieved. The second aim was to compare the Slovak with the Austrian discourses in this regard.

I identified various forms of depoliticization: spatial depoliticization, depoliticization through technological solutions, temporal depoliticization, depoliticization through the omission of agents, depoliticization through an explicit consensus invocation, and depoliticization through an inherently benign market. These included further subtypes of depoliticization that refine the typology.

The most common type of depoliticization present in both of the national discourses is achieved by focusing on the local level and ignoring other spatial levels and their respective power relations. The local is emphasized when one speaks about the reasons for poverty or when one proposes the instruments to solve the local problems. More specifically the access to market, to financial services, and to education are considered crucial elements on the way to development. A country or a region needs to break out of its isolation and connect itself economically to the rest of the world, despite the possibility that this connection already exists. To achieve a better life, people just need a bit of capital and education. That there might be conflicts between the lenders and borrowers and that education need not alter social immobility is often disregarded in the discourse. In this discourse, the market is, in general, not problematized and is most often represented as a benign place full of opportunities. Finally, local solutions are legitimized through local legitimation within the framework of the participation or partnership discourses.

The respondents also depoliticized unequal power relations by emphasizing technological solutions to problems that might be political. Technologies were regarded in a rather positive light by the Slovak respondents, but the respondents from Austroprojekt were more prudent in their position toward technologies.

The practices of a return to the past through environmental determinism, a focus on the future rather than the present, and representing the present as just fine, use different temporal contexts to disregard conflicts and unequal power relations. By focusing on the environment, one disregards colonialism; by focusing on the future, one postpones development as if an engagement here and now could not politically achieve changes right now; and by focusing on the present and believing that present-day actors already deal with various issues in a sufficient way, one disengages from the necessary action. The first two types of temporal depoliticization were to be found mainly among the Slovak respondents. A belief in the future in relation to education was present in both of the national discourses.

Both Austrians and Slovaks sometimes represented social actions as occurring without anyone's agency. Even though such a structuralist approach might be welcomed by Marxists, this approach avoids the political question of the conflict of interest between various actors in relation to, for example, the financial crisis or climate change. The actors responsible for the spread of HIV/AIDS were not named either, and various other negative phenomena in Kenya seem to be present without anyone causing them.

However, actors were also represented as acting together for the common good without conflicts. Texts and respondents from both of the national development apparatuses engaged in this type of depoliticization. Respondents and texts from Austria and Slovakia perceived the market in a positive way, but there was also a strong politicization in this respect, especially, but not uniquely, among the Austrian respondents.

These and other politicizations are analyzed in the next section, which also shows in greater detail the difference between the Slovak and Austrian respondents in regard to politicization. Depoliticization brought more similarity than differences between the two national apparatuses.

Forms of politicization

The opposite of depoliticization is politicization. I defined politicization at the beginning of this chapter as a political practice of including the friend-enemy element in a particular issue. Whereas depoliticization suppresses or disavows conflictive issues, politicization brings them to light. One can imagine cases of depoliticization that may, for example, smooth conflicting relations between nations and thereby contribute to the prevention of unnecessary violence. However, in general, a problematic depoliticization dominates the development discourse, and the focus on political issues should therefore be praised by those trying to push for emancipatory approaches.

Politicization is sparsely distributed in the analyzed texts. Political issues are voiced to a much greater extent in the interviews. The comparison between the Slovak and Austrian development apparatuses is therefore confined mainly to the last section, which focuses on the strongest forms of politicization stated by the respondents. Other sections show politicizing attempts coming from the development apparatuses in both countries.

This section begins by discussing the unused potential good governance and policy coherence for development provide for the politicization of a government that is, in general, portrayed as a benign force. However, as the evidence shows, the coherence is still lacking and the good governance discourse still depoliticizes to a much greater extent. Second, the analysis shows that education can depoliticize, as the previous chapter shows, but it can also politicize. At the same time, cultural politics in the form of global education may have both depoliticizing and politicizing consequences. Third, the chapter shows that unequal gender relations are strongly politicized in development discourse, however, this politicization may contribute to the depoliticization of other unequal power relations. Finally, I will argue that there are quite a few politicizing instances in the analyzed texts and interviews that are either weak or overwhelmed by instances of depoliticization, but a few respondents mainly (but not only) from Austria employed strong forms of politicization. The Slovaks politicized unequal power relations as well, but to a lesser extent than the Austrians.

The benign government and the potential for politicization through the good governance and policy coherence discourses

James Ferguson in 1991 assumed that in order for a "less developed country" to be part of development discourse there has to be an assumption of *a neutral effective government* (Ferguson 1994: 71–72). In his view, an analysis that suggests that "the national government is part of the problem (not a neutral instrument for its solution) […] has no place in 'development' discourse …" (ibid.: 69). Only such a depiction could lead to an apolitical, technical development intervention in 1991.

Whereas I believe that Ferguson's insight is still valid in many ways, the discourse has changed. Since good governance entered the development discourse, the perspective that "[t]he state itself […] tends to appear as a machine for implementing 'development' programs, an apolitical tool for delivering social services and agricultural inputs and engineering economic growth" (Ferguson 1994: 65) no longer holds.

A whole apparatus of knowledge has been created in order to evaluate states' governance, which is not a priori neutral or effective anymore, but can now be "good" or "bad." Institutions can be "sound" (or not), and "regulatory quality" can vary (Erkkilä and Piironen 2009: 134; see also Doornbos 2001: 94 for the same argument). Simply put, the government can be a part of the problem.

The good governance discourse has been criticized for depoliticizing governance through its technocratic and neoliberal understanding of governance. Instead of focusing on the political issues in the government, this discourse presents a view in which the government becomes a mere administrative institution, and the term "good" can be equated with "neoliberal." According to Hout, "[t]he dominant understanding of (good) governance in policy circles fails to recognise the essentially political character of governance issues, which relate to existing power relations in society" (Hout 2010: 3). It is still understood in predominantly technocratic terms, as such an understanding seeks to ensure efficiency in public administration and public finance management, rule of law, decentralization, and regulation of corporate life, including competition laws and anti-corruption watchdogs, etc. (ibid.: 2).

This is most visible in the construction of the good governance indices. Four out of six indicators from the World Bank Operations Policy and County Services, such as the quality of budgetary and financial management or the quality of public administration, are "highly technically and administratively oriented" (ibid.: 42). Erkkilä and Piironen conclude that, out of the World Bank's six World Governance Indicators, only one – "voice and accountability" – clearly measures democratic aspects of governance; however, this indicator is "more or less overwhelmed by the economic dimensions of governance" (Erkkilä and Piironen 2009: 138). Also, four criteria out of the six "treat governance as an instrument for ensuring functioning markets" (ibid.: 139).

In their latest research, these authors confirm the abovementioned findings (Erkkilä and Piironen 2014). However, there is a growing awareness of some of the problems related to governance indices, and the OECD offers a space for politicization (ibid.). The awareness of the problem that good governance might be depoliticizing unequal power relations led to serious attempts to change the existing situation in the World Bank, in the British Drivers of Change framework, and in the Dutch Strategic Governance and Corruption Analysis (Hout 2012). Even though Hout shows that these attempts failed, the reason for including good governance in the section on politicization is that good governance contains a potential for politicization.

In relation to particular projects, Tania Murray Li observes that the "detailed and site-specific project planning seems to bear little resemblance to the scenario in Lesotho described by Ferguson in the 1970s, in which ahistorical generic descriptions were used to characterize 'underdeveloped' countries ..." (Li 2007: 125–126). But Ferguson's analysis remains pertinent:

> Yet despite the attention to detail, the programs ... retained two fundamental features of the development problematic Ferguson identified. First, they reposed political-economic causes of poverty and injustice in terms amenable to technical solution. Second, they highlighted only those problems for which a technical solution could in fact be proposed – sidelining much of the data so painstakingly collected.
>
> (Ibid.)

Thus, the problems of depoliticization may have been recognized in the development apparatus, but the potential for politicization in good governance or in project management is not being used.

That the government can today still be "seen as a machine for delivering services; but never as a way of 'governing' people, a device through which certain classes and interests control the behavior and choices of others" (Ferguson 1994: 225), is most visible in Austroprojekt's Plan of Operation. In it, decentralization is, for example, understood as a smooth process that "is far from being completed," and this indicates a "lack of capacity within the central organs" (NDC-Austroprojekt and Orgut 2002: 16) rather than, e.g., a process that would be full of political conflicts. The government is also perceived as a somehow naturally benign instrument, as it is "determined to improve the welfare and health of the population... " (ibid.: 13, see also ibid.: 82).

Governance as a smooth, benign process is also mirrored in the perception of management. One can read in the Austrian Three-Year Program that "[t]he number of migrants to fertile areas is growing, calling for tighter management to prevent soil degradation" (BMEIA 2012: 56) or that, due to the growing pressure on water, "resource management and conservation play an increasing role" (ibid.: 23). An apolitical management is expected to solve political issues that may involve important conflicts between various groups of people over resources. The (political) reasons for migration or for the growing pressure on water are not discussed.

Even though depoliticization is clearly part of the good governance discourse, the main aim of this section is to show the potential for politicization in this discourse. There are numerous instances, especially in the texts from the state level, of trying to politicize development by focusing on good governance (e.g., MFEA 2013: 10). The objectives mentioned in the Austrian Federal Act on Development Cooperation from 2002 (amended 2003) contain the promotion of democracy, rule of law, human rights, and good governance (Nationalrat 2003). The Austrian Strategy further specifies that "ensuring the rule of law is one of the key functions of government" (ibid.: 30) and that "weak institutions and deficits in public administration" become one of the "main obstacles to sustainable development" (ibid.: 34). Whereas one could argue that the understanding of good governance in the official Austrian and Slovak discourse focuses on nonpolitical administration rather than on securing an equal representation of the people in connection with political issues, there is a potential in good governance to include political issues. It thus may have ambivalent effects, as it works as a rather empty signifier that can be used also, for example, as a reason for poverty (see, e.g., Interview No. 5 2013).

Some respondents offered such potentially politicizing views on good governance: "most governments failed to hand over power from one person to another person in a [...] democratic way. So I think this is a very good indicator of how democratic and people-driven the governance [is]" (Interview No. 23, 2013). A respondent from Pontis offered a similar perspective:

> Of course, the public administration is important [...] but at the same time it is extremely important for the citizens to be active, to be informed, to know how they can participate in case they have a particular interest in an issue that is being decided upon.
>
> (Interview No. 5, 2013)

The participatory approach here leads to a redefinition of good governance from a predominantly technocratic and administrative issue to an issue of people's participation in public decisionmaking. Herein lies the potential offered by the good governance approach informed by a participatory perspective.

There is little doubt that other respondents would also agree with the interpretation of the quotes in the previous paragraphs, but the potential remains unused, as good governance is mostly included in the discourse as a buzzword without much detail, and its meaning is defined by the official non-political discourse. Despite the potential, depoliticization still prevails. This applies to the discourse of the Policy Coherence for Development to a much greater extent.

Politicization occupies a specific space within the overall bureaucratic institutional framework of the EU (and also of the OECD). The Policy Coherence for Development (PCD) represents development cooperation as a policy that is superior to other external policies, such as those pertaining to trade, agriculture or fisheries. This is an explicitly articulated obligation of the EU under the Lisbon Treaty, and it is thus not surprising that official documents in Austria and Slovakia follow this obligation in their national strategies.

In the Austrian Three Year Program, the policy coherence approach is one of the "precepts" (ibid.: 19): "We must [...] take account of the far-reaching consequences of our policies, at legislative and executive level" (BMEIA 2012: 19). Meanwhile, "[t]he principle of policy coherence for development" (ibid.: 8) is part of the Slovak Medium-Term Strategy. It is included in the section "Visions, goals and principles...."

The aim to focus on the differences between the sectoral policies of the EU and of the national members is thus clearly present in the official documents, and in this sense there is space for the politicization of unequal relations of power. Nevertheless, the question remains how well the policy coherence is implemented in the institutional practice of the EU or of the nation states.

In this regard, it is interesting to note first that the PCD does not just date back to the Maastricht Treaty (1992), but previously the Single European Act called on the EU to act as "a cohesive force in international relations" (Article 30.2[d] in Carbone 2008: 324). And, even before that, the Treaty of Yaoundé in 1964 "presaged the coherence principle" (Picciotto 2005: 315). It is quite striking that, even after such a long period of aiming to harmonize development policies with other policies, one can still speak of a "mission impossible" with regard to these aims (Carbone 2008, see also Carbone and Keijzer 2016). The European Commission actually acknowledged that the results of the PCD itself were only modest (European Commission 2007, 2009).

So far, the empirical evidence regarding the results of the PCD is mainly concerned with the EU level. Some progress has been made in the agricultural policy even if the now mostly decoupled support still distorts the market (Matthews 2008; see also Klavert, Engel and Koeb 2011). On the other hand, the current investment regime of the EU "protects corporate grabbing of resources and markets in the Global South with negative impacts on small-scale food producers' human right to adequate food" (CONCORD 2015a). The EU trade and development policy subordinates the developmental to commercial imperatives in the reform of the Global System of Preferences (Siles-Brügge 2014), and the same seems to apply to the Economic Partnership Agreement with West Africa (CONCORD 2015b). So far, no research on the PCD has been conducted in either Austria or Slovakia.

Thus, it can be said that the Policy Coherence for Development opens up a space for politicization, and the Sustainable Development Goals that introduce the policy coherence for sustainable development go even a step further in this regard. The NGO sector can demand from the government or the European Commission that they should stick to their own commitments. On the other hand, the empirical evidence so far shows that the rhetorical politicization does not lead to actual changes in the Global North–South relations. A similar ambivalence in terms of politicization and depoliticization is to be found in the educational realm.

Cultural depoliticization and politicization in archipolitics through education

Conflicts in a political system can be depoliticized through so-called archipolitics. Rancière traces this form of depoliticization to Plato, who replaces the democratic configuration of politics with the complete realization of the *arkhê* (the basic principle) of a community (Rancière 1999: 65). The open democratic decision-making – the space of politics – is replaced with the "ethos (morality, ways of being, character) of the community and of each of its members" (ibid.). *Krátos* (might) no longer matters, and the republic is based "on the education that constantly translates the law into its spirit" (ibid.: 68). Education becomes the crucial instrument to create a community with a single morality that will no longer need any politics. "The good city [...] is a city in which legislation is entirely resumed in education" (ibid.). In this sense, archipolitics becomes archipolicing, as here the way of being is defined with no place left for a political engagement.

On the one hand, Rancière's perspective seems legitimate: the public space should be a democratic space of equality in which everyone can engage in a political conflict. An image of a homogenized community with a single morality, in which everyone is assigned a particular place or a particular function, clearly goes against Rancière's notion of democracy.

On the other hand, one might employ two similar counterarguments. The first acknowledges archipolicing as a form of politics. As Rancière himself claims, "[p]olitics is the art of suppressing the political" (Ranciere 1995: 19). An attempt to try to replace politics with an educated citizen who will dispense with politics while opting for the morality s/he acquired at school or elsewhere in the public space is just as political as engaging in a class struggle or a race struggle. My argument is that, whereas Rancière is right in saying that archipolicing depoliticizes the struggle between various subjects, at the same time, it is necessary to recognize the possibility of competing *arkhai* that struggle against each other at a higher level. Such an archipolitics is then a legitimate form of politics. It, however, contains a very clear danger of depoliticization, as a success of one *arkhê* at the expense of another silences the basis of concrete political struggles.

The second counterargument is similar, as it turns an *arkhê* into an educational curriculum, and the citizen into a student. An attempt to change a school curriculum is simply an ideological fight just like any other. As already claimed, an attempt to influence fellow citizens or children is the gist of politics. In order to win political conflicts, one needs to find wider support within a democratic society. Such support can be gained through, among other things, a transformation of the ideological landscape or an ideological indoctrination of children. More importantly, such a transformation can also include a mere broadening of the school curriculum rather than its change into an instrument of policing the society and turning it into a homogenized community. With these objections in mind, it might still be worth pointing at the danger of depoliticization as well as at the potential for politicization that one may find in the global education in both Slovakia and Austria.

In the Slovak Medium-Term Strategy, one can read that the goal of the "[d]evelopment education and public awareness program" is to "integrate development cooperation into school plans and curricula at respective levels in Slovak schools" (MFEA 2013: 20) and to "increase public support for SlovakAid activities by providing information about the Slovak development cooperation as well as global issues and challenges of developing countries" (ibid.: 21). In Austria, the "[d]evelopment education [...] fosters awareness in the population" (BMEIA 2012: 17), and "global learning is [...] an essential contribution to modern general education, for (sic) a more aware and committed population that supports the concerns of development cooperation in an informed way" (ibid.).

Both policies might run the risk of depoliticization. Without a previous public consultation, the ministries in both countries are aiming at a substantial change in the school curriculum. Citizens do not decide about this change in a public deliberation or (at least) in an election. The decision is taken by unelected officials and does not involve the citizens whom it concerns the most. The political problem of who is supposed to decide about what the children are going to learn at school is avoided and thus depoliticized.

The aim of increasing public support for SlovakAid and for the Austrian development cooperation is equally problematic. The goal here seems to be to influence the public in a particular way. It is difficult to expect from the state that it will not be providing the public with one-sided information about its activities. However, at the rhetorical level, this is surprising. Usually the state claims neutrality in informing people about its activities and does not seek to *openly* gain their support for its own policy. Moreover, as claimed in the second chapter, this will is shaped according to the demands coming from outside of both societies. Development education aims to just confirm this outside influence. Otherwise the Slovak government would not need to "increase the public support for SlovakAid activities" (MFEA 2013: 21), or the Austrian government would not consider global learning to be "an essential contribution [...] for a more committed population that supports the concerns of development cooperation" (BMEIA 2012: 17).

This problem is also related to the way the development education and public awareness program is supposed to be evaluated: "The impact of public awareness activities is reflected in the EC Eurobarometer or in public surveys conducted in the [Slovak Republic]" (ibid.). The archipolicing here moves in a circle. The government tries to influence "its" population to support SlovakAid activities and then uses problematic surveys (see Profant 2018a) so that it would be able to say that the population indeed supports this policy. Yet, as already mentioned in Chapter 2, it is common knowledge that the Slovaks are not as generous as the surveys suggest (Beňáková 2011; Tichý 2015).

Even though I claim that archipolitics need not depoliticize conflicts and power relations, some of the respondents' answers pointed in this direction. Pike (2000) shows that global education can politicize unequal power relations to a greater extent, as in the UK and Canada, but also to a lesser extent, as in the USA, depending among other things on the national culture. The engagement of my respondents stayed at the personal and cultural level. One respondent from PiP thought that:

> the most important is the public education and gradual rise in awareness of at least a part of the population [...] the most important [practice is] to give people the information to be able to make decisions, and maybe one day it will come about that people will refuse certain things, certain types of goods

> [...]. If everyone were thinking [...] and demonstrated it with their consumer behavior, that would be great; it is just difficult to reach that [point] [...]. I at least try in my private life.
>
> (Interview No. 10 2013)

As the last section in this chapter will also show, this respondent individualizes her political actions. Collective political engagement is almost completely missing from her account of the possibilities one has as an activist. This is where the depoliticizing potential that Rancière writes about is visible. She becomes a subject of her own *arkhê* or global education – a responsible consumer – but she does not engage in a more explicit political fight (for a similar argument in relation to the British global education see Andreotti 2011, in relation to German global education, see Bendix, Danielzik, and Kiesel 2015).

In a similar fashion, a respondent from CARE, when asked about what he would do should he have much greater power, replied that he would "change the Lehrplan [curriculum], what children would learn, because what we need to change is the global learning" (ibid.). It needs to be emphasized here that this respondent strongly politicized unequal economic power relations (see the last section). At this point, I would like to stress that he also aims at transforming the Austrian culture by influencing children. This part of his strategy avoids a political conflict within Austrian society. I am not suggesting that this is somehow a deeply held apolitical perspective, but merely that, even though it clearly aims at unequal power relations, the method is non-political and fits well with archipolitics – inculcating a particular ethos into the members of a society.

The non-political character became clearer when I asked this respondent about how democratic it is to promote global learning at schools if it might be against citizens' (or parents') wishes. According to him, "it is democratic [...] because when you refer to migrant people, it's a question of tolerance [...] even if they don't like it" (Interview No. 26 2013). When I suggested that children influenced by global learning may wish to wear Fair Trade t-shirts and demand this from their parents, who may be too poor to afford it, the respondent defended himself by saying that he does not

> give advice on what to buy; I just [...] ask where it is from [...] it's based on exploitation mostly [...] I would do it because then there would be discussion [...]. Even if it might not seem so democratic, it is democratic, because you are free to say what you think.
>
> (Ibid.)

His

> opinion is that people need some kick in the ass to think, and this is pressure, of course [...] that is what I learned in offices wherever I worked – that people need to be taught this and this or need a kick in the ass to do things.
>
> (Ibid.)

On the one hand, exposing others to different perspectives or opening up discussions is hardly problematic, and it can have serious politicizing consequences; on the other the danger of depoliticization lies in not letting the citizens decide about the legitimate ways information should be spread to youngsters.

Moreover, buying Fair Trade might be a moral consumerist choice defining one's identity. The political problem that may occur in relation to a depoliticizing global education is precisely the question of Self and its relation to moral consumerist practices. It's not just that the representation of Fair Trade echoes the colonial practice of representation with all its hierarchies between the self and Other (Backes 2011). Of equal importance is the relation between the Northern (Western) middle class, which is capable of buying Fair Trade and thereby securing its moral self, and the Northern lower class, which is incapable of affording Fair Trade and therefore becoming an irresponsible problematic Other exploiting the poor deserving Other, who works hard for Fair Trade products and needs the help of the Self. In this way, Fair Trade as a consumer practice that is related to the construction of the Self may contribute to the division between the lower and the middle class in the Global North and global education may inadvertently contribute to this outcome by focusing predominantly on depoliticizing consumer practices (see also Varul 2011). This applies to the West as well as to the much smaller community of people who may engage, not only in buying Fair Trade, but also, for example, in buying organic food and enjoying feelings of superiority over those who do not engage in such moral consumerist practices.

Depoliticizing archipolitics can be found also in relation to the Global South in the attempts to change people's attitudes or their cultural practices. For example, according to Austroprojekt's Plan of Operation, the spreading of HIV/AIDS is made easier "by cultural practices among the pastoralist majority" (NDC-Austroprojekt and Orgut 2002: 45). The logical solution is then a change in these cultural practices. The Plan, however, does not address the political causes of the spreading of HIV/AIDS. Wilson claims that "since the 1990s, it has been increasingly widely accepted that higher levels of 'risky' behaviour cannot in themselves possibly explain the far more rapid spread of the virus in sub-Saharan Africa in comparison to other regions" (Wilson 2012: 104). Thus, rather than focusing on culture, a political-economic approach could focus on the decline in funding for health services and at the same time study neoliberal reforms that lead to an increase in commercial sex work (ibid.: 102–105).

I am not suggesting that informing the public about hazards of unsafe sex or promiscuous behavior is problematic in itself, but merely that such a nonpolitical approach can become problematic if it is so dominant in the discourse that it excludes or marginalizes analyses of political-economic causes or suggestions of political solutions.

It is not just global education that can lead to politicization of students as well as to their depoliticization, but the same applies to education in general. Whereas the section on education above showed that the education discourse can have depoliticizing effects, education itself can actually politicize conflicts and unequal power relations. There seems to be a threefold understanding of education in the texts. First, education is portrayed in a very general manner without a specified content; second, it is represented as particular skills and; third, it is represented as awareness raising. It was the third meaning that contained instances of politicization.

When education is represented as simply an effective means to fight poverty, it is entirely unclear what it is supposed to contain, and this (almost) empty signifier is close to the one used at the international level analyzed by Spitzl (2011, see above). In his analysis, education is, e.g., a key to progress, but its content is never specified.

This perspective on education is to be found among respondents who claim that a lack of education is one of the reasons for poverty (Interview No. 12 2013; Interview No. 13 2013; Interview No. 15 2014). According to one respondent from SAIDC, "frankly, we have to tell ourselves that if someone does not have an elementary education, s/he probably does not produce any values for the society" (Interview No. 12 2013; see also Wagner-Hager 2014; CARE 2014a; Wilke 2014).

On the other hand, CARE specified what education can mean in practice: "Who cannot read and write will remain caught in the poverty trap" (CARE 2005). In this second meaning, education is represented in terms of particular skills that the students or pupils can learn, such as "English, computer literacy, presentations and interview techniques" (CARE 2014c). This meaning of the term then is related to success in the labor market, as these skills "should increase the chances in the labor market" (ibid.).

Two respondents from Pontis even criticized the content of the education in Kenya by saying that it is not practical (Interview No. 7 2013, No. 5 2013). Whereas the first meaning depoliticizes unequal power relations at a very general level (see above), this second meaning can depoliticize the problems related to the labor market, as it assumes that the market is just waiting for better prepared workers to enter it and find a job.

The third meaning of education is related to awareness raising in the Freirian sense (Freire 1996), and it means teaching about political issues such as people's rights. According to one respondent from CARE Austria, education for everyone would substantially reduce poverty "because people would stand up; they would think about what the reason for poverty is [and] charge, test and attack the power holders" (Interview No. 26 2013; see also Interview No. 25 2013).

One respondent from Slovak NGDO Pontis thought that, through education, students should "understand the context of the environment in which they live" (Interview No. 4 2013). It should "explain to them why they are poor and how they can remove poverty from their lives" (ibid.) – for example, "how they can improve their consuming practices, what they spend money for and how they can spend more effectively, and how to earn money," but also "why their society is poor," and "this question [...] leads to wider relations, not only inside Egypt, but somewhere further" (ibid.). Here the depoliticizing discourse of one's own responsibility for one's poverty continues into the discourse that politicizes wider international relations.

The Freirian understanding of education was not present in the analyzed texts, but only among respondents from CARE and Pontis. The depoliticizing consequences of the way education (including Global Education) was conceptualized in both the Austrian and Slovak discourses were thus dominant. There was a similar ambivalence in the politicization of unequal gender relations, which is analyzed in the next section.

Depoliticization through politicization of unequal gender relationships

Even though it might seem counterintuitive, politicization of some unequal power relations can lead to a depoliticization of other unequal power relations. There are two issues that politicize unequal power relations, but since they do so at the household and local levels, their effect might be a depoliticization of unequal power relations in different social fields (e.g., the economy) and also at different spatial levels. This is the case of the participatory approach and projects that aim at gender equality. I will focus on the latter here.

According to Sarah White (2006: 58–59), "[t]he tendency has thus been for gender and poverty to occupy all the space available for 'social issues', eclipsing, rather than enabling the recognition of other dimensions of inequality." When it comes to gender awareness, "gender […] is magnified and constituted as the primary power relation" (ibid.: 60). The problem is that the exploration of other power relations can be blocked by this focus on gender. One of the more critical respondents from ADA makes a similar claim: "We discuss power relations between men and women. We are very obsessed with these micro power relations because we are unable to address the really important power relations" (Interview No. 22 2013; for a similar claim see Gütermann 2014).

Within the Marxist approach, these arguments are elaborated upon by Jameson's cultural logic of late capitalism as he criticizes postmodernism, namely theories of information society and post-industrial society that perceive late capitalism as not obeying the laws of classical capitalism: "namely the primacy of industrial production and the omnipresence of class struggle" (ibid.: 55). Jameson's argument can also be used in relation to feminism, as the gender struggle can become so dominant that the class struggle is replaced rather than just complemented by it.

It may seem to be clearly laudable to help oppressed women in distant places (if these women articulate their will for a change). This means a clear politicization of relations of power. At the same time, however, such projects add to the mass of other projects on the local level that depoliticize unequal relations of power at the national and international levels related to different issues. Such a claim can be only based on the argument of the amount of politicizing gender-related projects that displace other projects or on the attention gender relations get in the development discourse.

Gender equality is a cross-cutting issue in the Slovak Medium-Term Strategy with an "emphasis on women's empowerment" (MFEA 2013: 11), and the

Austrian Three-Year Program also contains the usual politicization of gender inequality (ibid.: 22) with the aim of "strengthening the role of women and their participation in organisational and decision-making processes" (ibid.: 31).

A more specific field that emphasizes gender relations is microfinance. Microfinance has "given women a new-found confidence […] increased their purchasing power, [as they are now] obtaining goods formerly owned by men […] and enhanced their level of decision-making power within the household" (Plan UK, CARE International UK and Barclays 2013: 12). Simply put, "[m]icrofinance groups are […] an important instrument for the improvement of women's situation" (CARE 2006b). Gender relations are thus politicized as decision-making power within the household or the society is addressed. However, the focus on gender through microfinance also weakens the attention that could be given to larger issues of power beyond the household.

The focus on gender was also important for the respondents. According to one respondent from CARE, "we believe that you have more than a proportional impact on the development aspect if you work especially for women, or girls" (Interview No. 28 2014; see also Interviews Nos. 25 and 26 2013 and Interview No. 27 2014). However, as I will show in the last section of this chapter, some of these respondents also sharply criticized other relations of power. Thus, while the focus on power relations between men and women can limit one's focus on other relations of power and have depoliticizing effects, as some of these interviews show, it need not.

One can also find a somewhat clearer instance of a neglect of non-gender unequal power relations. Here, the argument is not based on showing yet another text focusing on gender and contributing to the domination of gender power relations in development discourse at the expense of other political issues. One can see the neglect in this case in a more direct way. The readers of the Banking on Change report learn that, "[i]n Africa, for example, women own just one per cent of [all the] agricultural land" (Plan UK, CARE International UK and Barclays 2013: 11). Not only is the 1% figure problematic (Doss et al. 2013), but nowhere else in the text can one read about a part of the population of both men and women that owns as much as 1% of all the agricultural land[4] and that this could be connected to other people owning the rest. Whereas the inferior economic position of women is mostly represented in relation to the superior position of men, the same relation between the rich and the poor does not figure in the report. The projects, reports or strategies that target household and local power relations thus depoliticize power relations at the international level and in the different fields of power.

Still, the politicization of gender and other local unequal power relations is clearly laudable. One may find a solution to the unequal power relations problem in combining various spatial levels in order not to ignore the other important power relations. A more political approach from the Austrian (as well as the Slovak) respondents will be shown in the next section.

Weak and strong politicization

The politicization of unequal power relations in the analyzed texts was very weak. Apart from the already mentioned instances of politicization, occasionally a conflict between various actors was admitted to, but these were exceptions in a rather non-political corpus. Due to the instances of politicization being sparsely scattered throughout the texts, I will present them here in a rather haphazard manner in order to give a glimpse of the nature of the politicization in the texts, as the instances of it were very similar in their non-significance in both the Slovak and the Austrian texts. There were two rather systematic but not strong forms of politicization. One was achieved due to the effort to avoid hierarchization and the other one was related to the household (see above). I will first focus on the weaker type of politicization. After analyzing the texts, I will show the instances of politicizations being overwhelmed by depoliticization, which occurred especially in the Slovak interviews. The more politicizing interviews with mainly (but not only) Austrian respondents are analyzed in the later part of this section.

The omission of agents, which is interpreted here as a way to deal with the problem of hierarchization (see Chapter 3), actually enabled a weak politicization. As already mentioned, there were instances of negative representations whose negativity was weakened by the omission of the agents behind the actions. The negativity did not connote the agent. Regarding depoliticization, these soft negative representations can have two opposite effects. They can either depoliticize potential or existing conflicts related to the mentioned negativity by omitting the agents, or they can politicize these conflicts in a weak way by focusing on their structural causes and by not making the poor responsible for them.

As argued in Chapter 3, "they" (e.g., the poor) are represented (abstracted) as, e.g., a "high population density […] high unemployment, a high HIV/AIDS ratio […] [or] gender inequality." (PiP 2009) "They" are thus portrayed in a less negative way than "they" would be if one would say, e.g., "they" are unemployed or "they" have AIDS. On the other hand, the agent behind the causes of the unemployment or the spread of AIDS is missing. These phenomena simply exist, and the lack of a cause depoliticizes the conflicts that lead to the increase in unemployment or AIDS. The reader does not learn what social actions enacted by particular agents contribute to the prevalence of AIDS or unemployment.

A weak politicization then occurs when there is a cause behind these and similar phenomena, even though the representation of that cause omits its agents. One can thus read that "*Poverty* and Kenya's east coast inhabitants' *insufficient income* cause uncontrolled woodcutting of precious mangrove trees in Kilifi" (italics by author, PiP 2012b; see also CARE 2005, 2014b). It is not the poor people who are causing the uncontrolled wood cutting, but their poverty and insufficient income. Such a representation shows a potential for politicization, as one may ask how the poverty comes about, and it seems that the poor are not responsible for their poverty; otherwise one could just say that the poor are cutting down the trees. Thus there might be something else, and it is not the poor people's choice to cut down the trees. A whole political field for discussion is thereby opened. However, the politicization here is not as strong as it could be, as the causes of the poverty and insufficient incomes are not discussed at all.

This structural approach goes one step further in another article, as, in it, the destruction of nature is again caused by poverty. This time "they" will not get out of the cycle of poverty "without access to education" and "without help" (Zorád 2013). If these two aspects are lacking, no one can stop "them" from looting nature. In the first step of the argument, it is not "them," but poverty, that causes the destruction of nature. In the second step, the causes of the poverty are clarified as well. Again, it is not "them" who is responsible for the poverty, but the lack of help and the lack of access to education. The reader still does not know who causes this lack, but it is certain that the poor are not to be blamed.

The explanation here goes in a depoliticizing direction, as the cause of the poverty is the lack of education and the lack of aid, and it is not a problem of power inequality. Education would make people realize how important the environment is and offer them alternative ways of making a living. One can thus again speak only of a weak form of politicization in this case. Poverty is to be solved through education and aid. I should emphasize, however, that not only can education be political, but a non-political education can also be useful in tackling social problems.

Further instances of politicization varied, and here they will be presented in an order based on the analyzed actors, beginning with the Austrian actors. Reasons for poverty in Austroprojekt's Plan of Operation were sometimes politicized (as in cases of, e.g., border conflicts, land grabbing, or conflicts between agriculturalists and pastoralists; NDC-Austroprojekt-Orgut 2002: 50, 58), but they were almost uniquely related to Tanzania and not to other places.

Hints of politicization were present in the Austrian Three Year Program via the passages on corporate social responsibility (BMEIA 2012: 28, 29). One could also read in it that " 'unfair' power relations should be broken and rights as well as obligations should be equally distributed" or that "we seek to make a contribution to [...] a fair global economy" (ibid.: 6) and "debt relief" (ibid.: 17). Again it is unclear who should be doing what, but the aim is clear – to address unequal economic relations.

There were also instances of politicization in the *Weltnachrichten*, which spoke about "structural inequality in the countries [of the Global South]" (Rabitsch 2013). Again, these instances were very rare and not so strong, and one would need to seriously elaborate on the abovementioned issues in order to engage in a discussion about particular conflicts of interests related to these issues.

Politicizations of unequal power relations were included not only in the texts, but also in the interviews, but they were often overwhelmed by instances of depoliticization. For example, three respondents from the Slovak Agency for International Development and Cooperation mostly depoliticized unequal power relations, but occasionally also politicized them. A very rough count shows ten instances of politicization and 22 instances of depoliticization (of varying strength) by them.

All three of these respondents depoliticized unequal power relations by mentioning natural conditions (Interview No. 12 2013; Interview No. 13 2013; Interview No. 15 2014) as one of the conditions for reaching development. Another important element in reaching development was education (Interview No. 12 2013; Interview No. 13 2013; Interview No. 15 2014).

These same respondents also offered contradictory statements that contained instances of politicization of various levels of strength. To a direct question about the world market, one respondent answered: "This is maybe a question of some kind of neocolonialism [...] strong Western companies [can be], of course, a plus, but obviously this has its negative side. The globalization certainly has a negative influence on those countries" (Interview No. 13 2013). This respondent, however, also stated that he is "for a liberal approach to the market ... [and] for the least possible regulation" (ibid.). This respondent thus politicized the relation between the Western companies and poorer countries, but also depoliticized these relations by arguing for the least possible regulation.

A similar pattern was to be found in the two other respondents from this organization (Interview No. 12 2013; Interview No. 15 2014; see also Interview No. 8 2013).

Some of the Austrian respondents also engaged in weak politicizations that were overwhelmed by depoliticization. Regarding the role of the market, one respondent from ADA offered a weak politicization as he emphasized the need for the market to work efficiently and meant "that there are no monopolies" in such a case (Interview No. 23 2013). Yet, he considered globalization "unavoidable [...]. There's no right of politicians or any other group not to allow this" even though it "also [is] a threat for a lot of people" (ibid., see also Interview No. 24 2014).

All in all, depoliticization of unequal power relations prevailed in these and other respondents' answers, even if they all mentioned them as problematic, and this was a significant contradiction in their responses. They weakened their politicizations by strongly supporting free trade, by proposing small-scale projects as a solution or simply by mentioning political relations only after several questions related to this topic had been asked. They thus differed from the more politically oriented respondents in ADA, Austroprojekt and CARE Austria, but also from three of their Slovak colleagues. The most politicized interviews are analyzed below.

The aim here is not only to show the strongest forms of politicization, which occurred almost exclusively in the interviews, but also to compare the Austrian and Slovak respondents with regard to politicizations of unequal relations in the interviews.

Two respondents from CARE were very strong in politicizing unequal power relations at the local, national, and international level, including gender issues. They clearly distinguished between the local and the global level. When answering the question of how to achieve development, one respondent first spoke of participation: "It is necessary to have a good project design where the partner organizations and also the people agree on what is best for them" (Interview

No. 26 2013). Then he moved on to talking about power up to the national level: "I think it's very important to gain local, regional and national power holders and opinion leaders for the cause. And if you don't get them into the boat you could forget it. That is a reason for many failures." (ibid.) After that, he focused on the global level:

> sometimes it is frustrating; you do this and you do that, but if you don't put hold to the financial capitalism […] this madness […]. My opinion is that we have to change the superstructure of capitalism or economics [… in order] to better the life of the poor people, wherever they might be. We have to change the logic of the economy.
>
> (Ibid.)

As the reasons for poverty, this respondent gave "unequal distribution, absolute power, corruption, exploitation and also exploitation from the West" (ibid.). This respondent even connected Northern wealth with Southern poverty: "the wealth of the West […] greatly depends on poverty" (Interview No. 26 2013; see also Interview No. 27 2013; Interview No. 25 2013).

This respondent and his colleagues also offered a substantial self-critique of CARE, focusing on international power relations and their connection with CARE's advocacy work. According to one of them,

> we [CARE] are not so strong in negotiating with and in engaging in these trade treaties, [in] how they are set up, how private investors do business, what is the law [for running] business development and doing business in a country.
>
> (Interview No. 25 2013; see also Interview No. 26 2013)

CARE also organizes climate change symposia, invites opinion leaders, and raises awareness among journalists: "Some of the speakers we invite are actually criticizing turbo-capitalism. Or I would when I am moderating or facilitating" (Interview No. 26 2013).

There were also mixed responses criticizing capitalism as part of the reason for poverty, but at the same time expecting business to help poor communities (Interview No. 27 2013).

One respondent also criticized microfinance, as "people 'deassetify' themselves, […] selling their assets to cover the loans" (Interview No. 27 2013). She politicized the relation between the lenders and borrowers by describing it, not in terms of service, cooperation or harmony, but in terms of exploitation: "the private sector often acts badly, and that's why you have these incredible interest rates, which are meant to cover the risk […] but often I find that they are exploitative" (ibid.).

These three respondents responded positively to a critical question that problematized a causal relation between education and social mobility and agreed that "people from a higher background with money, they know how to put their children in another place [...]. Not always, not everywhere, but more or less, yes" (Interview No. 26 2013; see also Interview No. 25 2013; Interview No. 27 2013). None of the Slovak respondents responded in this way.

Christoph Gütermann from Austroprojekt also publicly politicized

> the global framework that disadvantages the Third World and the farmers there. The agriculture in Burkina Faso cannot protect itself from cheap imports. The farmers there cannot compete at the world market, because the European and the US agriculture protect themselves massively.
>
> (Gütermann 2006)

According to him, the last 30 years of development cooperation "serve nothing if the fundamentals of the situation remain the same" (ibid.).

Another respondent from Austroprojekt, after being asked a direct question about the role of market in development, offered a clear politicization of the market power relations, finding them very one-sided in favor of the countries of the North (Interview No. 17 2013).

Three respondents in the Austrian Development Agency were quite political in their responses as well. For the already mentioned respondent who criticized the focus on the micro power gender relations, the reason for poverty was the "uneven distribution of power" (Interview No. 22 2013):

> For me it's not technical. It is political [...]. If the poor people of the world would not accept their fate, if they would fight for their own rights, but this is a political measure, you see, and you cannot press the button and say: "Now a revolution is on." It needs a social movement. It needs a social protest, a social engagement to reverse this situation.
>
> (Ibid.)

I also asked her whether ADA is doing anything about the power relation she talked about before. According to her,

> We keep discussing questions like this, and we know that in other development cooperation agencies and the European Union they are discovering political economy [...] but [...] it is still a more theoretical approach, and I think we cannot talk openly or too openly about power relations.
>
> (Ibid.)

She went on by talking about what can be done: "We are a governmental institution, and we cannot turn a governmental institution into a leftist movement (laughing). This is not possible. It is not mainstream to think in power relations" (ibid.).

In this regard, she offered an explanation of her critical perspective: "not everybody is [as] outspoken [as] me. And there is a difference if you are 35 [...] if you are younger, you are more careful" (ibid.).

Other respondents from ADA were somewhat less political, but two of them still included many politicizing responses (Interview No. 20 2013; see also Interview No. 22 2013).

There were fewer Slovak respondents who would engage in strong as well as not so strong politicizations of unequal power relations. One respondent from Pontis considered the following as the reason for poverty: "a combination of certain geopolitical and trade relations, in which the given country is situated in combination with some kind of historical evolution that could have been influenced by, e.g., some colonial past or some military conflicts" (Interview No. 4 2013).

This respondent also offered an explanation as to why Pontis does not deal with these issues to a greater extent. Apart from claiming that these issues are dealt with within the field of development education in Pontis, he also said the following:

> [W]e are trying to be an apolitical organization on the outside. This is, I think, the most important reason. And also […] because our people do not perceive this [as an] element of poverty. If you talk to them about it in greater detail […] then […] they would admit […] that the trade relations are bad, that they are wrongly regulated, but it would not be something that would be important for their decisions about some strategic direction of their work. So why is it not so in Pontis? Because Pontis' leadership has a strategy, and this is not included in that strategy.
>
> (Ibid.)

I asked him further why he worked for Pontis then if he considered this to be important and Pontis does not deal with it. He replied that Pontis does other stuff that he considers important – for example, development education. Another important thing was the mindset of the people working there – their way of looking at the world – and also the flexible way the organization works.

A respondent from SAMRS also focused on power relations. She put herself on the side of the theories that say that "we got into the situation in which we are now because developing countries became some kind of a provider of cheap labor and minerals, and this led to the accumulation of wealth in the rich states" as opposed to neoliberal theories (Interview No. 14 2014).

Apart from the accumulation of wealth, she criticized the conditionality of loans that forced countries to offer tax breaks to foreign investments, tax policies of the Western states, and the whole deregulation of financial markets (ibid.).

In the next step, I asked her how it is possible that deregulation was adopted in the given case, and she replied that "this is politics, this is neoliberalism" (ibid.). In her reply to a follow up question – what she means by politics in this context – she said that the situation arose because of "political parties who put this global political system in place" (ibid.). And I asked, "How was this possible?" She hesitated, and then gave the following answer:

> Because they were elected? Well, yes, this is questionable [...] today it is difficult to assess whether power is in the hands of the politicians who were entrusted with it [...] or whether political power is not in the hands of transnational corporations, people who have money. If they have money they have influence.
>
> (Ibid.)

To the hypothetical question about what she would do if she had the possibility to change things, she replied that she would change the whole financial architecture, the "one dollar – one vote" principle. She would also change the Western trade policies. Foreign aid, according to her, is then "only a small component that cannot change the whole system" (ibid.).

A respondent from PiP, in her politicization of unequal power relations, problematized the corporate power, but to a great extent individualized her political strategy, almost completely excluding the possibility of a collective action. She thus engaged in politics on a personal level, perceiving other levels as unreachable. According to her,

> powerful countries and powerful corporations rule the world [...] but this cannot be undone. We do not have the power. As an individual I cannot abolish Tesco or McDonald's [...] but I can talk about it, and I can try, as a consumer, to behave in one way or another and not support companies about whom I know that they cause harm [...] but I, as a person, do not know how to change that.
>
> (Interview No. 10 2013)

She also tries to engage in debates at the Ministry of Foreign Affairs or bigger fora where decision-makers participate. In her personal life she, e.g., buys chicken from a nearby farm and not at Tesco. A politicization of the corporate power in her case thus turns into the helplessness of an individual who cannot do anything except for conscious shopping and occasionally taking part in discussions. This is not unsimilar to what CARE actually does, despite the much greater political imagination of some of the respondents from this NGO.

As this section shows, there were respondents who offered clear politicizations of unequal relations of power. These were related not only to the local, but also to the national as well as to the global arenas. The conflict that these respondents articulated was between the wealth of the Global North and the poverty of the Global South, or between the powerful corporations and the much less powerful smaller producers, who are competing unfairly on the market. Another question of power concerned the relationship between the two sides of microfinance as well as the loans from the IFIs. The question of the relation between education and social mobility was politicized as well. The inequality in the power relations was ascribed to politics, in particular to the politicians influenced by money. It was stated that grassroot organizations and social movements should be supported in order to change the current situation. However, three respondents admitted that their organizations (Pontis, CARE and ADA) do not act very much in this regard. They engage in the discussions with the public and with people from the ministries.

There were more respondents from Austria (8) who strongly engaged in the politicizations of unequal power relations than from Slovakia (3). The language of some of the Austrian respondents was also more expressive than the language of the Slovaks, as the former subsumed the issue of power relations under terms such as "turbocapitalism," "madness," "revolution," or "parasitic relationship." Overall, however, the difference is one of degree and not of substance. There were some Slovak respondents who expressed the same concern with unequal power relations as their Austrian counterparts. All of the respondents then differed from the analyzed texts that politicized power relations to a substantially lesser degree.

The analyzed texts were dominated by depoliticization, despite a few instances of politicization. The attempts to avoid hierarchization resulted in the focus on structural causes of problematic phenomena in the Global South, which offered a potential for politicization.

Conclusion

This chapter showed that the respondents as well as the analyzed texts engage in the politicization of unequal power relations. Even though depoliticization is dominant in what they say, several respondents were very critical of the conflicts that exist between the Global North and Global South. The most obvious finding of the analysis of (de)politicization is that the respondents were much more political than the PR articles were. A few texts that one could put into the "critical development" genre are analyzed in the next chapter.

The depoliticization was achieved through the focus on the local level – local reasons for poverty and local instruments to solve local problems. These instruments included education and microfinance, or more specifically an access to a market that is considered to be inherently benign. Furthermore, the focus on technological solutions also contributed to the depoliticization of unequal power relations and so did the omission of agents responsible for various social processes. Depoliticization was also achieved by focusing on the past regarding the question why some countries are developed and others are not, by focusing on the future rather than the present situation and by being content with the present situation.

The potential for the politicization of unequal relations of power is to be found in the good governance discourse. Despite its representation of the government in technocratic and administrative terms, there is a growing awareness of the problem of depoliticization, not only in organizations such as the OECD, but also among some of the respondents, who were aware of the way the governments functioned as political institutions. There is thus a potential for a repoliticization of the term governance.

To a much greater extent than good governance, the Policy Coherence for Development is supposed to politicize the conflicts between the values of development policy and those of other policies. Even though such a politicization occurs and is clearly present in the discourse in Austria and Slovakia, the results of the PCD are modest at most.

Apparatuses from both countries politicized gender inequality, but this politicization, as one Austrian respondent also observed, may lead to an ignorance of other forms of inequality and thereby cause depoliticization. As the last section shows, however, this need not be the case.

This chapter showed that education can have important depoliticizing consequences if understood as an empty signifier or as skills to be used in the labor market. However, it can be a very political tool if understood as a way to learn about one's unequal position and as a way to change that inequality. More Austrians were aware of this possibility than Slovaks.

The way culture and global education are understood is also ambiguous. On the one hand, global education can be promoted in a non-political manner through bureaucratic procedures rather than through democratic decision-making. It can also serve the aims of the state to promote development cooperation rather than more political awareness raising. On the other hand, the content of global education can spread awareness of political issues among the population. Still, this awareness may result in individualized actions, such as choices in consumer shopping, rather than collective political interventions into the society. An interview with one of the more politicizing Slovak respondents showed this well.

The instances of a clear articulation of a conflict between different parties in the texts were quite rare apart from the ones mentioned above and the attempts to avoid hierarchization that emphasized the role of structural forces such as poverty. Most of the respondents engaged in some kind of politicization, though. However, most of the Slovaks spoke of political issues only to a limited extent, and, when they did, they more often mentioned non-political solutions to the problems of development. Some of the Austrian respondents expressed their views in similar patterns, but quite a few spoke about power inequality in a very strong way. This was the starkest contrast between the Slovaks and the Austrians. But again, the difference was only in the degree and the amount of politicization, and there was no substantial difference. After all, several Slovaks also politicized unequal power relations to a considerable extent.

Notes

1 There is one hint of a view that is critical of the way microcredit functioned since the 1990s in the report co-authored by CARE Austria: "[S]ome irresponsible credit lending by profit-oriented institutions has seen the sector called into question" (ibid.: 3).

2 One should note that one of the already mentioned respondents from PiP praised technology, but also thought that "technologies would not solve every problem" (Interview No. 8 2013). He had in mind geo-engineering – huge mirrors that would reflect solar radiation – and called it a sci-fi utopia.

3 My critique goes against the systemic (Marxist) perspective in which actors act the way they do because of the systemic pressure. I would agree to a certain extent with this perspective, but it does not mean that the actors lack agency completely, and more importantly, it does not divest them of responsibility for their deeds.

4 For example, in the Western Cape in South Africa, black people own less than 1% of all the Cape farms (Villette 2015).

Bibliography

Abrahamsen, Rita 2000: *Disciplining Democracy. Development Discourse and Good Governance in Africa*. London and New York: Zed Books.

Adams, W. M. 2009: *Green Development. Environment and sustainability in a developing world*. London and New York: Routledge.

Adelle, Camilla and Jordan, Andrew 2014: Policy Coherence for Development in the European Union: Do New Procedures Unblock or Simply Reproduce Old Disagreements? *Journal of European Integration* 36(4), 375–391, doi:10.1080/07036337.2013.845180.

Amsden, Alice, H. 1989: *Asia's Next Giant. South Korea and Late Industrialization*. New York and Oxford: Oxford University Press.

Andreotti, Vanessa de Oliveira 2011: *Actionable Postcolonial Theory in Education*. New York: Palgrave Macmillan.

Andreotti, Vanessa de Oliveira 2014: *The Political Economy of Global Citizenship Education* (1st edition). London and New York: Routledge.

Annan, Kofi 2003: Literacy is key to a future of freedom and hope for mankind, www.un.org/press/en/2003/sgsm8606.doc.htm.

Backes, Martina 2011: Das Wunder von Fern – Bildsprache in Produkten des Fairen Handels. *Von Trommlern und Helfern. Beiträge zu einer nicht-rassistischen entwicklungspolitischen Bildungs – und Projektarbeit*. Berlin: Berliner entiwcklungspolitischer Ratschlag e.V., 36–39.

Barthes, Roland 1972: *Mythologies*. New York: The Noonday Press.

Bateman, Milford 2010: *Why Doesn't Microfinance Work? The Destructive Rise of Local Neoliberalism*. London and New Jersey: Zed Books.

Beck, Ulrich 2003: Toward a New Critical Theory with a Cosmopolitan Intent. *Constellations* 10(4), 453–468, doi:10.1046/j.1351-0487.2003.00347.x.

Beňáková, Nora 2011: Ochota Slovákov pomáhať? Radšej sa ľutujú (Rozhovor Karola Sudora). sme.sk, www.sme.sk/c/6151200/nora-benakova-ochota-slovakov-pomahat-radsej-sa-lutuju.html.

Bendix, Daniel, Danielzik, Chandra-Milena, and Kiesel, Timo 2015: Education for sustainable inequality? A postcolonial analysis of materials for Development Education in Germany. *Critical Literacy: Theories and Practices* 9(2), 47–63.

Blaut, James 1993: *The Colonizer's Model of the World. Geographical Diffusionism and Eurocentric History*. New York and London: Guilford Press.

BMEIA 2012: Three-Year Programme on Austrian Development Policy 2013–2015. Federal Ministry for European and International Affairs, Directorate-General for Development Cooperation, www.entwicklung.at/fileadmin/user_upload/Dokumente/Publikationen/3_JP/Englisch/2013-2015_3-YP.pdf.

Bourdieu, Pierre 2002: Against the Policy of Depoliticization. *Studies in Political Economy* 69 (Autumn), 31–41.

Bowles, Samuel and Gintis, Herbert 1976: *Schooling in Capitalist America. Educational Reform and the Contradictions of Economic Life*. London and Henley: Routledge and Kegan Paul.

Bowles, Samuel and Gintis, Herbert 2002: Schooling in Capitalist America Revisited. *Sociology of Education* 75(1), 1–18.

Brigg, Morgan 2001: Empowering NGOs: The Microcredit Movement Through Foucault's Notion of Dispositif. *Alternatives: Global, Local, Political* 26(3), 233–258.

Brockington, Dan 2014: *Celebrity Advocacy and International Development*. London and New York: Routledge.

Burtscher, Robert 2013: Sauberes Wasser allein genügt nicht. *Weltnachrichten. Information der österreichischen Entwicklungszusammenarbeit* 1(2013), 3–4.

Carbone, Maurizio 2008: Mission Impossible: the European Union and Policy Coherence for Development. *Journal of European Integration* 30(3), 323–342, doi:10.1080/07036330802144992.

Carbone, Maurizio and Keijzer, Niels 2016: The European Union and policy coherence for development: reforms, results, resistance. *European Journal of Development Research* 28(1), 30–43.

CARE 2005: CARE: Analphabetismus ist weiblich. CARE, www.care.at/news/presseaus sendungen/care-analphabetismus-ist-weiblich/.

CARE 2006a: Friedens-Nobelpreis: CARE gratuliert Muhammed Yunuz. CARE, www.care.at/news/presseaussendungen/friedens-nobelpreis-care-gratuliert-muhammed-yunuz/.

CARE 2006b: Das Woman-CARE-Statement: Armut ist weiblich. CARE, www.care.at/news/news/das-woman-care-statement-armut-ist-weiblich/.

CARE 2012: Ein Dorf zieht an einem Strang. CARE, www.care.at/news/news/ein-dorf-zieht-an-einem-strang/.

CARE 2013a: Bankensektor ignoriert 2,7 Milliarden potenzielle KundInnen. CARE, www.care.at/news/presseaussendungen/bankensektor-ignoriert-ueber-2-milliarden-potenzielle-kundinnen/.

CARE 2013b: Tansania: Ex-Präsident Clinton besucht Mikrofinanzprojekt. CARE, www.care.at/news/news/tansania-ex-praesident-clinton-besucht-mikrofinanzprojekt/.

CARE 2014a: Syrische Flüchtlingsmädchen: Hochzeitskleid statt Schuluniform. CARE, www.care.at/news/presseaussendungen/syrische-fluechtlingsmaedchen-hochzeitskleid-statt-schuluniform/.

CARE 2014b: Nepal: Zugang zu Bildung für benachteiligte Mädchen. CARE, www.care.at/projekte/nepal-zugang-zu-bildung-fuer-benachteiligte-maedchen/.

CARE 2014c: Südkaukasus: Aufbau von Bildungszentren. CARE, www.care.at/projekte/suedkaukasus-aufbau-von-bildungszentren-fuer-fluechtlinge/.

Causa, Orsetta and Johansson, Åsa 2010: Intergenerational Social Mobility in OECD Countries. *OECD Journal: Economic Studies* 2010, 1–44.

CONCORD 2015a: Investing for Development? Examining the Impacts of the EU's Investment Regime on Food Security, the Right to Food and Lan Governance. European NGO confederation for relief and development, http://library.concordeurope.org/record/1633/files/DEEEP-REPORT-2016-007.pdf.

CONCORD 2015b: The EPA between the EU and West Africa: Who benefits? Coherence of EU Policies for Development. European NGO confederation for relief and development, http://library.concordeurope.org/record/1589/files/DEEEP-PAPER-2015-045.pdf.

Crewe, Emma and Harrison, Elizabeth 2002: *Whose Development? An Ethnography of Aid*. London and New York: Zed Books.

Crouch, Colin 2004: *Post-Democracy*. Cambridge, Malden: Polity.

Danielzik, Chandra-Milena, Kiesel, Timo, and Bendix, Daniel 2013: Bildung für nachhaltige Ungleichheit; Eine postkoloniale Anlyse von Materialien der entiwicklungspolitischen Bildungsarbeit in Deutschland. glokal, www.glokal.org/wp-content/

uploads/2018/03/Glokal-e-V_Bildung-fuer-nachhaltige-Ungleichheit_Barrierefrei-Illustrationen-26-03-2013.pdf.

Diamond, Jared M. 1997: *Guns, Germs, and Steel: The Fates of Human Societies*. New York: W. W. Norton & Company.

Dogra, Nandita 2014: *Representations of Global Poverty. Aid, Development and International NGOs*. London and New York: I.B. Tauris.

Doornbos, M. 2001: "Good Governance": The Rise and Decline of a Policy Metaphor? *Journal of Development Studies* 37(6), 93–108, doi:10.1080/713601084.

Doss, Cheryl, Kovarik, Chiara, Peterman, Amber, Quisumbing, Agnes R., and van den Bold, Mara 2013: Gender Inequalities in Ownership and Control of Land in Africa: Myths versus Reality. IFPRI Discussion Paper 01308. International Food Policy Research Institute, www.ifpri.org/sites/default/files/publications/ifpridp01308.pdf.

Easterly, William 2013: *The Tyranny of Experts: Economists, Dictators and the Forgotten Rights of the Poor*. New York: Basic Books.

Erkkilä, Tero and Piironen, Ossi 2009: Politics and Numbers. The Iron Cage of Governance Indices. *Ethics and Integrity in Public Administration. Concepts and Cases*. New York and London: M.E. Sharp, 125–145.

Erkkilä, Tero and Piironen, Ossi 2014: (De)Politicizing Good Governance: the World Bank Institute, the OECD and the Politics of Governance Indicators. *Innovation: The European Journal of Social Science Research* 27(4), 344–360, doi:10.1080/13511610.2013.850020.

Escobar, Arturo 1996: Construction Nature. Elements for a Post-Structuralist Political Ecology. *Futures* 28(4), 325–343.

European Commission 2007: EU Report on Policy Coherence for Development. COM (2007) 545, https://ec.europa.eu/europeaid/sites/devco/files/report-eu-policy-coherence-development-2007_en.pdf.

European Commission 2009: EU 2009 Report on Policy Coherence for Development. SEC (2009) 1137, https://ec.europa.eu/europeaid/sites/devco/files/report-eu-policy-coherence-development-2009_en.pdf.

Fairclough, Norman 2003: *Analysing Discourse. Textual Analysis for Social Research*. London and New York: Routledge.

Fairclough, Norman 2007: *Language and Globalization*. London and New York: Routledge.

Feldman, Shelley 2003: Paradoxes of Institutionalisation: The Depoliticisation of Bangladeshi NGOs. *Development in Practice* 13(1), 5–26, doi:10.1080/0961452022000037955.

Ferguson, James 1994: *The Anti-Politics Machine: "Development," Depoliticization, and Bureaucratic Power in Lesotho*. Minneapolis: University of Minnesota Press.

Ferguson, James 2006: *Global shadows: Africa in the neoliberal world order*. Durham and London: Duke University Press.

Fernando, Jude L. 2006b: Mcirocredit and empowerment of women: visibility without power. In: Fernando, Jude L. (ed.): *Microfinance. Perils and Prospects*. Oxon and New York: Routledge, 187–238.

Findl, Gertraud and Gruber, Reinhold 2014: Bildung als globale Herausforderung. *Weltnachrichten. Information der österreichischen Entwicklungszusammenarbeit* 3(2014), 3–4.

Flinders, Matthew and Buller, Jim 2006: Depoliticisation: Principles, Tactics and Tools. *British Politics* 1(3), 293–318, doi:10.1057/palgrave.bp.4200016.

Foucault, Michel 2002: The Political Technology of Individuals. *Power. Essential Works of Foucault 1954–1984* 3, London: Penguin Books, 403–417.

Freire, Paulo 1996: *Pedagogy of the oppressed*. London: Continuum.
Geosits, Christian and Gruber, Claudia 2014: Auf dem Weg zur Wissensgesellschaft. *Weltnachrichten. Information der österreichischen Entwicklungszusammenarbeit* 3, 2014, 20.
Gutenbrunner, Manuela 2014: Zehn Jahre ADA –ein Grund zum Feiern? *Weltnachrichten. Information der österreichischen Entwicklungszusammenarbeit* 2(2014), 3–4.
Gütermann, Christoph 2006: Nach wie vor marginalisiert. *Südwind. Magazin für internationale Politik, Kultur und Entwicklung*, Juni, 2006, www.suedwind-magazin.at/start.asp?ID=236426&rubrik=31&ausg=200606.
Gütermann, Christoph 2014: AW: comment, email communication, 1.8.2014.
Harris, John 2001: *Depoliticizing Development: The World Bank and Social Capital*. New Delhi: Leftword Books.
Hartmeyer, Helmuth 2012: Globales Lernen vernetzt Europa. *Weltnachrichten. Information der österreichischen Entwicklungszusammenarbeit* 4(2012), 14.
Hout, Wil 2010: Governance and Development: changing EU policies. *Third World Quarterly* 31(1), 1–12, doi:10.1080/01436590903557298.
Hout, Wil 2012: The Anti-Politics of Development: donor agencies and the political economy of governance. *Third World Quarterly* 33(3), 405–422, doi:10.1080/01436597.2012.657474.
Hout, Will and Robinson, Richard 2009: *Governance and the Depoliticization of Development*. Abington: Routledge.
Interview No. 3 2013: Interview with the respondent from the Pontis Foundation. 25.6.2013, personally in Bratislava.
Interview No. 4 2013: Interview with the respondent from the Pontis Foundation. 26.6.2013, personally in Bratislava.
Interview No. 5 2013: Interview with the respondent from the Pontis Foundation. 3.7.2013, personally in Bratislava.
Interview No. 7 2013: Interview with the respondent from the Pontis Foundation. 15.7.2013, personally in Bratislava.
Interview No. 8 2013: Interview with the respondent from PiP. 15.7.2013, personally in Bratislava.
Interview No. 9 2013: Interview with the respondent from PiP. 13.8.2013, personally in Bratislava.
Interview No. 10 2013: Interview with the respondent from PiP. 15.8.2013, personally in Bratislava.
Interview No. 11 2013: Interview with the respondent from PiP. 19.8.2013, personally in Bratislava.
Interview No. 12 2013: Interview with the respondent from SAIDC. 8.8.2013, personally in Bratislava.
Interview No. 13 2013: Interview with the respondent from SAIDC. 15.8.2013, personally in Bratislava.
Interview No. 14 2014: Interview with the respondent from SAIDC. 26.2.2014, personally in Bratislava.
Interview No. 15 2014: Interview with the respondent from SAIDC. 11.6.2014, personally in Bratislava.
Interview No. 16 2013: Interview with the respondent from Austroprojekt. 7.10.2013, personally in Vienna.
Interview No. 17 2013: Interview with the respondent from Austroprojekt. 6.10.2013, personally in Vienna.

Interview No. 20 2013: Interview with the respondent from ADA. 19.11.2013, personally in Vienna.
Interview No. 22 2013: Interview with the respondent from ADA. 20.11.2013, personally in Vienna.
Interview No. 23 2013: Interview with the respondent from ADA. 26.11.2013, personally in Vienna.
Interview No. 24 2014: Interview with the respondent from ADA. 11.2.2014, personally in Vienna.
Interview No. 25 2013: Interview with the respondent from CARE. 20.11.2013, personally in Vienna.
Interview No. 26 2013: Interview with the respondent from CARE. 26.11.2013, personally in Vienna.
Interview No. 27 2013: Interview with the respondent from CARE. 27.11.2013, over Skype.
Interview No. 28 2014: Interview with the respondent from CARE. 11.2.2014, personally in Vienna.
Jaeger, Hans-Martin 2007: "Global Civil Society" and the Political Depoliticization of Global Governance. *International Political Sociology* 1(3), 257–277, doi:10.1111/j.1749-5687.2007.00017.x.
Kamat, Sangeeta 2014: The New Development Architecture and the Post-Political in the Global South. *The Post-Political and Its Discontents. Spaces of Depoliticisation, Spectres of Radical Politics*. Edinburgh: Edinburgh University Press, 67–85.
Kapoor, Ilan 2012: *Celebrity Humanitarianism: The Ideology of Global Charity*. Routledge.
Karim, Lamia 2011: *Microfinance and its Discontents. Women in Debt in Bangladesh*. Minneapolis and London: University of Minnesota Press.
Kim, Linsu 1997: *Imitation to Innovation: The Dynamics of Korea's Technological Learning*. Boston: Harvard Business School Press.
Klavert, Henrike, Engel, Paul and Koeb, Eleonora 2011: Still a thorn in the side? The reform of the Common Agricultural Policy from the perspective of Policy Coherence for Development, Discussion Paper Np. 126. European Centre for Development Policy Management, http://ecdpm.org/wp-content/uploads/2013/10/DP-126-Reform-Common-Agricultural-Policy-Coherence-for-Development.pdf.
Landes, David S. 1999: *The Wealth and Poverty of Nations: Why Some Are So Rich and Some So Poor*. New York: W. W. Norton & Company.
Latour, Bruno 1993: *We Have Never Been Modern*. Cambridge: Harvard University Press.
Lazar, Sian 2004: Education for Credit: Development as Citizenship Project in Bolivia. *Critique of Anthropology* 24(3), 301–319, doi:10.1177/0308275X04045423.
Leeuwen, Theo van 2008: *Discourse and Practice. New Tools for Critical Discourse Analysis*. Oxford: Oxford University Press.
Li, Tania Murray 2007: *The Will to Improve. Governmentality, Development, and the Practice of Politics*. Durham: Duke University Press.
Löwenheim, Oded 2008: Examining the State: a Foucauldian perspective on international "governance indicators." *Third World Quarterly* 29(2), 255–274, doi:10.1080/01436590701806814.
Manji, Firoze 1998: Depoliticisation of Poverty. *Development and Rights*. Oxford: Oxfam Publishing, 12–33.
Marx, Karl 2012: *On the Jewish Question*. Aristeus Books.

Matthews, Alan 2008: The European Union's Common Agricultural Policy and Developing Countries: the Struggle for Coherence. *Journal of European Integration* 30(3), 381–399, doi:10.1080/07036330802141998.

Mawdsley, Emma 2012: *From Recipients to Donors. Emerging Powers and the Changing Development Landscape*. ZED Books.

MFEA 2013: Medium-Term Strategy for Development Cooperation of the Slovak Republic for 2014–2018. Ministry of Foreign and European Affairs of the Slovak Republic, https://issuu.com/slovakaid/docs/strednodoba_strategia_oda_sr_2014-2_83963017c1b288.

Mouffe, Chantal 2005: *On the Political*. London and New York: Routledge.

Murdoch, Jonathan 2000: The Microfinance Schism. *World Development*, 28(4), 617–629.

Nationalrat 2003: Federal Act on Development Cooperation (2002), including its Amendment (2003), www.oe-eb.at/en/dam/jcr:82518ac8-d1e8-4e22-a407-5569a159bb5d/Development-Cooperation-Act.pdf.

NDC-Austroprojekt and Orgut 2002: Plan of Operation for Ngorngoro District Development Programme. Phase 1. Ngorngoro District Council and Austroprojekt and Orgut Consortium.

Nelson, Richard R. and Pack, Howard 1999: The Asian Miracle and Modern Growth Theory. *The Economic Journal* 109(457), 416–436, doi:10.1111/1468-0297.00455.

Öppinger-Walchshofer, Brigitte 2013: Lebensquell Wasser. *Weltnachrichten. Information der österreichischen Entwicklungszusammenarbeit* 1(2013), 2.

Perez, Francisco 2014: Why are affected West African states so spectacularly ill-prepared to deal with Ebola. *Africa is a Country*, https://africasacountry.com/2014/09/why-are-affected-west-african-states-so-spectacularly-ill-prepared-to-deal-with-ebola/.

Pettit, Phillip 2004: Depoliticizing Democracy. *Ratio Juris* 17(1), 52–65.

Picciotto, Roberto 2005: The Evaluation of Policy Coherence for Development. *Evaluation* 11(3), 311–330.

Pike, Graham 2000: Global Education and National Identity: In Pursuit of Meaning. *Theory Into Practice* 39(2), 64–73, doi:10.1207/s15430421tip3902_2.

PiP 2009: Podpora podnikania vidieckych žien v západnej Keni (2008–2009). People in Peril, https://clovekvohrozeni.sk/podpora-podnikania-vidieckych-zien-v-zapadnej-keni-2008-2009/.

PiP 2011: Obnova ekosystému Mau forest cez aktívne zapojenie miestnych komunít. People in Peril, https://clovekvohrozeni.sk/obnova-ekosystemu-mau-forest-cez-aktivne-zapojenie-miestnych-komunit/.

PiP 2012a: Už ďalšie štyri školy majú výživnejšiu stravu. People in Peril, https://clovekvohrozeni.sk/uz-dalsie-styri-skoly-maju-vyzivnejsiu-stravu/.

PiP 2012b: Poľnohospodárstvo rozvíjame aj na východnom pobreží Kene. People in Peril, https://clovekvohrozeni.sk/polnohospodarstvo-rozvijame-aj-na-vychodnom-pobrezi-kene/.

PiP 2012c: Mladí farmári sa tešia na nový prístup k internetu. People in Peril, https://clovekvohrozeni.sk/mladi-farmari-sa-tesia-na-novy-pristup-k-internetu/.

Plan UK, CARE International UK and Barclays 2013: Banking on Change: Breaking the Barriers to Financial Inclusion, www.care.org/sites/default/files/documents/Banking_on_Change_Breaking_Barriers__April2013.pdf.

Pogge, Thomas 2002: *World Poverty and Human Rights. Cosmopolitan Responsibilities and Reforms*. Cambridge: Polity press.

Pomeranz, Kenneth 2000: *The Great Divergence: China, Europe, and the Making of the Modern World Economy*. Princeton and Oxford: Princeton University Press.

Pontis 2010a: more than 200 students came to lectures on kenya. Pontis Foundation, www.nadaciapontis.sk/article/more-than-200-students-came-to-lectures-on-kenya/276.

Pontis 2010b: slovak teachers taught their colleagues from kenya how to use information technologies. Pontis Foundation, www.nadaciapontis.sk/article/slovak-teachers-taught-their-colleagues-from-kenya-how-to-use-information-technologies/277?lang=en_US.

Profant, Tomáš 2018a: The Social Construction of Slovakia as a Donor and its Power Effects. *Europe–Asia Studies* 70(3), 365–387, doi:10.1080/09668136.2018.1453486.

Profant, Tomáš 2018b: The Slovak NGDO Pontis Foundation's depoliticizing development discourse. *Journal of Contemporary Central and Eastern Europe* 26(1), 69–85, d oi:10.1080/25739638.2017.1405900.

Qorban 2005: Afghanistan: Brot und Bildung – der Weg in die Zukunft. CARE, www.care.at/news/news/afghanistan-brot-und-bildung-der-weg-in-die-zukunft/.

Rabitsch, Waltraud 2013: Entwicklung neu (über)denken. *Weltnachrichten. Information der österreichischen Entwicklungszusammenarbeit* 4(2013), 3–4.

Rabitsch, Waltraud and Sötz, Elisabeth 2013: Nachhaltig zusammenarbeiten. *Weltnachrichten. Information der österreichischen Entwicklungszusammenarbeit* 4(2013), 10–11.

Rancière, Jacques 1995: *On the Shores of Politics*. London and New York: Verso.

Rancière, Jacques 1999: *Disagreement: Politics and Philosophy*. Minneapolis: University of Minnesota Press.

Rankin, Katharine N. 2001: Governing Development: Neoliberalism, Microcredit, and Rational Economic Woman. *Economy and Society* 30(1), 18–37.

Rist, Gilbert 2008: *The History of Development: From Western Origins to Global Faith*. London and New York: Zed Books.

Rodney, Walter 1981: *How Europe Underdeveloped Africa*. Washington D.C.: Howard University Press.

Rose, Nikolas 2004: *Powers of Freedom: Reframing Political Thought*. Cambridge: Cambridge University Press.

Rössler, Daniel 2014a: Financial Literacy für Entwicklung. *Weltnachrichten. Information der österreichischen Entwicklungszusammenarbeit* 1(2014), 22.

Rössler, Daniel 2014b: Lehrjahre statt Leerjahre. *Weltnachrichten. Information der österreichischen Entwicklungszusammenarbeit* 3(2014), 19.

Sachs, Wolfgang 1992a: Environment. In: Sachs, Wolfgang (ed.): *The Development Dictionary. A Guide to Knowledge as Power*. London and New Jersey: Zed Books, 26–37.

Sachs, Wolfgang 1992b: One World. In: Sachs, Wolfgang (ed.): *The Development Dictionary. A Guide to Knowledge as Power*. London and New Jersey: Zed Books, 102–115.

Schmitt, Carl 2007: *The Concept of the Political*. Chicago and London: Chicago University Press.

Shihata, Ibrahim F. I. 1986: Towards a Greater Depoliticization of Investment Disputes: The Roles of ICSID and MIGA. *ICSID Review* 1(1), 1–25, doi:10.1093/icsid-review/1.1.1.

Simmel, Georg 2009: Sociology. *Inquiries into the Construction of Social Forms* 1, Leiden and Boston: Brill.

Siles-Brügge, Gabriel 2014: EU trade and development policy beyond the ACP: subordinating developmental to commercial imperatives in the reform of GSP. *Contemporary Politics* 20(1), 49–62, doi:10.1080/13569775.2014.881604.

Spitzl, Karlheinz 2011: "Education" – Zauberwort, Universalschlüssel, Allheilmittel. In: Profanter, Annemarie (ed.): *Kulturen im Dialog II*. Frankfurt am Main: Peter Lang, 55–79.

Swanson, Jacinda 2008: Economic Common Sense and the Depoliticization of the Economic. *Political Research Quarterly* 61(1), 56–67, doi:10.1177/1065912907306469.

Swyngedouw, Erik 2011: Depoliticized Environments: The End of Nature, Climate Change and the Post-Political Condition. *Royal Institute of Philosophy Supplements* 69, 253–274, doi:10.1017/S1358246111000300.

Teivainen, Teivo (2002): *Enter Economism, Exit Politics: Experts, Economic Policy and the Political*. London: Zed Books.

Thiard-Laforet, Susanne 2013: Die reichen Gaben Demeters. Weltnachrichten. Information der österreichischen Entwicklungszusammenarbeit 4(2013), 12.

Tichý, Braňo 2015: Pomáhajme utečencom (aj) u nich doma. *Pravda.sk* 5.8.2015, http://nazory.pravda.sk/osa/clanok/362751-pomahajme-utecencom-aj-u-nich-doma/.

UNESCO 1996: 50 Years for Education, n.d., www.unesco.org/education/nfsunesco/brochure/E00.PDF.

Van Ausdal, Shawn 2001: Development and Discourse among the Maya of Southern Belize. *Development and Change* 32(3), 577–606.

Varul, Matthias Zick 2011: The Fear of the Fair Trade Consumer – An Informed Guess on a Form of Consumer Anxiety, Post-colonial Guilt and Anti-conquest, http://blogs.exeter.ac.uk/unfinishedbusiness/blog/2011/06/19/the-fear-of-the-fairtrade-consumer-%E2%80%93-an-informed-guess-on-a-form-of-consumer-anxiety-post-colonial-guilt-and-anti-conquest/.

Wade, Robert H. 1990: *Governing the Market: Economic Theory and the Role of Government in East Asian Industrialization*. Princeton, New Jersey: Princeton University Press.

Wagner-Hager, Andrea 2014: Nur wer Frauen stärkt, kann Armut bekämpfen. CARE, www.care.at/news/news/nur-wer-frauen-staerkt/.

Weber, Heloise 2002: Global governance and poverty reduction. The case of microcredit. In: Wilkinson, Rorden and Hughes, Steve (ed.): *Global Governance: Critical Perspectives*. London: Routledge, 132–151.

Weber, Heloise 2006: The global political economy of microfinance and poverty reduction: locating local "livelihoods" in political analysis. In: Fernando, Jude L. (ed.): *Microfinance. Perils and Prospects*. Oxon and New York: Routledge, 43–63.

Weber, Max 2005: *The Protestant Ethic and the Spirit of Capitalism*. London and New York: Routledge.

White, Sarah 1996: Depoliticising development: the uses and abuses of participation. *Development in Practice* 6(1), 6–15.

White, Sarah 2006: The "Gender Lens": A Racial Blinder? *Progress in Development Studies* 6(1), 55–67, doi:10.1191/1464993406ps127oa.

Wilke, Sabine 2014: Kenia: Ismails Traum. CARE, www.care.at/news/news/kenia-ismails-traum/.

Williams, Glyn 2004: Evaluating Participatory Development: Tyranny, Power and (Re)Politicisation. *Third World Quarterly* 25(3), 557–578, doi:10.1080/014365904200 0191438.

Wilson, Japhy and Swyngedouw, Erik (eds.) 2014a: *The Post-Political and Its Discontents. Spaces of Depoliticisation, Spectres of Radical Politics*. Edinburgh: Edinburgh University Press.

Wilson, Japhy and Swyngedouw, Erik 2014b: Seeds of Dystopia: Post-Politics and the Return of the Political. *The Post-Political and Its Discontents. Spaces of Depoliticisation, Spectres of Radical Politics*. Edinburgh: Edinburgh University Press, 1–22.

Wilson, Kalpana 2012: *Race, Racism and Development: Interrogating History, Discourse and Practice*. London and New York: Zed Books.

World Education Forum 2000: Education for All: Learning lies out of reach for 125m of the world's poorest children. *Guardian*. 31.1.2000, www.theguardian.com/education/specialreports/readtheworld/story/0,,130490,00.html.

Ziai, Aram 2007: *Globale Strukturpolitik? Die Nord-Süd-Politik der BRD und das Dispositiv der Entwicklung im Zeitalter von neoliberaler Globalisierung und neuer Weltordnung*. Münster: Westfälisches Dampfboot.

Žižek, Slavoj 1999: *The Ticklish Subject: The Absent Center of Political Ontology*. London and New York: Verso.

Žižek, Slavoj 2008: *Violence. Six sideways reflections*. New York: Picador.

Zorád, Lukáš 2011a: Sucho na rovníku, alebo prepíšeme učebnice geografie?!? *blog.sme.sk*, http://zorad.blog.sme.sk/c/260659/Sucho-na-rovniku-alebo-prepiseme-ucebnice-geografie.html.

Zorád, Lukáš 2011b: Zo života na rovníku: Ako prežiť sucho? *blog.sme.sk*, http://zorad.blog.sme.sk/c/262683/Zo-zivota-na-rovniku-Ako-prezit-sucho.html.

Zorád, Lukáš 2011c: Južný Sudán: dva týždne v bubline. *blog.sme.sk*, http://zorad.blog.sme.sk/c/282300/Juzny-Sudan-dva-tyzdne-v-bubline.html.

Zorád, Lukáš 2011d: Zo života na rovníku: Potravinovo sebestační? *blog.sme.sk*, http://zorad.blog.sme.sk/c/271950/Zo-zivota-na-rovniku-Potravinovo-sebestacni.html.

Zorád, Lukáš 2012: TEDx@Nairobi 2012: prezentácia modernej „Afriky." *blog.sme.sk*, http://zorad.blog.sme.sk/c/298467/TEDxNairobi-2012-prezentacia-modernej-Afriky.html.

Zorád, Lukáš 2013: Ako učíme „lenivých černochov" chytať ryby. *blog.sme.sk*, http://zorad.blog.sme.sk/c/319119/Ako-ucime-lenivych-cernochov-chytat-ryby.html.

5 (De)Legitimization of development

One of the crucial effects of any discourse is a legitimization of social practice. One could in this sense speak of a legitimizing function that "the discourse under study must carry out in a field of non-discursive practices" (Foucault 2002b: 75). The aim of this chapter is to analyze the legitimizing effects of the development discourse.

The most substantial form of legitimization in this case is achieved through the positive connotation of the term development itself. Despite the positive connotation, very different, even contradictory, elements can be subsumed under this term. "It is an empty word that can be filled by any use to conceal any hidden intention, a Trojan horse of a word" (Frank 1997: 263). Its contours are thus "about as precise as those of an amoeba. It is now a mere algorithm whose significance depends on the context in which it is employed" (Esteva 1992: 10).

The discussion about the meaning of development has been a crucial part of the wider postdevelopment debate. On the one hand, there was this amoeba definition of an imprecise word or even an empty word, and, on the other, Crush claims that, by wanting to dismantle the development mental structure and wanting to write an obituary to development, Sachs at the same time "implicitly suggests that it is possible to arrive at an unequivocal definition" (Crush 1999: 3; see also Ziai 2004a).

According to the critics of the homogenization of development discourse, "it is convenient to talk of there being several coexistent discourses of development" (Cooper and Packard 1997: 10; see also Hobart 1993: 12; Unnithan and Srivastava 1997).

> Indeed, if we are to take a postmodern approach to development and reveal it as discourse we have to show how it involves multiple and ever changing realities and narratives, for to construct it as bounded and internally homogeneous is theoretically contradictory.
>
> (Gardner and Lewis 2000: 18)

It is true that, when postdevelopment speaks about "an essence [of development]" (Esteva 1992: 17), a development paradigm (Rahnema 1997: xiv; Ziai 2004b), or about the development discourse (Escobar 1995), it may ignore many rhetorical changes. However, an analysis of a discourse focuses on a deeper unity within the discourse. Despite an existence of differing statements within one discursive formation, these statements are united by their rules of formation, and therefore one can find a certain unity between them (Foucault 2002b).

Wherein lies this unity? Regarding the question of the meaning of development, this unity has been traced in the positive connotation of the term. "Though development has no content, it does possess one function: it allows any intervention to be sanctified in the name of a higher goal. Therefore, even enemies feel united under the same banner" (Sachs 1992: 4). "The word always implies a favorable change … from the inferior to the superior, from worse to better" (Esteva, 1992: 10).

The term can thus be defined by its two main characteristics – its unclear meaning and its positive connotation – as an "empty plus" (Ziai 2009: 197), "a signifier without a signified" (Laclau 2007: 36) that legitimizes anything it denotes.

The positive connotation and the unclear meaning of the term results in definitions of development such as those analyzed by Gilbert Rist. He quotes the Report of the South Commission presided by Julius Nyerere, which defines development as "a process which enables human beings to realize their potential, build self confidence, and lead lives of dignity and fulfilment … " (in Rist 2008: 8). A development project, then, by definition becomes a project that leads to the realization of the potential of human beings, builds self-confidence, etc. The problem with most of such "pseudo-definitions" is "that they are based upon the way in which one person (or set of persons) pictures the ideal conditions of social existence" (ibid.:10). Rist makes an analogy with the definition of Christianity, which could be defined from the inside as "a religion based upon love of one's neighbor which seeks to establish peace and justice among men" (ibid.: 19). A definition of religion from the outside perceives it as a set of indisputable truths which are to be followed rather than as a true exercise of love towards one's neighbor. The same can be said about development. A definition from the inside would be different to a definition from the outside. One wishes development to be something which it need not be. Nonetheless, this does not change the way the term development is understood or used. It always implies a favorable change, and it always adds a positive connotation to any noun to which it is added as an adjective. This is its discursive effect in the field of non-discursive practices.

I will, however, not go in the direction proposed by Rist and his own definition of development.[1] Rather than actually attempting to define any activity denoted as development, one may prefer to remain at the level of discourse and define it as an "empty plus" (Ziai 2009: 197). This does not mean that development is an empty signifier waiting to be filled within a hegemonic struggle, even if it is "a signifier without a signified" (Laclau 2007: 36). This struggle has, according to Ziai, long been lost: "[I]n the light of the scale of knowledge production of the development business, any subversive attempt to redefine 'development' is most likely to be a losing battle" (Ziai 2007: 71). Development is thus, from this perspective, one of those privileged discursive points, the nodal points, which fix the current hegemonic formation in such an almost absolute closure.

The closure may in fact be stronger where development is to be applied in practice. As already Escobar (1995: 51) noted, the Afro-Colombian farmers "tend to become ardent advocates of development." One could find a similar acceptance of the positive notion of development in the countries that can still strive for development. The empty plus that turns everything it touches into an element worth supporting cements the division of Europe between East and West as the embodiment of (demi-)Orientalism. At the same time, the East–West slope in the opposite direction reinforces the positive connotation of the term "development" as it becomes evident in the development discourse the what is developed is better. The tautology thus goes both ways and, as the hierarchy between the Self and Other supports whatever is denoted as development, the empty plus supports the hierarchy as it is filled with the Western norm. The East thus becomes locked in its belief in development, yet, as this chapter shows, incoherencies exist.

The aim of this chapter is to analyze the closure of the discursive formation and, at the same time, demonstrate the "subversive attempts to redefine 'development' " (ibid.), while comparing the discourses of old and new donors. Whereas the hegemonic notion is to be found mainly in the analyzed texts, various subversive attempts to redefine the term come from the respondents. The analyzed term is often understood in its "usual meaning" (Interview No. 3 2013) without being given any definition, or as a general progress, which is sometimes specified in particular ways, including by pointing to economic growth. Development cooperation is legitimized also through other forms of legitimation. The most common "subversion" from the respondents' perspective is to be found in the meaning that has been dominant for more than a decade – that of a partnership. However, a whole critical genre is emerging that casts doubt on the positive connotation of the term development. Critical, but also not so critical, perspectives have been articulated in relation to sustainable development that complement the analysis of the (de)legitimization of development. In the final section, the respondents explain why they use the term the way they do and contribute to the critical reflection of development.

There is no difference between the Austrian and Slovak analyzed texts regarding the meaning of development and other forms of legitimization; however, the Austrian respondents offered a more critical perspective on the use of the term development than the Slovaks. Still, a few Slovaks also engaged in a significant criticism of it, and the difference was thus one of degree and not of substance. The research results in many ways confirm extant research that analyzes the meaning of development and how development workers use the term (Heron 2007).

The usual understanding of development and development as progress

The PR texts in the corpus in general did not problematize the term development or its derivatives. The term was mainly treated as self-evident without a definition or explanation of it and with a clear positive connotation. For example, the title of one of the texts claimed that "[w]e are developing agriculture on the East coast of Kenya," or in the PR texts from SAIDC, the term was mostly used together with other words in phrases such as "development project," "development aid," "development cooperation," "developing countries," "development day," "development organizations," "countryside development," or "development needs." The same applies to the PR texts from ADA and similar terms are used in the Austrian Three-Year Program. It is expected that the term is self-evident to the reader. On the PiP website, it is not questioned in any way when it is used in the title "Development Cooperation," which is the title of a whole section. It is also used without any questioning in several articles (PiP 2009, 2010, 2011, 2012a, 2012b, 2012c). One can thus infer that no doubt was cast on the meaning of the term in most of the analyzed texts and that it usually had the effect of an empty plus. The connotation of the term seems to be positive and there is no discussion about the meaning of the term.

The most abstract positive representation of development as an empty plus was present in the interviews when it was understood according to its "usual understanding" (Interview No. 3 2013) as a respondent from the Slovak Pontis Foundation put it. This was followed by a circular argument defining development as "a socio-economic development" (ibid., see also Interview No. 12 for a similar circular reasoning).[2] Also in regard to this matter, one respondent from the Slovak Agency for International Development Cooperation stated that her position in the Agency is not about "philosophizing, but about working performance" (Interview No. 12 2013, see Interview No. 13 2013 for a similar response).

The "usual understanding" of the term could be found also in answers that invoked official definitions. According to one respondent (from ADA), "[t]he term is defined by the Austrian Cooperation Act" (Interview No. 24 2014), and according to another, "we [i.e., ADA] made all this public" (Interview No. 21 2013). The first respondent went on to talk about "a catalog, a list of objectives," that one can find in the act, and this list includes "eradication of poverty […] gender equality, responsible treatment of resources […] good governance, [and] human rights" (Interview No. 24 2014). Another respondent offered a similar set, but also responded in a tautological manner: in Georgia or Kosovo, "[development] means support of social development, how this can be done through different measures" (Interview No. 23 2013).

The following responses from both countries emphasized the positive meaning of development. In the most abstract sense of an empty plus, development is "a movement to […] a qualitatively better state" (Interview No. 4 2013), or it is "an advancement forward, or a progress in something" (Interview No. 5 2013; see also Interview No. 10 2013). A respondent from SAIDC was most explicit in this regard: "I do not see any negative connotation in [the term development], because for me the word has a positive touch" (Interview No. 24 2014; see also Interview No. 27 2013).

Development thus was understood, on the one hand, as a self-evident term without the need for a definition, which occasionally resulted in tautologies or the invocation of official definitions, and, on the other hand, the term was understood as having a positive touch – a movement to a qualitatively better state without a negative connotation. Both these meanings of development legitimize the actions undertaken in the name of development and reinforce the dominant notion of the term.

However, the positive touch was also specified in less abstract terms. The least specific element of development as a movement to a qualitatively better state was, in the words of a respondent from Austroprojekt, related to "a change in social standard of a certain population" (Interview No. 16 2013). In a similar manner, according to one SAIDC employee, development meant "the improvement of the living conditions of the people [in developing countries]" (Interview No. 13 2013; see also Interview No. 15 2013).

This still rather general perspective was complemented with more particular issues that are often related to MDGs and their main goal – poverty reduction. A respondent from ADA understood development in general as "reducing poverty because we all support MDGs" (Interview No. 21 2013; see also Interview No. 15 2014). A similar pattern was offered by a respondent from Austroprojekt: it means also "economic enhancement [...] social infrastructure like hospitals, schooling [...]" (Interview No. 16 2013). Simply put, "it's very vast" (ibid.).

Indeed, development can contain numerous meanings and thereby be ideologically productive. By containing all those meanings it effectively negates any substantial criticism as whatever criticism there is can be absorbed into the very meaning of development. In this sense, development cannot be rejected. Every criticism of it can be turned into a solvable problem, and such a problem-solving approach (Cox 1981) assures further acceptance of development. This particular feature makes sense in both North and South, as well as East and West, and the term effaces any controversies that the practice of development may cause between donors and recipients, as well as between different donors.

The term can even mean one of the most fundamental human values – freedom. One respondent from Slovak NGDO PiP followed Amartya Sen by claiming that development means the capacity to "fulfill one's own vision of development [...] it is a freedom to decide what one perceives as an improvement of oneself, one's family, one's property" (Interview No. 9 2013).

The official definitions in the Austrian and Slovak development cooperation acts (NRSR 2007; Nationalrat 2003) offered two meanings – a positive change (e.g., "sustainable improvement," NRSR 2007) and then an array of more practical meanings similar to the ones already mentioned.

An important element of development is the already mentioned economic enhancement or economic growth. The theory of human development (Haq 1995; Sen 1999) was supposed to replace the focus on growth with a focus on the people themselves, especially human capabilities and factors that prevent humans from achieving their full potential. The theory of human development was an important correction of the unfettered belief in economic growth and diverted the attention of development scholars to issues other than growth and modernization. One of the results of this new theory was the adoption of the Human Development Index by the UN, which ranked countries according to, not only economic growth, but also longevity and school attendance. The analyzed texts as well as interviews follow this discursive change.

Austroprojekt's Plan of Operation sets "the overriding goal" to be "poverty alleviation" (NDC-Austroprojekt and Orgut 2002: 6); however, the section entitled "Tanzania's Overall Development Policies" (ibid.) pushes the meaning towards the economic dimension of GDP growth, as here the "improvement in recent years" means, among other things, that "the average annual GDP growth rate has stabilised at a relatively high level (5.6% in 2001)" (ibid.).

Several respondents implicitly or explicitly defined development as economic growth. A respondent from PiP, in relation to sustainable development, spoke of a growth "that will be maybe slower, but [...] will be self-financed [...] and enable the future generation to continue with the trend" (Interview No. 9 2013). Similarly, as soon as one respondent from Pontis started to talk about economic issues during the respective interview, he stopped using the term development and replaced it with "growth," eventually claiming that what China and Korea achieved during the last 50 years "certainly is [development]" (Interview No. 7 2013).

The growth was not understood only as a goal in itself, but also as a means to reach a more substantial aim, or was somehow related to several different aims in some cases. One can infer from the Austrian Federal Act on Development Cooperation, amended in 2003, that development means, among other things, "sustainable economic activity and economic growth combined with structural institutional and social change" (Nationalrat 2003). According to a respondent from Pontis, development means "raising the economic indicators and the subsequent improvement of the standard of living" (Interview No. 15 2014). According to a respondent from PiP, Kenya is number one "in the economic development sense and the inhabitants' standard of living" (Interview No. 11 2013). For another respondent from the same organization, "economic growth certainly is important, because jobs are being created" (Interview No. 8 2013).

In sum, development as progress was in general perceived as a higher quality of living, and, in more particular terms, as poverty reduction and improvements in healthcare, schooling, human rights, gender equality, freedom, etc. Economic growth is still an important element, but to a noticeable extent it is important as a means to a better life.

Development was thus understood, not only in strictly abstract terms, but also in more particular ways. These reflect the dominant strand in the development discourse and contribute to the legitimization of development cooperation. Other forms of legitimization of development are analyzed in the next section.

Other constructions of legitimation in the analyzed texts

The analysis of discursive constructions of legitimation in the examined texts again did not bring any noteworthy difference between the Austrian and the Slovak NGDOs and state actors. Every text had its own specific forms of legitimations, but all the texts included many of the legitimations found in the whole corpus. In this sense the texts served the main aim of the development discourse – to legitimize development cooperation. Just as the word development as an empty plus legitimizes these interventions, so do the PR articles, plans, reports, and national strategies.

One of the more general forms of legitimation was moral tales in which protagonists are "rewarded for engaging in legitimate social practices" (Leeuwen 2008: 117). One such tale about the possibility of achieving progress was included in an article from Pontis. The gist of the story is in sentences 20–22:

> Before the Slovaks came to Kenya, teachers at Rukanga did not know how to work with [PowerPoint], however after only three days of the training, they were able to create their own presentation of a very good quality [...]. On Wednesday they saw PowerPoint for the first time and already on Saturday they had a presentation about the school ready for the parents that lasted almost six hours.
>
> (Pontis 2010)

The problem in Kenya is, according to the text, the lack of ICT. The narrative of the development cooperation thus takes the usual path. The knowledgeable Self comes to help the Other, who lacks knowledge. After the training – i.e., the engagement in legitimate social practices – the knowledge is transferred and the teachers are now developed, as they are capable of having a presentation.

But, the story follows the development discourse even more closely. The theoretical insight brought about by Bhabha is present here as well. The reformed Other becomes a "subject of a difference that is almost the same, but not quite" (Bhabha 2004: 122). The difference is minimized to show success, yet maintained to keep the raison d'être of the existence of the whole apparatus. There is always something to improve. "[The visit of Kenyan teachers to Slovakia] should take place in November of this year, and while in Slovakia, the teachers from Kenya will further improve their PC skills" (Pontis 2010). The project can continue. The institutional interests of the Pontis Foundation are thus secured. Similar moral tales were based on the following legitimate social practices: financial training, aid to vulnerable members of the same community, and the creation of saving groups. The reward for the legitimate actions was a subsequent success in microfinance (PiP 2012a; CARE 2012).

The reformed Other in the Global South that is almost the same but not quite is reflected in the new donor, who is almost the same or, more specifically, not quite the same yet. However, unlike the recipient, the new donor gains a specificity of its own that now complements the Self. The hierarchy is minimized as the new donor is accorded formal equality, not only in the capacity to learn (or develop), but also in the capacity to engage in development, the only difference being that the new donor's field of engagement is very specific.

However, the specificity of that field is where the equality is disrupted. The new donor is good at transition, i.e., at a particular type of development from an authoritarian to a democratic regime. The question is, why not accord this knowledge to traditional donors, i.e., old democracies? They were also originally authoritarian regimes (monarchies) and only later became democracies. The difference is the period since this transition. Some of the new donors were authoritarian until 1989 and therefore their knowledge of authoritarianism and transitioning from it should still be fresh (unlike that of old donors, including Portugal, which ceased being authoritarian in 1974). This fresh experience puts CEE donors closer to the countries of the Eastern Partnership and here they can claim their expertise related to their specific position – the closeness in terms of development. The development ladder keeps its importance in this specificity. The new donors' recent development (democratic transition), as well as their not only geographical, but also political, closeness to "less developed" countries in the Eastern Partnership, builds on the basic assumption that the new donor is still the Other of the old donor Self in terms of development. But this Other is very much reformed – so reformed that it even became a donor. Still, it is almost the same, but not quite.

The new donor can engage in the traditional fields of aid such as education or microfinance, but in the self-Orientalizing move, the dominant field of action promoted by the state is the sharing of the transition experience. There is still a way to go before the donor can engage in the equal endeavor of aid or cooperation in the traditional field and will not base its complementarity to old donors on development discourse. The hybrid identity of the new donor on the postcolonial crossroads embodies the complexities of the global development apparatus with its multiple hierarchies (see also Profant 2018).

There are further legitimations in development discourse. A moral tale can be extended with a prediction that legitimizes a social action on the basis of a positive expectation. Thus, within the framework of microfinance, "small saving groups will go on even when a drought comes again [...]. There will always be small trade [...]. We know how to overcome poverty in the future" (CARE 2012; see also SAMRS 2013). In this case, the current actions within development cooperation are legitimized with a positive expectation of the future.

Behind the engagement abroad were not just moral tales, but also a helping imperative or the so-called "global obligation" behind this engagement (Heron 2007: 41). According to Heron, the obligation is based on the North–South civilizational distinction and the binaries of comfort and security vs. disorder, diseases, etc. In research of the white middle-class women engaged in development cooperation, these women generally respond to the media portrayals of global problems by feeling that "it is up to them to set right the wrongs of the world" (ibid.: 37). Such a perspective can be found in the analyzed texts, e.g., in legitimizations based on what is "our" concern.

For example, since the way out of poverty is difficult, "it is our priority concern to actively engage in LICs" (BMEIA 2012: 11), or we simply "want to make the best contribution we can" (ibid.: 13). In these (and several other) cases, there is a connection to a local or world problem that "we" want to, should, or must solve, and this willingness on "our" side seems sufficient to legitimize the engagement. There is thus a colonial continuity in the European subjectivity with the obligation of the civilizing mission.

Sometimes, "our concern" need not even be mentioned, as the situation in the Global South can be of such a problematic nature that a reaction to it is an obvious thing to do, and therefore the decision to help does not have to be mentioned. For example, when a text says, "[a]round 1.5 billion people [...] are affected by the results of the fragility" (BMEIA 2012: 11), there is no follow-up in the text saying that we should do something. The number of people affected is so huge that it is simply clear that this requires "our" action or that this is "our concern."

These kinds of negative representations of "them" were an important part of the PR articles. Apart from the negative representations, there were also positive representations of "us." Both of these types of representations were already mentioned in Chapter 3. "Their" negative representations include, for example, a "persisting significant poverty level" (MFEA 2013: 5) and a "bad" harvest (CARE 2012). These problems constitute "challenges" (MFEA 2013: 5), and "we" respond to such challenges, as "we" are, e.g., "innovative" (Pontis 2010), or "we" introduce "new agricultural methods" (PiP 2012a). The problems of the Global South can be solved with help from the positively connoted Global North.

The positive representation of "us" that legitimized the engagement in the projects was also achieved through analogies either with existing projects in Slovakia (Pontis 2010) or with similar projects in the countries of the Global South (CARE 2012). Thus, for example, the project "designed for the African continent [...] is based on experiences of a Slovak educational project – Innovative Teacher... " (Pontis 2010). The alleged success of previous projects legitimizes the engagement in new projects.

Further legitimation was achieved through the authority of experts and role models, a position assigned to "us" rather than "them." Development projects are legitimized on the basis of being run by people with legitimate knowledge. For example, the Ngorongoro Development Programme is supposed to be "assisted by technical advisors" (NDC-Austroprojekt and Orgut 2002: 4).

The authority of the local population and of partnerships is mentioned in Chapter 3. In connection with this, the projects are legitimized as their content is based on the acceptance of the project by the local population or is (co-)decided upon by "our" partners.

There were also quite a few instances of impersonal authority that legitimizes development cooperation on the basis of laws, rules, and regulations (Leeuwen 2008: 108). The European Consensus from 2006, and the resultant EU Code of Conduct on Division of Labour of 2007, "provide major action guidelines"

(BMEIA 2012: 11) for the promotion of human rights and democracy, which is legitimized also by the mentioning of the Universal Declaration of Human Rights. Furthermore, the Monterrey commitments and an EU binding phased plan legitimize the increase of ODA "despite the economic and financial crises" (ibid.). Also, MDGs "make up the binding global framework" and "we are committed to [them]" (ibid.).

The texts included scientific and experiential rationalizations explaining phenomena with the use of scientific evidence and common sense knowledge. In them, one can, for example, read that "[g]irls who go to school are three times better informed about how to protect themselves from AIDS than illiterate girls" (CARE 2006) or that

> [m]any HIV positive teachers cannot teach anymore, because they are sick and weak. These educational deficiencies lead again to a vicious circle: a person who is poorly educated knows little about AIDS and infects him- or herself more easily with the deadly virus.
>
> (Ibid.)

These rationalizations leigitimize the ensuing action by CARE: "CARE works against this vicious circle with a project for orphans ... " (ibid.), thereby completing the legitimizing pattern.

The analyzed texts include quite a few legitimations based on instrumental rationalizations. These stress the outcomes or the goals of actions, as it is their usefulness that counts.

One particular instrumental rationalization shows how the omission of the action's agent can have legitimizing effects. In the Slovak Mid-Term Strategy, one can read that "[t]he abovementioned challenges mean for development cooperation the need to seek effective solutions within the global partnership ..." (MFEA 2013: 5). The action of seeking effective solutions is here without an agent. According to Leeuwen, "the greater the power of a particular role in a social practice, the more often the agents who fulfill that role will be presented as intentional, as people who can decide to act on the world and succeed in this" (Leeuwen 2008: 114). Here, the effect of omitting the agent is precisely the opposite. Instead of representing the actor behind the development cooperation as intentional, it represents development cooperation as a means to an end and thereby naturalizes this response to all the challenges. The lack of agency makes the proposed response (development cooperation) look obvious, normal, or natural.

Finally, all the texts contained generalizations which put together social actions at a lower level into one general action. The legitimization is based on the possibility that the more specific micro-actions that make up the general action can consist of problematic elements covered by the generalized action. However, this simply need not be the case, and the analysis here remains at the rhetorical level.

One example of such a generalization is in a text from PiP (2012a), in which "we" are developing agriculture, food security, and economic self-reliance in cooperation with the local people, "we" set up the ponds and forest tree nurseries, "we" train "them," and "we" focus on the elementary and high schools. All of these social actions could be divided into smaller micro-actions, and this happens with some of these more general actions when "we" are showing "them" that by drying and conserving fruits "they" will be able to enrich "their" diet, and by selling them "they" will increase "their" income. This represents the food security, economic self-reliance, new agricultural methods, and alternative ways of making a living. Yet, it is unclear whether these practices will actually contribute to reaching the intended goals (e.g., food security).

Also, the cooperation between "us" and "them" is represented just as a cooperation, thereby implying a smooth process. The reader does not know what exactly is meant by the term "cooperation," which, in general, is positively connoted. What may happen is that both actors, "us" and "them," will be planting trees in *conflict* and *cooperation* over micro issues. The potential conflict within cooperation, that is by no means unusual, is hidden here, and the exclusively positive relationship between "us" and "them" legitimizes "our" engagement with "them" in the eyes of the reader.

The analysis of this last type of legitimation shows well one of the results of this section. PR articles serve PR needs to legitimize whatever their authors do. In this case, it is development. In this sense, my results regarding the analysis of legitimation are not surprising. Yet, they are important. They show that there is a whole apparatus trying to legitimize actions that, according to various scholars, might be problematic. Through the legitimizing discursive practices, the analyzed texts (PR articles, official strategies, the Plan of Operation, and a report on microfinance) achieve the crucial effect of the development discourse – the legitimization of development – despite its potentially destructive nature.

The legitimations (apart from the sectoral focus of the national development policies) were similar in all the Slovak and Austrian texts. The discourses of the new and the old donors are thus, in this regard, very much the same. The next section shows their critical perspectives on development.

The critical perspective: development as partnership, "real" development, Westernization, and sustainable development

The development apparatus is an ever evolving body of institutions and discourses. Self-criticism of the apparatus is an important element of this evolution. New approaches to development aid or cooperation emerge after old ones are criticized and abandoned as not working. This cycle is repeated continually. Within the cycle, first, a problem is identified that causes underdevelopment (see Chapter 3), and after that a solution to this problem can be suggested and implemented. This means that development in the form of projects follows the identification of a particular problem. Despite occasional successes, the projects never succeed to such an extent as to actually achieve development. A new problem within the implementation has to be identified. It is something new, something different from what the whole apparatus has been working on. Eventually, this hitherto neglected problem is dealt with in the same way. This way the cycle is repeated over and over, with problems and their proposed solutions being repeated, reconfigured, and reimplemented (Ziai 2016: 43–44). Most recently, the problem seems to be the lack of a comprehensive approach to development and of measurable goals that can achieve development.

Partnership as an approach is one such innovation dealing with the problem of equality, accountability, and the failures of previous approaches. Chapter 3 discusses this approach at length. In the next section, I will show that the idea of partnership is prominent in the understanding of development and that it may have legitimizing as well as delegitimizing effects on development cooperation. After that, I analyze the critical perspective on "real" development and on development understood as Westernization. The analysis focuses also on sustainable development.

In the understanding of development as partnership, "their" agency dominated the relationship; however, there were also cases that foregrounded the active Self as in "we, in some way, build their capacity in order for them to be able to use their potential" (Interview No. 9 2013; see also Interview No. 11 2013; Interview No. 21 2013). In this and a few other cases, "we" helped, motivated, built "their" capacity, and provided solutions and support, and "they" helped themselves or used "their" potential. "Their" agency was thus subordinated to "ours."

The partnership approach was, on the one hand, part of the meaning of development that did not contain any questioning of the term and, on the other hand, it was part of a critical approach to development as well.

Within the context of the former, development was represented as the likely meaning of the term for the partner. In one case, development was represented by a respondent from PiP as know-how; however, the know-how should not be "something that we think is developing them," but it "should be useful for them [...] according to themselves, not according to us" (Interview No. 10 2013; see also Interview No. 26 2013).

Most of the definitions that gave importance to the partner belonged to the critical perspective on development. The discourse of partnership enabled them to perceive themselves as critical actors who do not succumb to Orientalism in development discourse. Thus, according to a respondent from Austroprojekt, development as a change in social standards also meant that "the population itself has a say in what is being developed, what the priorities are, which was always very difficult to implement mainly because the donors already had their own ideas" (Interview No. 16 2013).

A respondent from PiP even criticized development for spreading the liberal or Christian ideology (Interview No. 10 2013) and a respondent from CARE put the term "developing countries" into quotation marks during the interview and explained it by saying:

> because I am aware [of the] discourse [...] that is coming from our Western side, from the North [to] the South. We never ask them if they would call themselves developing countries, or it might imply that we think we know it

> better and, you know, it's [...] this connotation that, I think, makes me put it like this.
>
> (Interview No. 25 2013; see also Interview No. 26 2013; Interview No. 28 2014)

A respondent from Pontis even tries not to use the term development

> because for our partners it is a very sensitive issue, since Tunisia is going through changes that the Tunisians themselves do not want to perceive as something that is concerned with the term development in its true sense, as [they see development as pertaining to] some Third World country.
>
> (Interview No. 5 2013)

The term development was thus criticized as part of an Orientalist discourse. For a few respondents, the non-Orientalist meaning of development as partnership was the unquestioned meaning of development, but for others this was a new meaning and it enabled them to distance themselves from the problematic discourse reminiscent of the colonial era and its discursive practices.

The criticism of development went beyond the embracing of partnership. On the one hand, there was a general unspecified critique of development and a distinction between the "reality" and "ideal development," and on the other, there was a more specific criticism of Westernization. This critique included the problem of hierarchization mentioned in the previous section and in Chapter 3, but it also problematized other elements of the classical development paradigm (Ziai 2004b) – the linear conception of development as well as environmental issues and the problem of economic growth.

Several Austrian respondents offered a rather unspecified criticism of development. As one respondent from CARE put it, "quite honestly [...] we are all kind of critical of development" (Interview No. 27 2013). According to a respondent from ADA, "if there were an open debate [in ADA], people would be critical of the traditional understanding of the word development" (Interview No. 20 2013; see also Interview No. 22 2013; Interview No. 26 2013).

This general criticism was complemented with a more specific distinction between "ideal development" and "reality." According to a respondent from Austroprojekt, this reality of development "is still development [...] development is a change," but "negative change is not a development" (Interview No. 16 2013). Despite the contradiction caused by the confusion in distinguishing development as a process from development as progress, the criticism of "negative change" is clear here. A similar position was voiced by a respondent from CARE: "we don't know if it always improves the situation" (Interview No. 25 2013; see also Interview No. 26 2013). Intentional development (Cowen and Shenton 1996: 4) in the form of various projects is thus criticized as having potentially negative effects. This criticism does not achieve its full potential as development is understood as immanent at the same time. The confusion that is created due to these two meanings attached to the term development is ideologically productive in softening the criticism of the intentional activity that goes under the name development.

Herein lies also the productivity of the term within the subjects. Ziai may be right in saying that differences in the definitions of development between different people "allow these people to cooperate without having to engage in conflict about their different assumptions and world views" (Ziai 2013: 133). However, the critical subjects themselves may in fact resort to different meanings of the term as they engage in the criticism of what they do. The conflict then occurs within one person and not just between different people.

A less ambiguous criticism was concerned with the understanding of development as "Westernization" (Interview No. 17 2013). A respondent from Austroprojekt was very confident in his criticism of it:

> Of course I know that development is a rather dubious concept, especially now that we found out that the whole Enlightenment [...] is no [longer] valid [...] we have many critics [of] development, which in the Austrian terms means progress, growth, Westernization and things like that. This is the ordinary concept [...]. Development is a teleological concept; there is [...] a linear conception.
>
> (Ibid.)

This respondent "personally [does not] believe at all in this kind of development" (ibid.); for him, real development is a sustainable development that, apart from local traditions, also respects the environment (ibid., see also Interview No. 16 2013; Interview No. 22 2013).

What was criticized was thus, not only the Orientalism in the development discourse that puts the Self above the Other, but also the linear concept of development problematizing the content of what the Self represents. This respondent and other respondents went beyond the focus on the representation of "us" and "them" toward a more substantial environmental criticism and the perspective that it is possible for everyone to follow the Western type of development.

Two Slovak employees from PiP were also critical regarding development. They spoke of the "so-called development" (Interview No. 8 2013), by which they meant dams that cause displacement of people and environmental degradation or building of hotels with similar consequences, and "anti-development" (Interview No. 10 2013), which meant flushing toilets. They thus also focused on the linear concept of development that contains the Western developmental model as an ideal and criticized the environmental problems as well as the Westernization that it brings.

The whole concept of development is considered "totally wrong" by one of them (Interview No. 10 2013) due to the Westernizing tendencies and also due to tied aid: "[...] in reality the aim is to sell our own products or place our companies on their market. This certainly is not development, because it does not develop anybody" (ibid.; see also Zorád 2012).

There was a specific contradiction in an article by one PiP employee, according to whom nobody believes in the linear model of developing countries following the developed ones (Fialová 2013). However, after this basically post-development critique, she drops the inverted commas and follows the big players (the UN, the EU) (but also small NGOs) in talking "about the need of effectiveness in development" (ibid.). Later in her text, she writes about "developing countries," thus putting them on the previously criticized evolutionary ladder. In the last paragraph, we can read that "development cooperation develops especially ourselves" (ibid.), as "we" can learn from other cultures. The positive representation of "development cooperation" then culminates in the opinion that "[d]evelopment cooperation teaches humbleness" (ibid.).

Whereas the term development is considered discredited at the beginning of the article, the critique is weakened as the term development is used in an unquestioned manner later in the text. Development is thus partly legitimized even in this most critical text.

Just as with depoliticization and hierarchization, the Austrian respondents were more critical of development and delegitimized it to a greater extent and in a stronger way than the Slovaks. Both groups criticized development in an abstract way, and in particular they criticized the Westernization, the linear concept of development, and environmental problems brought about by development. It is noteworthy that the unclear meaning of development enabled respondents to be critical of the term and at the same time accept it as a neutral process or change.

Apart from the discourses of microfinance and education in development analyzed especially in relation to depoliticization, I also focused on the sustainable development discourse. Just as the positive connotation of the term development legitimizes the practice of development, so do particular notions of sustainable development legitimize the practice of sustainable development.

Taken literally, sustainable development means "development that can be continued" (Lélé 1991: 609). The question then is "what is development?" (ibid.). Sustainability is, according to Lélé, understood as "ecological sustainability" (ibid.), but development in this conceptualization is a process of change "that has (ecological) sustainability added to its list of objectives" (ibid.: 608). Development with its traditional objectives comes first, and sustainability second. Thus, according to Lélé, the literal connotation, in which "sustainable" means sustaining anything, comes down to sustainable growth. The mainstream interpretation understands sustainable development as "achieving traditional objectives + ecological (& social?) sustainability" (ibid.: 608). "In this way sustainable is an adjective added to the substantive development" (Eblinghaus and Stickler 1996: 50), with the substantive dominating the adjective. It is understood as durability, but not of a nature that sets limits, but of the development itself (see Rist 2008: 192–193).

As the term development is ambiguous, so is the term sustainable development. There are various subtypes of sustainable development in the extant literature, mainly focusing on the belief in technology (technocentrism) on the one hand and on putting nature into the center of the approach (ecocentrism) on the other.

One respondent from PiP followed the mainstream sustainable development discourse as defined by Lélé (1991) to the letter. Whereas unsustainable development meant, according to this respondent, building roads and economic growth supported by too much debt and a destruction of the environment, sustainable development means “doing it the way that enables future generations to continue the trend” (Interview No. 9 2013, see Interview No. 11 2013 for a very similar response), and “[sustainable development] is growth with the use of certain conditions […] that does not cause irretrievable damage of the ecosystem. That means that you can cut the trees only to a certain extent … ” (ibid.). The term sustainable is an extra criterion:

> Economic growth is also the goal of the sustainable development. It is such a motivator – the end station, of course – but there is a certain extra criterion. It is not just a pure growth, but growth with conditions a, b, and c to make it sustainable.
>
> (Ibid.)

Another respondent from PiP called nature our mother, yet at the same time he said: “let’s use everything we have to the limit” (Interview No. 8 2013). Here, the more spiritual deep ecology was contradicted by a utilitarian approach that reflects the more elaborate answer of his colleague and is in accordance with the mainstream understanding of sustainable development.

An important element of the distinction between ecocentrism and technocentrism is the importance of economic growth. Growth has been a central element of development theories since its rise to prominence after the Second World War (see, e.g., Lepenies 2016). Especially, modernization theories in the 1950s emphasized the importance of economic growth. The failures of development led to the emergence of the theory of human development, which puts people at its center (see above) as opposed to more economic development theories. The controversy around economic growth was reflected also in the interviews, but not in the analyzed texts.

One respondent from Austroprojekt even considered himself “a crusader of the degrowth movement […] I don’t believe in growth” (Interview No. 17 2013). However, the respondent also claimed that poor countries “need some growth” (ibid.) in some aspects such as the health sector or agriculture. Another claimed that “everybody is telling us that we have to grow to be sustainable, but I cannot believe it […] you cannot grow indefinitely” (Interview No. 16 2013). This respondent also questioned the uncritical use of technologies.

In general, the respondents offered rather ecocentric definitions of sustainable development. More critical respondents from Austria criticized economic growth, and one of them also called for a cautious approach to technology. The Slovaks were less ecocentric than the Austrians. Still, the ecocentric approach was present among the Slovak respondents as well. The next section analyzes the respondents’ explanations of their discursive practices.

Explaining the discursive practice

Several respondents explained the reasons for how they use the term development already during the interviews when talking about the meaning of the term. Other respondents explained their discursive practices after reading my analysis. As the explanations of hierarchization and depoliticization complement the analysis, I include these explanations here as well.

The respondents explained the use of the term development by a lack of reflection with regard to the term and by the need to respect the apparatus dominated by official state institutions. They explained hierarchization by PR needs and emphasized the non-hierarchic relations in the field, and they explained the problematic discourse and depoliticization by the size of the PR texts and the complexity of development issues. Two respondents admitted to being part of a larger problematic whole and explained their persistence in their work by their occasional contributions to the improvement of people's lives. The reasoning used by the respondents was not dependent on their nationality in any way.

As has already been mentioned, development was defined through its "usual understanding." Several respondents offered a similar perspective and complemented this perspective by explaining the reasons for the way they use the term development in their everyday discursive practice. Development was defined by a respondent from Pontis as "a buzzword" (Interview No. 4 2013), i.e., a word that one uses "without thinking about what it actually means" (ibid.). A respondent from CARE said in a similar manner that "many times we use the word without having a complete understanding of what each individual thinks of that word" (Interview No. 27 2013; see also Interview No. 25 2013). A respondent from ADA complements the picture by claiming that "there is no great discussion in ADA" regarding the term (Interview No. 20 2013; for a similar claim see Interview No. 22 2013 and Interview No. 13 2013). Quite a few respondents thus admitted to having a vague understanding and use of the term development.

The use of this term and the lack of reflection over it were explained with a reference to external actors. According to a respondent from Pontis, the Ministry of Foreign Affairs demands particular development projects to be carried out, and the NGDO follows the direction of the project as it is set by the Ministry or by another donor.

> After that you are not concerned with whether development means for you this or that, and that you should now critically evaluate it during your work, but you are interested in whether you bought the plane tickets, whether you have a speaker for trainings, and whether your partner replies to you [...] and you take care of these types of things.
>
> (Interview No. 4 2013)

A respondent from Austroprojekt, in a similar manner, claimed outright that he uses "the term as it was used by our donors [...]. The Austrian government decides to do development and what they understand [as development is what] we have to apply" (Interview No. 17 2013). Another made a similar comment, reflecting also the non-participatory nature of the meaning of the way the term is used: if he talks

> about development in this special project [...] this was determined by the project documents, which were given to us as the framework in which we had to do our work, but it wasn't our own decision, nor the decision of the population [...] it was determined also by the selection of fields of interventions by the Austrian government.
>
> (Interview No. 16 2013)

The participatory approach is thus endangered by the top-down nature of the development apparatus. Even though development discourse emanates from the myriads of local sources and in this sense it is an anonymous field, at the same time there are dominant actors who influence the meaning of development from the top. These prevent the participation from taking place, while at the same time preaching it.

A respondent from the Austrian state agency also absolved his organization from responsibility of the use of the term. He did not even start his response with defining the term, but outright defensively claimed, "we use the term [...] because it is still the official term in the DAC language" (Interview No. 20 2013; see also Interviews 25 and 26 2013), and to correct my understanding that he has to use it, he said he uses it "not because I have to, not me personally, but this is the sort of common international agreement that this term is used in. I am not defending the term" (ibid.). The development discourse may be more autonomous than Dreyfus and Rabinow (1982) allow in their criticism of Foucault. It seems that the seriousness of particular speech acts is only a function of other speech acts (ibid.: 58). The "sort of common international agreement" is precisely such a speech act, as it is an agreement about which speech acts are serious and which are not. The source of development discourse then seems to be an anonymous development field. Clearly, there are actors more powerful than others which are capable of shaping this field to a greater extent than others, and in this sense power is both non-subjective and intentional, and subjective and intentional. The analysis of the non-subjective element of power among donors is, however, understudied within the academic sphere. The main point here is that, just as new donors are inferior to the autonomous discourse, so can old donors be inferior to it, and in this sense it may be better to distinguish between those subjects that dominate the discourse and those that are the points of transmission of the discourse.

Writing in a hierarchic manner inferiorizing the Other was also blamed on the PR needs:

> [Hierarchization] is often caused not by the fact that I think so, but because we do it to make it sound better. You basically need money from the people, and you write in order for them to understand a bit what you are doing, and

> therefore you have to say “we”, because we Slovaks are extremely generous, because we help them.[3]
>
> (Interview No. 18 2014)

The need to write in a particular way is thus supported by a particular image of the public:

> I do not think that it should be this way, and if I were to write for the professional part of the public, I would never dare to write that, but if I were to write the way one should, then nobody in Slovakia would understand it.
>
> (Ibid.)

Later this respondent continued by confirming the evident (but never publicly claimed) reason: “the website is a fundraising tool and this concerns also blogs and everything; you bow and scrape to those people […] I mean this does not reflect what I think at all” (ibid.; see also PiP respondent No. 8 2014).

The arguments of this respondent confirm Dogra’s finding that “there is a growing trend across INGOs to oversimplify the content in messages […] I was frequently told that ‘root causes’ of [the majority of world] issues are not ‘sexy enough’ to capture readers’ imagination” (Dogra 2014: 136). As is clear also from my analysis, “[a]ssumptions about audiences played a big role in these arguments” (ibid.). However, Dogra’s research shows that, especially the younger part of the audience, responds well to more critical messages (ibid.: 175).

There is one more explanation of Orientalism in the texts that is not present in the interviews. Pleasure is derived from superiority in the field, especially that of white middle-class women, who experience a different social position in the field than at home (see Heron 2007). One could speculate that such pleasure is present, not only in the field, but also behind the desk. Writing about the Other in a hierarchic manner may be just as pleasurable as meeting the Other in an asymmetrical situation.

Not only hierarchization, but also depoliticization, was blamed on the PR nature of the texts. A respondent from PiP said that “the way power relations are represented in the text is due to the text being a PR article” (Interview No. 19 2014; see also PiP respondent No. 8 2014). Next to the blaming of the PR department or of the PR nature of the analyzed texts was the perspective that more complex political issues do not belong in the PR texts, but elsewhere:

> the scope of articles does not allow for a more complex discourse on global power relations. Perhaps a specific forum can be established, but certainly not within the PR articles on the project, which themselves are very narrow in scope.... The information within articles on the project will never be broader than the projects themselves, as this discussion belongs to different fora.
>
> (PiP respondent No. 9 2014)

I have been to the fora the respondent writes about several times (but certainly not to all of them). Their nature is much closer to the PR found in the analyzed articles, with the PiP employees trying to sell the projects and persuade the public to support PiP and their projects. PiP did not engage in political actions related to the wider North–South relations in these fora. However, it should be noted that political issues were addressed by several movies played at the One World Film Festival organized by PiP. Further research in the field of global education would be necessary to offer more conclusive results in this regard. Research on German and British global education, as well as my own on the Czech national strategy, points to depoliticizing tendencies (Andreotti 2011; Bendix, Danielzik, and Kiesel 2015; Kunová, Sobotková, and Profant 2017).

Finally, two respondents in the interviews engaged in what could be called development or responsible cynicism. The respondents criticize the development apparatus, but at the same time feel compelled to participate in the field. An extract from an exchange of emails with one respondent after he read the analysis introduces the issue at hand:

> It is equally by no means astonishing that the two interviewees express differing views from those contained in the analyzed text: first, they have both retired in the meantime and are therefore more open to critical reflection also [on] what they have done themselves. Secondly, even at the time of its elaboration, the analyzed text did not necessarily express exactly the views of people responsible for its content: it reflects much more a working agreement between the ambitions and interests of the different actors in the whole process.
>
> (Gütermann 2014a)

> Such a programme – as the one analyzed – is a small wheel in the midst of a big machine and it is virtually impossible to change [the course of that machine]. "We", the relevant actors, know this and always knew it. [...] The need for eventual change lies much deeper – on a global level....
>
> (Gütermann 2014b)

In both these instances, the author represents himself as knowledgeable of the governmentality in which he participates and at the same time as a powerless cog in a machine that needs substantial changes. Such a position is close to the cynicism that Pieter de Vries, following Sloterdijk and Žižek, succinctly describes for the field of development cooperation: "They know very well that the development apparatus does not deliver what it promises, but still they play the game" (De Vries 2008: 168). It is the opposite of Marx's false consciousness ("They do not know it, but they are doing it," ibid.). Whereas in the "traditional" understanding of ideology, the subject does not know the true nature of reality and therefore participates in whatever oppressing actions that take place, in the understanding of ideology as working through cynicism, the subject is well aware of how problematic the whole apparatus might be from the recipient perspective, yet keeps on participating in it and reproduces it by publishing PR articles and by engaging in development projects. The development expert "is in fact the 'real believer', ready to invest in the official text of the development apparatus while disavowing the essentially political nature of development" (ibid.: 169). S/he perpetuates the machine by producing the texts and by pretending to take them seriously.

As is clear from Christoph Gütermann's final comments, he preferred to keep on working for and in the machine because he knew "that even with all the deficiencies in the system and the set-up one can improve the actual living conditions of local people [that he was] working with" (Gütermann 2014b). One possibly needs a typology of cynicisms, but this is not the "ironical distance" Žižek (in De Vries 2008: 169) writes about. The development machine offers something different from what is usually understood as "cynicism." Rather than just saying, "there is nothing I can do," this *development* or *responsible cynicism* is based on the premise "at least I am doing something."

A respondent from PiP offers a similar account. She claimed[4] that her opinion on development cooperation changed and that the whole development at the place where she works [in an NGO] is stupid. She said that "down there" [in the Global South] it makes sense, but with the global context "the whole thing" [development cooperation] is "bullshit." On the other hand, she said that, if you use some money to improve several people's lives, then it is not complete garbage (Interview No. 18 2014). The respondent thus distinguishes between development cooperation in general, which does not makes sense, and projects in the Global South, which are meaningful.

This approach is connected to a positive image of one's work and contradicts the usual understanding of cynicism. The positive perception of one's work then holds the moral Self from falling apart (Heron 2007: 134). The understanding that one is part of a problem could make the moral Self fall apart. In the case of Heron's respondent, Laura (and a few others), a new understanding actually led to the conclusion that she would not have become a development worker had she known then what she knows now (ibid.: 132). Here, the moral Self is saved through the positive small deeds achieved thanks to development projects. These respondents differ from Carol, whose "center cannot hold," for whom the contradictions of her positioning become unbearable as she perceives herself as implicated in the racialized domination. This domination is understood by my respondents, yet their moral Selves do not fall apart, since they are appeased by the positive outcomes of their projects. Their comments are thus similar to Vickie's, who claims: "In the big picture, I was part of the problem. In the day-to-day affairs I was useful in a limited way" (ibid.: 129). Heron's research confirms the similarity among donors regardless of age. Similar positions of development workers can be found in the Canadian and Austrian, but also the Slovak, development apparatuses.

Conclusion

The aim of this chapter was to analyze the legitimizing and delegitimizing effects of the development discourse with regard to development. The overall finding is that, whereas the written development discourse represented here by the PR articles, national strategies, national laws, NGO reports, and a plan of operation legitimizes the practice of development, personal blogs and one editorial that one could put into the critical development genre included important delegitimizing instances. The workers of the development apparatus offered serious subversive attempts, not only with regard to the positive representation of the Other, but also with regard to the legitimacy of development.

These findings apply to the written discourse from both countries and, to a certain extent, also to the respondents' discourse. Here, however, more Austrians were critical than Slovaks, and they were also critical in a stronger way than the Slovaks. Still, several Slovaks engaged in important delegitimizing discursive practices, and the difference between them and the Austrians is thus one of degree and not of substance.

The legitimization of the development discourse was achieved through the unquestioned positive connotation of the term development, which was found in most of the analyzed texts as well as in the interviews with most of the respondents. Development was understood by the respondents in an abstract way without being actually given any specific definition. This understanding most likely contributes to the dominant use of the term. It was understood also as a positive touch, as an unspecified progress, and as an improvement in a social standard, and then it was understood through an array of meanings such as poverty reduction, improved basic education, healthcare, infrastructure, economic growth (improving the standard of living), freedom, etc. In all these cases, the dominant – positive – meaning of the term was secured.

Development was further legitimized through an array of legitimizing discursive practices that included moral tales, predictions, a helping imperative, "their" negative and "our" positive representations, analogies, authority of experts, authority of the local population, impersonal authority, scientific, experiential, and instrumental rationalizations and generalizations. All these forms served the need to legitimize development projects.

Such findings are not surprising. Yet, it is important to repeat this, as it is through the legitimization of development that the problems in the practice of development get to be ignored or overlooked. The development discourse legitimizes social activities that ought to be seriously questioned.

A further contribution of this analysis is the distinction of the legitimizing practices from a critical perspective that, to various degrees, delegitimizes development. This has been done with the invocation of the partnership discourse, which enabled the respondents to distance themselves from the Orientalism of the development discourse. More abstract criticism of the term development further made it possible for respondents to assume a critical position of actors who are aware of problems within the development apparatus.

The ambivalent meaning of development as progress and as a neutral process at the same time, however, produced the possibility for subjects to defend and criticize development simultaneously, thereby securing their personal integrity. A similar ambivalence was also present in the development or responsible cynicism through which the respondents thoroughly criticized, but at the same time also defended, the practice of development.

Further criticism focused on the distinction between ideal and real development that enabled the problematization of Westernization, the linear understanding of development, the environmental issues caused by development, and the economic growth. Whereas one respondent offered the dominant understanding of sustainable development as a growth with an extra criterion, other respondents were critical of economic growth and also presented a cautious approach to new technologies.

Finally, the respondents explained why they use the term development the way they do, why they hierarchize "us" over "them," and why they depoliticize unequal power relations. They blamed their Ministries and the IOs for the way they use the term development. They blamed their PR departments and the PR nature of the texts their organizations produce for the hierarchization. They also expressed assumptions about the audience, which allegedly makes them write in the problematic way they do. They questioned the depoliticizing thesis, claiming that politicization belongs to other fora and that the projects' limited focus is not problematic. The respondents claimed that political issues are certainly addressed in the field and that, despite the problematic workings of the big development machine, it is still meaningful to engage down there in the Global South.

Notes

1 According to Rist,

> "Development" consists of a set of practices, sometimes appearing to conflict with one another, which require – for the reproduction of society – the general transformation and destruction of the natural environment and of social relations. Its aim is to increase the production of commodities (goods and services) geared, by way of exchange, to effective demand.
>
> (Rist 2008: 13)

2 I can only reproduce here the exact, yet very unclear, response (translated into English) to a follow-up question asking what exactly the respondent means by socio-economic development: "That means that regarding the finances or livelihood, people can secure their subsistence, plus have access to education, healthcare, services that are, for us, maybe automatic. Also some kind of a position toward the environment belongs there" (Interview No. 3 2013). This respondent later defined development also as "a neutral process that is happening in all the countries of the world" (ibid.).

3 The respondent refers to "we" in the "we-they" distinction and talks about how PiP needs to represent Slovaks, and it is not so that she would actually think that the Slovaks are generous.

4 I did not have the recorder turned on when the respondent was talking about this, and I only turned it on later in the interview. I am thus reporting what was stated in the interview at this point from my notes. We started to talk about my analysis as soon as I entered the room.

Bibliography

Andreotti, Vanessa de Oliveira 2011: *Actionable Postcolonial Theory in Education*. New York: Palgrave Macmillan.

Bendix, Daniel, Danielzik, Chandra-Milena, and Kiesel, Timo 2015: Education for sustainable inequality? A postcolonial analysis of materials for Development Education in Germany. *Critical Literacy: Theories and Practices* 9(2), 47–63.

Bhabha, Homi 2004: *Location of Culture*. London and New York: Routledge.

BMEIA 2012: Three-Year Programme on Austrian Development Policy 2013–2015. Federal Ministry for European and International Affairs, Directorate-General for Development Cooperation, www.entwicklung.at/fileadmin/user_upload/Dokumente/Publikationen/3_JP/Englisch/2013-2015_3-YP.pdf.

CARE 2006: CARE: AIDS bewirkt Bildungsmissstände. CARE, www.care.at/news/presseaussendungen/care-aids-bewirkt-bildungsmissstaende/.

CARE 2012: Ein Dorf zieht an einem Strang. CARE, www.care.at/news/news/ein-dorf-zieht-an-einem-strang/.

Cooper, Frederick and Packard, Randall 1997: Introduction. In: Cooper, Frederick and Packard, Randall (ed.): *International development and the social sciences: essays on the history and politics of knowledge*. Berkeley, Los Angeles and London: University of California Press, 1–41.

Cowen, Michael P. and Shenton, Robert W. 1996: *Doctrines of development*. London and New York: Routledge.

Cox, R. W. 1981: Social Forces, States and World Orders: Beyond International Relations Theory. *Millennium – Journal of International Studies* 10(2), 126–155, doi:10.1177/03058298810100020501.

Crush, Jonathan 1999: Introduction. In: Crush, Jonathan (ed.): *Power of Development*. London and New York: Routledge, 3–23.

De Vries, Pieter 2008: The Managerialization of Development, the Banalization of Its Promise and the Disavowal of "Critique" as a Modernist Illusion. In: Cooke, Bill and Sadhvi, Dar (ed.): *The New Development Management. Critiquing the Dual Modernization*. London and New York: Zed Books, 150–176.

Dogra, Nandita 2014: *Representations of Global Poverty. Aid, Development and International NGOs*. London and New York: I. B. Tauris.

Dreyfus, Hubert and Rabinow, Paul 1982: *Michel Foucault: Beyond Structuralism and Hermeneutics*. Chicago: Harvester Wheatsheaf.

Eblinghaus, Helga and Stickler, Armin 1996: *Nachhaltigkeit und Macht. Zur Kritik von Sustainable Development. Mit einer Dokumentation der Debatte um die Studie "Zukunftsfähiges Deutschland."* Frankfurt am Main: IKO – Verl. für Interkulturelle Kommunikation.

Escobar, Arturo 1995: *Encountering Development. The Making and Unmaking of the Third World*. Princeton: Princeton University Press.

Esteva, Gustavo 1992: Development. In: Sachs, Wolfgang (ed.): *The Development Dictionary*. London and New Jersey: Zed Books, 6–25.

Fialová, Zuzana 2013: Koho alebo čo vlastne rozvíjame? *SME* 15. 3. 2013.

Foucault, Michel 2002a: The Political Technology of Individuals. *Power. Essential Works of Foucault 1954–1984* 3. London: Penguin Books, 403–417.

Foucault, Michel 2002b: *Archaeology of Knowledge*. London: Routledge.

Frank, Leonard 1997: The Development Game. In: Rahnema, Majid and Bawtree, Victoria (ed.): *The Post-Development Reader*. London and New Jersey: Zed Books, 263–273.

Gardner, Katy and Lewis, David 2000: Dominant Paradigms Overturned or "Business as Usual"? Development Discourse and the White Paper on International Development. *Critique of Anthropology* 20(1), 15–29, doi:10.1177/0308275X0002000106.
Gütermann, Christoph 2014a: Interview with Christoph Gütermann led by Tomáš Profant.
Gütermann, Christoph 2014b: AW: comment, email communication, 1.8.2014.
Haq, Mahbub ul 1995: *Reflections on Human Development*. New York and Oxford: Oxford University Press.
Heron, Barbara 2007: *Desire for Development. Whiteness, Gender, and the Helping Imperative*. Waterloo: Wilfrid Laurier Univ. Press.
Hobart, Mark 1993: Introduction: The Growth of Ignorance? In: Hobart, Mark (ed.): *An anthropological critique of development: the growth of ignorance*. London and New York: Routledge, 1–30.
Interview No. 3 2013: Interview with the respondent from the Pontis Foundation. 25.6.2013, personally in Bratislava.
Interview No. 4 2013: Interview with the respondent from the Pontis Foundation. 26.6.2013, personally in Bratislava.
Interview No. 5 2013: Interview with the respondent from the Pontis Foundation. 3.7.2013, personally in Bratislava.
Interview No. 7 2013: Interview with the respondent from the Pontis Foundation. 15.7.2013, personally in Bratislava.
Interview No. 8 2013: Interview with the respondent from PiP. 15.7.2013, personally in Bratislava.
Interview No. 9 2013: Interview with the respondent from PiP. 13.8.2013, personally in Bratislava.
Interview No. 10 2013: Interview with the respondent from PiP. 15.8.2013, personally in Bratislava.
Interview No. 11 2013: Interview with the respondent from PiP. 19.8.2013, personally in Bratislava.
Interview No. 12 2013: Interview with the respondent from SAIDC. 8.8.2013, personally in Bratislava.
Interview No. 13 2013: Interview with the respondent from SAIDC. 15.8.2013, personally in Bratislava.
Interview No. 15 2014: Interview with the respondent from SAIDC. 11.6.2014, personally in Bratislava.
Interview No. 16 2013: Interview with the respondent from Austroprojekt. 7.10.2013, personally in Vienna.
Interview No. 17 2013: Interview with the respondent from Austroprojekt. 6.10.2013, personally in Vienna.
Interview No. 18 2014: Interview with the respondent from PiP about this chapter. 14.8.2014, personally in Bratislava.
Interview No. 19 2014: Interview with the respondent from PiP about this chapter. 14.8.2014, personally in Bratislava.
Interview No. 20 2013: Interview with the respondent from ADA. 19.11.2013, personally in Vienna.
Interview No. 21 2013: Interview with the respondent from ADA. 20.11.2013, personally in Vienna.
Interview No. 22 2013: Interview with the respondent from ADA. 20.11.2013, personally in Vienna.

Interview No. 23 2013: Interview with the respondent from ADA. 26.11.2013, personally in Vienna.

Interview No. 24 2014: Interview with the respondent from ADA. 11.2.2014, personally in Vienna.

Interview No. 25 2013: Interview with the respondent from CARE. 20.11.2013, personally in Vienna.

Interview No. 26 2013: Interview with the respondent from CARE. 26.11.2013, personally in Vienna.

Interview No. 27 2013: Interview with the respondent from CARE. 27.11.2013, over Skype.

Interview No. 28 2014: Interview with the respondent from CARE. 11.2.2014, personally in Vienna.

Kunová, Anna, Sobotková, Lenka and Profant, Tomáš (2017): Závěrečná zpráva z vyhodnocení projektů zahraniční rozvojové spolupráce ČR realizovaných v rámci dotačního titulu „globální rozvojové vzdělávání a osvěta" (Příloha 1: Hodnocení dotačního titulu a procesních otázek). Evaluation4Action a MZV ČR, www.mzv.cz/file/2647276/Priloha_1___Hodnoceni_dotacniho_titulu.pdf.

Laclau, Ernesto 2007: *Emancipation(s)*. London: Verso.

Leeuwen, Theo van 2008: *Discourse and Practice. New Tools for Critical Discourse Analysis*. Oxford: Oxford University Press.

Lélé, Sharachchandra M. 1991: Sustainable Development: A Critical Review. *World Development* 19(6), 607–621.

Lepenies, Philipp 2016: *The Power of a Single Number: A Political History of GDP*. New York: Columbia University Press.

MFEA 2013: Medium-Term Strategy for Development Cooperation of the Slovak Republic for 2014–2018. Ministry of Foreign and European Affairs of the Slovak Republic, https://issuu.com/slovakaid/docs/strednodoba_strategia_oda_sr_2014-2_83963017c1b288.

Nationalrat 2003: Federal Act on Development Cooperation (2002), including its Amendment (2003), www.oe-eb.at/en/dam/jcr:82518ac8-d1e8-4e22-a407-5569a159bb5d/Development-Cooperation-Act.pdf.

NDC-Austroprojekt and Orgut 2002: Plan of Operation for Ngorngoro District Development Programme. Phase 1. Ngorngoro District Council and Austroprojekt/Orgut Consortium.

NRSR 2007: Zákon o oficiálnej rozvojovej pomoci a o doplnení zákona č. 575/2001 Z. z. o organizácii činnosti vlády a organizácii ústrednej štátnej správy v znení neskorších predpisov. Zbierka zákonov č. 617/2007, www.zakonypreludi.sk/zz/2007-617.

PiP 2009: Podpora podnikania vidieckych žien v západnej Keni (2008–2009). People in Peril, https://clovekvohrozeni.sk/podpora-podnikania-vidieckych-zien-v-zapadnej-keni-2008-2009/.

PiP 2010: Podpora zamestnanosti a komunitnej participácie v Západnej Keni (2010–2011). People in Peril, https://clovekvohrozeni.sk/podpora-zamestnanosti-a-komunitnej-participacie-v-zapadnej-keni-2010-2011/.

PiP 2011: Zvyšovanie potravinovej bezpečnosti v Keni (2011–2012). People in Peril, https://clovekvohrozeni.sk/zvyovanie-potravinovej-bezpenosti-v-keni-2011-2012/.

PiP 2012a: Poľnohospodárstvo rozvíjame aj na východnom pobreží Kene. People in Peril, https://clovekvohrozeni.sk/polnohospodarstvo-rozvijame-aj-na-vychodnom-pobrezi-kene/.

PiP 2012b: Slovenskému veľvyslancovi v Keni chutia čerstvé rajčiny zo školskej záhrady. People in Peril, https://clovekvohrozeni.sk/slovenskemu-velvyslancovi-v-keni-chutia-cerstve-rajciny-zo-skolskej-zahrady/.

PiP 2012c: Mladí farmári sa tešia na nový prístup k internetu. People in Peril, https://clovekvohrozeni.sk/mladi-farmari-sa-tesia-na-novy-pristup-k-internetu/.

PiP respondent No. 8 2014: Email from the PiP respondent.

PiP respondent No. 9 2014: Comments to this chapter. (email).

Pontis 2010: slovak teachers taught their colleagues from kenya how to use information technologies. Pontis Foundation, www.nadaciapontis.sk/article/slovak-teachers-taught-their-colleagues-from-kenya-how-to-use-information-technologies/277?lang=en_US.

Profant, Tomáš 2018: The Social Construction of Slovakia as a Donor and its Power Effects. *Europe–Asia Studies* 70(3), 365–387, doi:10.1080/09668136.2018.1453486.

Rahnema, Majid 1997: Introduction. In: Rahnema, Majid/Bawtree, Victoria (ed.): *The Post-Development Reader*. London and New Jersey: Zed Books, ix–xix.

Rist, Gilbert 2008: *The History of Development: From Western Origins to Global Faith.* London and New York: Zed Books.

Sachs, Wolfgang 1992: Introduction. In: Sachs, Wolfgang (ed.): *The Development Dictionary*. London and New Jersey: Zed Books, 1–5.

SAMRS 2013: SlovakAid podporí produkciu bio-kešu orechov v Keni. *SlovakAid*, www.slovakaid.sk/en/node/110.

Sen, Amartya Kumar 1999: *Development as Freedom*. Oxford and New York: Oxford University Press.

Unnithan, Maya and Srivastava, Kavita 1997: Gender Politics, Development and Women's Agency in Rajasthan. In: Grillo, R. D. and Stirrat, R. L. (ed.): *Discourses of Development. Antrhopological Perspectives*. Oxford and New York: Berg, 157–181.

Ziai, Aram 2004a: The ambivalence of post-development: between reactionary populism and radical democracy. *Third World Quarterly* 25(6), 1045–1060.

Ziai, Aram 2004b: *Entwicklung als Ideologie? Das klassische Entwicklungsparadigma und die Post-Development Kritik zur Analyze des Entwicklungsdiskurses*. Hambrug: Deutsches Übersee-Institut.

Ziai, Aram 2007: The Meaning of "Development": A critical Perspective. *Journal Für Entwicklungspolitik* 2, 67–79.

Ziai, Aram 2009: "Development": Projects, Power, and a Poststructuralist Perspective. *Alternatives: Global, Local, Political* 34(2), 183–201.

Ziai, Aram 2013: The discourse of "development" and why the concept should be abandoned. *Development in Practice* 23(1), 123–136, doi:10.1080/09614524.2013.752792.

Ziai, Aram 2016: *Development Discourse and Global History: From Colonialism to the Sustainable Development Goals*. Oxon and New York: Routledge.

Zorád, Lukáš 2012: Zo života na rovníku: Každý musí utiecť, ako vie! *blog.sme.sk*, http://zorad.blog.sme.sk/c/300203/Zo-zivota-na-rovniku-Kazdy-musi-utiect-ako-vie.html.

6 Conclusion

This book has shown that there is a great similarity between new and old donors – which were represented here by Slovakia and Austria, respectively – which casts doubt on the distinction between them based on age. The aim of this conclusion is to summarize the main result and answer the research questions. Another aim is to explain the differences between the Slovak and Austrian development apparatuses, especially with regard to the old-new distinction, and further contemplate about the representativeness of the results and possible avenues for future research.

The analysis and the comparison

The analysis and the comparison of rather material issues in the Austrian and Slovak development apparatuses show striking similarities between them. Both donors had their development aid induced from the outside after they lost in a war – Austria after the Second World War, and Slovakia (again) after the Cold War. In the two cases, this was, for them, one of the ways to become part of the victorious part of the world. One can observe in the two cases a lack of commitment to aid on the side of the respective governments through the low ODA levels in Austria and Slovakia and also through the low levels of popular support for the aid in the two countries. Here, however, it should be noted that the popular support in Austria is probably higher than the popular support in Slovakia. The regional interests of the two countries, however, offer a similarity between them as the two donors direct their aid to their neighboring countries by following their national interest rather than the needs of the poorest. In the two cases, the national interest may be concealed by the discourses of effectiveness and of complementarity and coordination of donors. The motivation to give in both countries moves between altruism and egoism, but the Slovak respondents differed from the Austrians by emphasizing their professional interest more than the Austrians, who offered stronger moral reasoning. Finally, the nongovernmental spheres in both countries are rather similar – they are too close to the government and consist of small, private organizations that compete with each other instead of cooperating. All these similarities show that distinguishing between Slovakia and Austria by seeing them as a new and an old donor respectively is problematic, and maybe they should be put together into a group of donors focused on the countries in the neighborhood of the EU, a group of followers of other donors, a group of donors without a colonial past, or simply a group of donors who give because this has been traditionally expected of them from the more powerful countries which formulate development discourse and also shape the appropriate behavior of other so-called developed countries in the world.

The analysis of hierarchization shows that the Austrian and Slovak development discourses still put "us" above "them." Despite the mainstreaming of the postcolonial insights with regard to the criticism of Orientalism, the Self remains above the Other. There is a clear continuity of the colonial discourse that is still present even today. However, there are significant disruptions of the hierarchy in the discourse. The main similarity between Austrians and Slovaks is in the hierarchies between "us" and "them" that they construct. The difference between them then lies in the amount and strength of the deliberate disruptions of the hierarchy through positive representations of the Other.

Almost all the analyzed texts implicitly or explicitly followed the general law of development that puts "us" above "them" in a logocentric pattern. A few Slovak respondents offered a stronger hierarchy, in one case even one of civilizational difference. None of the Austrians engaged in such a strong hierarchization. Nevertheless, not so strong hierarchic representations of "us" and "them" gained various forms – but mainly they represented "us" in a positive way and "them" in a negative way. Discourses in both countries adhered to this pattern. Another form of hierarchization was achieved through one-way interactions between "us" and "them" as "we" interact with "them," but "they" do not interact back. This feature was also shared by texts from both countries, and even the most positive articles about "them" contained this pattern of interaction. The analysis of the enunciations showed that the subaltern are not silent, but when they speak they mostly express "their" gratitude or satisfaction with what "we" do, whereas "we" explain various phenomena. "Their" enunciations thus fit the dominant development discourse in Austria and Slovakia, confirming Spivak's (1994) famous argument that the subaltern cannot speak for the texts that I analyzed. Finally, power operates not only through hierarchization of "us" and "them," but also through one project's plan of operation that I analyzed. The analysis shows the way power structures the field of action for the Other using conditionality instead of coercion, sensitization trainings, and self-discipline.

The main finding with regard to the difference between the Austrian and Slovak development discourse was visible in the analysis of deliberate positivism. In a few instances, one could find a reversal of the logocentric pattern as "they" were represented as superior to "us." Less strong disruptions of the hierarchy between "us" and "them" were to be found in attempts to soften "their" negative representations either directly or through impersonalizations, in explicit attempts to fight negative stereotypes, in their "positive" representation outside and within the development discourse, and in a refusal to generalize and compare societies. A difference between the Slovak and Austrian texts was to be found in the Slovak representations of "them" as learning and sometimes as having learned something, and the Austrian representations of "them" as knowing rather than learning. Still, the Austrians also represented "them" as "only" learning. Another difference was in the toning down of "their" negative representations by Slovaks, and "their" direct positive representation by Austrians. In the interviews, the Austrians were slightly more critical toward the Global North than the Slovaks, and one Austrian respondent offered a very positive representation of "them."

However, overall, both Slovaks and Austrians mostly hierarchized, and both groups also weakened or disrupted the hierarchizations. They both thus contribute to the incoherence of the development discourse. The difference between them is one of degree and not of substance, which casts doubt on their differentiation on the basis of age. The Austrians engage in very much the same problematic hierarchic representations as the Slovaks, and so do other old donors, as the extant research shows (see, e.g., Kiesel and Bendix 2010; Wilson 2012; Goudge 2003; Eriksson Baaz 2005). The positively represented deserving Other is also present in the discourses of both old and new donors (Dogra 2014; Lidchi 1999). The next section offers a tentative explanation of the difference between the Austrian and Slovak representations in terms of hierarchy between "us" and "them."

The analysis of depoliticization shows similar results. The relations of power were depoliticized in almost all the texts regardless of their country of origin. The difference between the nationalities in this area was to be found in the interviews. More Austrians depoliticized than Slovaks, and they did so in a stronger way as well.

The most common type of depoliticization was spatial. By focusing on the local, the texts as well as some of the respondents ignored upper spatial levels. The actors often found the reasons for poverty to be at the local and not at the global or national level; the solutions then were also to be found at the local level, as was the legitimation of engaging in projects demanded by the local population. The solutions to the problems of poverty contained securing of an access to market that included access to financial services through microfinance and the capacity to succeed in the market competition, which was supposed to be enhanced through the education of the locals. Microfinance not only individualizes and thereby depoliticizes poverty, but it also legitimizes a financial globalization that should financially connect everyone in the world. The depoliticization of the access to market is deepened as the market is considered to be inherently benign. Several respondents considered the market as something that simply works rather than as a political space full of conflict.

Technological solutions such as collection of rain water were another way through which depoliticization occurred. A drought in such a perspective is not a political problem, but a problem of a lack of appropriate technology. Depoliticization often had its temporal dimension in the texts and interviews as well. Mainly Slovak respondents focused on the reasons for poverty, and these were connected, for example, with natural conditions; other respondents claimed that, in the present, everything is going well and we only need to fine-tune the details.

Finally, a very strong depoliticization is achieved through a belief in the future related to education as a key to a better future. Unequal power relations were depoliticized also through an omission of agents engaged in power struggles. As things such as an economic crisis simply happen, there is no space in the discourse to deal with those who are responsible for the crisis. Finally, the (potential) conflicts between actors were disregarded as a consensus between them seemed to be common, because we all want the same.

Depoliticization continued into the topics that offered a space for politicization. Good governance is part of the three-year strategies of both countries, and if politicized it could lead to an engagement with unequal relations of power. The same applies to the Policy Coherence for Development. In the two cases, however, the empirical record shows that neither of these policies leads to actual politicization of unequal power relations. The politicization of gender relations deals with unequal relations between men and women, but these micro-power relations lead to an omission of other power relations at different spatial levels. Whereas education can lead to depoliticization, it may also educate people in a way that will lead to a questioning of unequal power relations. This applies to the Global South as well as to the Global North in the form of the global development education.

The differences between the Slovaks and Austrians lay in the strength and the amount of politicization voiced by the respondents. Whereas the Slovaks depoliticized by invoking natural conditions in the past as a reason for poverty and by perceiving that enough is being done in the current situation with regard to sustainability, none of the Austrians did so. This does not mean that none of the Slovaks politicized unequal power relations, though. Quite a few of them engaged in politicization, but they more often depoliticized unequal power relations than politicizing them. There were some Austrian respondents who offered a similar incoherence in their responses as well. But more Austrians than Slovaks engaged in a strong politicization of unequal relations between North and South and they did so in a stronger way. This was the main distinction with regard to politicization, and again the difference was one of degree and not of substance.

The analyzed texts had almost exclusively the effect of legitimization of development and of development cooperation regardless of their country of origin. Only a few texts that could be put into the critical development genre delegitimized development. The respondents themselves, however, were much more critical than the texts their organizations produce. The legitimization was achieved by the invocation of the positively connoted term development, by defining it as progress, as an improvement of living conditions or as poverty reduction, education, human rights, etc. In all these instances development served as the empty plus gaining different positive meanings. Development cooperation was further legitimized through various other means such as moral tales, analogies, predictions, authority of experts, authority of the local population, and authority of impersonal actors, and through rationalization as well as through generalizations. In sum, the texts served the main function of the development discourse – to legitimize development cooperation.

Several respondents delegitimized development and distanced themselves from it by presenting a non-Orientalist perspective as an alternative to development. More Austrian respondents than Slovak ones criticized the actual practice of development from the environmental perspective and also focused on Westernization and the linear concept of development. The difference was again one of degree and not of substance, though, as some of the Slovaks also included a more ecocentric perspective.

Overall, this result holds for all three analyzed categories. Most of the actors hierarchize "us" above "them," depoliticize unequal power relations, and legitimize development, and do so in the texts as well as in the interviews. However, some of the actors engage in oppositional discursive practices and these are to be found to a greater extent in Austria than in Slovakia. The difference between them in this respect is not substantial, though, and the similarity casts doubt on the temporal distinction between new and old donors. The lack of substantial difference points to different factors at play, but the old-new distinction could also be related to power relations and to the Orientalist discourse that constructs an ideological hierarchy between East and West. Development cooperation is simply yet another field in which the East should be lagging behind the West. The question remains why there are the differences that I found between the Austrian and Slovak actors. In the next section, I offer a tentative explanation for some of the differences.

A tentative attempt at explaining some of the results

The aim of this final section is to offer a tentative attempt to explain some of the differences between Austria and Slovakia as donors by pointing at the differences between these two societies. Chapter 5 already offered a mainly institutional explanation of the discursive practice. My research shows that the Ministry of Foreign Affairs, together with international organizations, shapes the discourse of the NGDOs and of the state agencies. Another factor that contributes to the particular form (and content) of the analyzed discourse is the PR nature of the texts connected with the assumptions about the targeted audiences. These factors may explain the similarity in the discursive practices. The question is, what can be said about the difference with regard to hierarchic representations, depoliticized representations, sustainable development representations, microfinance representations, and the representations of education?

The first difference that requires an explanation is the difference with regard to depoliticization. Whereas the texts from both countries to a great extent depoliticized unequal power relations, more Austrian respondents than Slovak respondents politicized these and they did so in a stronger way than Slovak respondents. Still, even the scant Slovak politicization in the form of a critique of unequal economic power relations was a novelty in the Slovak ideological landscape.

There is no research about the political preferences of the Slovak nongovernmental (non-Christian) elite, but apart from being liberal in cultural issues, this group, throughout the 1990s and 2000s, seemed to be supporting neoliberal economic policies, or at least centre-right political parties (while at the same time claiming to be non-political).

The origin of this position is, in my mind, to be found in a general turn away from anything that could in any way be considered "leftist" after the Velvet Revolution in 1989. Despite the debt crisis and other problems related to the policies associated with the Washington consensus, at that time this approach was uncritically accepted among the (Czecho-)Slovak liberal elites and especially in the dominant Slovak non-tabloid media (see, e.g., Bockman and Eyal 2002). Those who disagreed were often labeled authoritarian or as looking towards the East if not the past. Even though Czechoslovak opinion polls from the end of 1989 actually show a preference for either socialism or something between socialism and capitalism, the following years were characterized by a strong neoliberal orientation. This has changed since then. The era of post-communism and the dominance of the anti-state and anti-communist approach seems to be crumbling. In my opinion it is too early to declare anti-communism dead, but there are signs that suggest that the end of the anti-communist hegemony is approaching (Barša 2012).

As the neoliberal discursive hegemony that seemed solid in Slovakia just a few years ago started to crumble, so have the liberal elites, in this case the employees of important Slovak NGDOs, who changed their neoliberal perspective by moving it slightly to the center. If the neoliberal hegemony was one of the major post-communist features, then we are indeed entering a different era in which social democracy and market regulation are becoming respected positions in the discourse. This is visible also in the formerly neoliberal media, which now strongly criticize the leader of the neoliberal party, Richard Sulík, for his racism.

Having gone through the interviews, I decided to ask five of the Slovak respondents who made it clear that they do not embrace a completely free market a question about the evolution of their political position and what were the reasons that led to the changes. All of them admitted that in the past they were on the right side of the political spectrum in economic questions. One of them claimed that she cannot theoretically elaborate on this and stressed values such as human dignity or respect for nature. Three of the four remaining respondents (the fourth one was too young) claimed that the fight against the semi-authoritarian leader Vladimír Mečiar until 1998 was a formative experience for them and that this fight was connected to their political orientation. According to one of them, "When I was around 16, I was mostly formed by the mass media when Mečiarism was falling" (PiP respondent No. 9 2015). According to another one, after 1998 (the year when Mečiar lost), "the right wing [economic] policy was a symbol of social progress [...] the right-wing government symbolized also a definitive break away from the communist/Mečiar clientelism, corruption and orientation to Russia" (Pontis respondent No. 4 2015). The third respondent was confronted with social issues by his father, who worked as a lawyer on employee protection issues, yet this respondent was on the right side of the spectrum. His teenage right-wing orientation was due to the continual repetition of the need for reforms in the television and newspaper mainstream.

> In that media mainstream, there was no left-wing response to those calls [for reform] – basically, nobody represented the left; therefore the only "reform" solution was right-wing … and the only fighters against Mečiar were also on the right (apart from [the Slovak Democratic Left] that was, for me, at the time an unreliable party consisting of people from the previous regime).
> (PDCS Respondent No. 1 2015)

I would not be surprised to find many other NGO workers with a similar formative experience; I myself went through such an experience as well (but such experiences, of course, might not be as common in other social milieus, e.g., rural or Christian milieus, those of people without a university degree, poor areas, etc.). All four respondents, however, turned to the center to various degrees. This was due to what they learned at universities in Slovakia, but also abroad, due to what they read (e.g., Žižek, Rodrik, Foucault, and Brubaker), due to their interest in "Third World" issues, or due to their own work in international development cooperation. Clearly, many factors contributed to the change in their perspective.

Still, one of them claims that he is "more or less consistently on the right side of the political spectrum" (PiP respondent No. 9 2015), and in the words of another one, "I don't claim that I moved to the left (but neither that I have not), just that the right-left perspective is not relevant for me anymore" (Pontis respondent No. 4 2015). The two remaining respondents did not make clear where they stand, even if they talked about changes in their political-economic orientation.

It should also be repeated that the Slovak respondents who embraced the free market made an exception when they started talking about microfinance. Lower rates distorting the market were in this particular case all right, at least temporarily, since they would make the start for the poorest easier. As if the concept of equal chances for everyone at a neutral market was suddenly not valid anymore.

The same happened in relation to a direct (suggestive) question about the role of the market and of the state in sustainable development. The respondents stated that the free market became unable to deal with environmental problems, and the state thus has to step in.

Still, only some of the Slovak respondents were in favor of some kind of market regulation and these mostly preferred the regulation to be weak. This points to a shift from the post-communist neoliberal orientation to a less unequivocal orientation as the post-communist era seems to be crumbling. One certainly cannot speak about a dominance of the left, but the discursive hegemony of neoliberalism that was connected to an anti-communist ethos is falling apart.

What would one find in Austria with regard to political economy among development workers? On the one hand, there was a very different political evolution there that comprised the more political 1960s and 1970s, which were then partly replaced by the neoliberal dogma from the 1980s. All this was happening during an era of governments usually consisting of the main center-right and center-left parties, which also divided the NGDOs. Thus, whereas there might have been a turn toward the depoliticization of unequal market power relations with the ascendancy of neoliberalism in Austria, the Austrian left has never been as weak as the left in Slovakia after 1989.

The Austrian development workers might have followed the non-political trends in the development discourse that dominated at least until the formulation of the MDGs (see, e.g., Ziai 2011), but the norms articulating social struggles may have coexisted with these trends in other forms in the Austrian society, and these norms are being pronounced today, almost ten years since the last economic crisis. Thus, the explanation of the difference with regard to the politicization of unequal power relations could be traced back to the anti-left sentiment that was dominant in the Slovak society and into which the respondents were socialized by the media and the surrounding society. The crumbling of the post-communist era may lead to a greater convergence between the two countries. Thus the difference, in my opinion, has nothing to do with the ages of the donors, but with the two countries' ideological evolutions that differed due to the communist or socially democratic past.

There was another difference in the interviews related to depoliticization. The texts from the two countries all hailed education as a key to a better future, but whereas the Austrians lost faith in education after being asked a quite suggestive critical question,[1] the Slovaks mostly still believed in its power with regard to social mobility despite the suggestiveness of the question. Whence may come this difference? A higher number of students and citizens with tertiary education can lead to the realization of the people in question that, if everyone is educated, education may cease to be the ladder for social mobility. Whereas, there is a rapidly growing number of graduates in Slovakia, this number is still lower than the corresponding number in Austria. The difference in the perspectives on education and social mobility thus need not be related to the ages of the donors, but it could simply be related to the different numbers of graduates in the respective countries who have problems finding a good job. Importantly, the belief in education as a key to a better future, which was disrupted in the interviews, goes uncontested in the written discourse of the NGDOs as well as the state agencies.

Several factors might have contributed to the difference between how the Austrian and Slovak texts and how the Austrian and Slovak respondents represented "us" and "them." The liberal anti-racist elites in Austria might be much stronger than their counterparts in Slovakia, which may translate into a greater awareness of the issue of race among Austrian development workers. However, it should still be noted that research shows that the prevailing racial stereotypes are also in the Austrian media (see below).

Another difference might be in the discussion of representations that began in development studies after the Ethiopian famine in 1984. Whereas the Austrian NGOs were active already then and the whole NGDO field in Austria was exposed to this discussion, in Slovakia, only a limited number of NGDO workers seriously engage with the related questions, and there are quite a few (e.g., from among the Christian NGDOs) who reject the meaningfulness of the discussion, pointing at the material gains humanitarian pornography brings (Profant 2013). This does not mean that one would not encounter such a perspective in Austria, but merely that some of the NGDOs, including those that I analyzed, are more sensitive to the issue of hierarchic representation.

But, is this due to the ages of the donors? I doubt that there was any discussion of the Eurocentric representations before 1989 in either Austria or Czechoslovakia. The discussion may have started in Austria as it followed other Western donors, and the same may have happened (later) in Slovakia. The important difference that should be emphasized, though, is the emergence of development studies in Austria at the Institute of Development Studies of the University of Vienna in 2002. The emergence of this institute may be due to very particular circumstances and the enthusiasm of a few people. There might also have been a need for development studies to emerge in Austria with its larger development cooperation and also with the boom of this field across various universities around the world. Thus, there certainly is a greater potential for anti-racist education in Austria with the Department of Development Studies in Vienna. However, this is not due to the age of the donor, but to its size and maybe also to the interest of the students in development studies, which again is probably not related to the age of the donor, but maybe it is related to the "post-materiality" of the issue as young people in richer countries tend to focus on issues such as the environment or human rights to a greater extent than young people in poorer countries.

There was also a difference between the Austrian and Slovak respondents in relation to sustainable development. The Austrians were more ecocentric than the Slovaks. First, however, it should be noted that there was one equally ecocentric respondent among the Slovaks. The greater focus on technologies among the other Slovak respondents can, in my mind, be related not only to the prevailing neoliberal technocentric discourse, but, more importantly, to the cautious approach in Austria, especially to nuclear technology. Whereas, in Slovakia, nuclear technology is generally not problematized in the media, Austria is known for its anti-nuclear stand. The public debate on technologies there differs substantially from the Slovak public debate. My argument here is the same again: this has nothing to do with the age of the donor, but is related to one particular social issue on which the two societies differ. Another reason may be related to the levels of wealth of the two societies. Ecology is still a postmaterial issue that is more popular in richer countries, with the strength of the Green Party in Austria and its counterpart's weakness in Slovakia confirming this general observation (to which, nevertheless, one could find exceptions around the world). The difference in the two countries' discourses on sustainability thus may also be related to the levels of wealth of the societies and not to the ages of the donors.

Finally, there was a difference between the Slovak and Austrian respondents with regard to microfinance, and this difference could indeed be related to the question of experience of the workers in the field. However, not only were there respondents from Austria with a similar perspective on microfinance as those in Slovakia, but the one respondent who was more critical of microfinance than her colleagues and also the Slovaks was not from CARE Austria, but from CARE International. This issue shows that a difference between donors or between parts of national development apparatuses may be related to the age of these apparatuses and to the experience gained in the past. I argue, however, that this difference does not apply substantially to the difference between Austria and Slovakia.

In sum, the differences between the donors in their development discourses may be attributed to various contributing factors, and the ages of the respective donors need not play a substantial role in these differences. More importantly, the similarities between the donors were much greater than the differences between them. This research thus questions the division of donors into old and new donors and offers the possibility to formulate a question: Why does the distinction prevail?

On the representativeness of the results and suggestions for further research

This research focused on small parts of the Austrian and Slovak development apparatuses, and it was my aim to make relevant arguments, not about whole Slovak and Austrian discourses, but about parts of the discourses in Austria and Slovakia as an old and a new donor. Still, it is worth comparing the results of my research with the extant post-colonial research on the Slovak and Austrian development discourses.

Whereas Maral-Hanak (2003), examining PR texts from Austrian NGDOs, and Prinz and Kuyumji (2002), examining Austrian newspapers, found hierarchizing racial stereotypes *15 years ago*, I found in both countries instances of deliberate positivism that are much more in accordance with the current research on (visual) representations in the UK (Dogra 2014). According to Maral-Hanak, in charity campaigns, the unequal relation is often based on a godfather-like sponsorship. On the one hand, there is poverty, helplessness, and passivity on the side of the recipient, and on the other there is the capacity to act decidedly on the side of the organization or the individual donor. The paternalist approach is thus followed here (Maral-Hanak 2003: 105). Her analysis of texts from Austrian NGDOs that included fundraising advertisements in the media, homepages, and brochures shows an infantilization of the Other, racist and sexist stereotypization, objectification through anonymization, speaking for the Other, and simplifications (Maral-Hanak 2003: 104).

According to Prinz and Kuyumji (2002), representations of foreign aid and development cooperation in Austrian newspapers contain reproduction of clichés that give the message that the rich states are urged to give something to the poor. The interaction between the "partners" is seriously neglected here due to the attributed stereotypical roles of active donors and passive receivers. Furthermore, it is the views of the politicians, NGOs, and individuals from the North that are most presented in the articles. My research from 15 years later, though, shows that the Other is also active.

Ondrej Gažovič (2014) conducted postcolonial research among the Slovak NGDOs and Ministry of Foreign Affairs employees focusing on the representations of development and the Self and the Other. One noteworthy finding of his thesis is that respondents who represented development cooperation as problematic were to be found exclusively on the non-governmental level, and at this level they have done so "often" (ibid.: 100; see also Ziai 2004 for the same argument in the German context). This partly confirms my analysis and applies even more so after one particularly critical respondent from SAIDC left the agency. I also found that those who problematized unequal power relations were in the lower echelons in their respective organizations. Their superiors always focused on development projects and the local level and did not point at the Self and its problematic actions towards the Other.

My results differ from Gažovič's with regard to the critical perspective on development of the NGDO workers. The notion of "critical" is very vaguely applied here, but it seems that the exclusion of Slovak Christian NGDOs from my analysis may have contributed to the difference between our results as the Christian NGDOs use stereotypical images such as those of African babies that the NGDOs that I interviewed avoid. The difference between Christian and non-Christian NGDOs with regard to the representation of the Global South also became clear in a discussion on representations that I attended (Profant 2013). I would thus argue that, if I were to include respondents from Christian NGDOs, the proportion between more and less critical respondents would be different.

Regarding the Austrian respondents, a different composition of respondents would also probably alter the results. As has already been mentioned, the inclusion of retired employees from Austroprojekt and one senior figure in ADA increased the proportion of rather critical responses. Moreover, according to an (anonymized) academic who deals with the Austrian development cooperation professionally, responses from younger employees in ADA would be less critical than those I gained from more senior figures there, and an inclusion of respondents from the Ministry of Finance and the Austrian Development Bank would lead to a critique of ADA for dealing too much with poverty reduction and not enough with risk reduction and private entrepreneurship. According to this academic,

> the linear understanding of development with all the implications you mentioned is more and more characteristic for young urban professionals in the BMF [Ministry of Finance], the BMEIA [Ministry of Foreign Affairs] and ADA. It is amazing that, in particular, young well educated people coming from university (mostly mainstream economists) dropped a critical approach. On the other hand young people coming from university [from the International Development deparment] refuse the idea of development [completely] (post developmentalism).
>
> (Anonymized 2015)

What would be the results if one tried to engage in an analysis of the whole Austrian and Slovak apparatuses? With regard to the texts, the results would most likely be very much the same, except for the inclusion of more texts belonging to the "critical development" genre that come mainly from a part of the academics, students, and some NGDO workers.

With regard to the interviews, it is likely that there would be greater congruence with the classical development paradigm. The inclusion of the people working in the Ministries in both Austria and Slovakia, and also the inclusion of the people from the private sector in Austria, would result in a less critical approach towards the development discourse. It also seems to me that the inclusion of the Slovak Christian NGDOs might have a similar result.

These contemplations suggest a need for a more quantitative research that would be able to deal with a much larger corpus as well as a much greater group of workers. Another field of research that needs to be studied, especially in relation to depoliticization, is that of global education in Austria and Slovakia. Studies from elsewhere suggest that a claim like "ok, maybe we depoliticize with the projects, but we critically focus on political issues in global education" does not hold (Danielzik, Kiesel, and Bendix 2013).[2] Such a research is missing in both these countries.

The research that is lacking the most and that would reply to an important objection would deal with the audience. How do we know that hierarchization and depoliticization actually have negative social effects? Are they unquestioningly accepted or even actively sought by the audience? And, if yes, what is the result? And what is the result if the audience is exposed to anti-stereotypical and politicizing representations?

Another topic worth investigating that I only touched upon in this research is the efforts to understand the various personal trajectories and their influence on the current political preferences among development workers. Finally, post-development research that is already going on should also focus on the practice of post-development. This might mean analyzing discourses among the supporters of de-growth and other alternative movements, but also analyzing more material practices of those who want to overcome the current development model.

Notes

1 What do you think of the critique that people think that, if they are educated, they will reach a higher standard of living, but the fact is that mostly those with rich parents reach high standards of living?

2 According to Bendix et al., the problem with the options for political acting that the German Development Learning offers is that it does not consider privileges of the people from the North as privileges and also excludes social movements, unions, and political campaigns as possibilities for engagement. It is more common to expect shopping (e.g., for bio products) as the way to engage the given problems (ibid.: 47).

Bibliography

Anonymized 2015: AW: Critical respondents overrepresented? Email communication.

Barša, Pavel 2012: Sbohem postkomunismu. *Lidové noviny* 7.1.2012.

Bockman, Johanna and Eyal, Gil 2002: Eastern Europe as a Laboratory for Economic Knowledge: The Transnational Roots of Neoliberalism. *American Journal of Sociology* 108(2), 310–352.

Danielzik, Chandra-Milena, Kiesel, Timo, and Bendix, Daniel 2013: Bildung für nachhaltige Ungleichheit; Eine postkoloniale Anlyse von Materialien der entiwicklungspolitischen Bildungsarbeit in Deutschland. glokal, www.glokal.org/wp-content/uploads/2018/03/Glokal-e-V_Bildung-fuer-nachhaltige-Ungleichheit_Barrierefrei-Illustrationen-26-03-2013.pdf.

Dogra, Nandita 2014: *Representations of Global Poverty. Aid, Development and International NGOs*. London and New York: I.B. Tauris.

Eriksson Baaz, Maria 2005: *The Paternalism of Partnership: a Postcolonial Reading of Identity in Development Aid*. London: Zed Books.

Gažovič, Ondrej 2014: *V zajatí paradoxov. Diskurzívna analýza rozvojovej spolupráce SR* (Dizertačná práca). Univerzita Komenského, Bratislava.

Goudge, Paulette 2003: *The Whiteness of Power: Racism in Third World Development and Aid*. London: Lawrence And Wishart.

Kiesel, Timo and Bendix, Daniel 2010: White Charity: Eine postkoloniale rassismuskritische Analyse der entwicklungspolitischen Plakatwerbung in Deutschland. *Peripherie: Zeitschrift für Politik und Ökonomie in der Dritten Welt* 120, 482–495.

Lidchi, Henrietta 1999: Finding the right image. British development NGOs and the regulation of imagery. In: Skelton, Tracey and Allen, Tim (ed.): *Culture and Global Change*. London and New York: Routledge, 87–101.

Maral-Hanak, Irmi 2003: Entwicklung kommunizieren: Öffentlichkeits - und Bildungsarbeit. In: Gomes, Bea, Maral-Hanak, Irmi and Schicho, Walter (ed.): *Die Praxis der Entwicklungszusammenarbeit. Akteure, Interessen, Handlungsmuster*. Wien: Mandelbaum, 89–111.

PDCS Respondent No. 1 2015: Facebook Communication.

PiP respondent No. 9 2015: RE: Ešte jedna otázka. (email).

Pontis respondent No. 4 2015: RE: SNR a kniha. (email).

Prinz, Vanessa and Kuyumji, Lonita 2002: Entwicklungszusammenarbeit als Zeilenfüller? Inhaltliche und begriffliche Darstellung in österreichischen Printmedien. *Stichproben. Wiener Zeitschrift für Afrikanstudien* 3, 97–110.

Profant, Tomáš 2013: Týždeň s Markízou. JeToTak.sk.

Spivak, Gayatri Charkravorty 1994: Can the Subaltern Speak? In: Williams, Patrick – Chrisman, Laura (ed.): *Colonial Discourse and Post-colonial Theory: A Reader*. New York: Columbia University Press, 66–111.

Wilson, Kalpana 2012: *Race, Racism and Development: Interrogating History, Discourse and Practice*. London and New York: Zed Books.

Ziai, Aram 2004: *Entwicklung als Ideologie? Das klassische Entwicklungsparadigma und die Post-Development Kritik zur Analyse des Entwicklungsdiskurses*. Hambrug: Deutsches Übersee-Institut.

Ziai, Aram 2011: The Millennium Development Goals: back to the future? *Third World Quarterly* 32(1), 27–43.

Index

For Product Safety Concerns and Information please contact our EU representative GPSR@taylorandfrancis.com
Taylor & Francis Verlag GmbH, Kaufingerstraße 24, 80331 München, Germany

www.ingramcontent.com/pod-product-compliance
Ingram Content Group UK Ltd.
Pitfield, Milton Keynes, MK11 3LW, UK
UKHW022128190926
475702UK00013B/1690

* 9 7 8 0 3 6 7 7 8 6 7 7 9 *